PORTUGUESE STUDIES

VOLUME 31 NUMBER 2
2015

In Medieval Mode:
Collected Essays in Honour of
Stephen Parkinson on his Retirement

Founding Editor
HELDER MACEDO

Guest Editors
CLÁUDIA PAZOS ALONSO
CLAIRE WILLIAMS

Editors
FRANCISCO BETHENCOURT
PAULO DE MEDEIROS
PAUL MELO E CASTRO
HILARY OWEN
JULIET PERKINS
LÚCIA SÁ
CLAIRE WILLIAMS

Editorial Assistant
RICHARD CORRELL

Production Editor
GRAHAM NELSON

MODERN HUMANITIES RESEARCH ASSOCIATION

PORTUGUESE STUDIES

A peer-reviewed biannual multi-disciplinary journal devoted to research on the cultures, literatures, history and societies of the Lusophone world

International Advisory Board

DAVID BROOKSHAW
JOÃO DE PINA CABRAL
IVO JOSÉ DE CASTRO
THOMAS F. EARLE
JOHN GLEDSON
ANNA KLOBUCKA

MARIA MANUEL LISBOA
KENNETH MAXWELL
LAURA DE MELLO E SOUZA
MARIA IRENE RAMALHO
SILVIANO SANTIAGO

Portuguese Studies and other journals published by the MHRA may be ordered from JSTOR (http://about.jstor.org/csp).

The **Modern Humanities Research Association** was founded in Cambridge in 1918 and has become an international organization with members in all parts of the world. It is a registered charity number 1064670, and a company limited by guarantee, registered in England number 3446016. Its main object is to encourage advanced study and research in modern and medieval European languages, literatures, and cultures by its publication of journals, book series, and its Style Guide. Further information about the activities of the Association and individual membership may be obtained from the Membership Secretary, Dr Jessica Goodman, Clare College, Trinity Lane, Cambridge CB2 1TL, UK, email membership@mhra.org.uk, or from the website at: **www.mhra.org.uk**

Disclaimer: Statements of fact and opinion in the content of *Portuguese Studies* are those of the respective authors and contributors and not of the journal editors or of the Modern Humanities Research Association (MHRA). MHRA makes no representation, express or implied, in respect of the accuracy of the material in this journal and cannot accept any legal responsibility or liability for any errors or omissions that may be made.

Parts of this work may be reproduced as permitted under legal provisions for fair dealing (or fair use) for the purposes of research, private study, criticism, or review, or when a relevant collective licensing agreement is in place. All other reproduction requires the written permission of the copyright holder who may be contacted at rights@mhra.org.uk.

ISSN 0267–5315 (print) ISSN 2222–4270 (online)
ISBN 978–1–78188–210–8

© 2015 The Modern Humanities Research Association
Salisbury House, Station Road, Cambridge CB1 2LA, United Kingdom

PORTUGUESE STUDIES VOL. 31 NO. 2

In Medieval Mode:
Collected Essays in Honour of
Stephen Parkinson on his Retirement

CONTENTS

Preface	147
Introduction CLÁUDIA PAZOS ALONSO and CLAIRE WILLIAMS	148
Sanctity and Social Alienation in Twelfth-Century Braga as Portrayed in the *Vita Sancti Geraldi* STEPHEN LAY	153
Seeing is Believing: The Miniatures in the *Cantigas de Santa Maria* and Medieval Devotional Practices KIRSTIN KENNEDY	169
Early Modern Marginalia in the *Cancioneiro da Ajuda* ANDRÉ B. PENAFIEL	183
The Manuscript Tradition of the *Regula Benedicti* in Portuguese IVO CASTRO	195
Service, not Subservience: Chapter 98 of Dom Duarte's *Leal Conselheiro* JULIET PERKINS	209
Rui de Pina, *Crónica de D. Afonso V* and Bodleian MS Don. c. 230 T. F. EARLE	222
Damião de Góis's *Livro de Linhagens*: An Untold (Hi)Story CATARINA BARCELÓ FOUTO	235
Lusophone Studies: A Cumulative Area Bibliography, 2013–15 Compiled by EMILCE REES	250
Abstracts	265

NOTES FOR CONTRIBUTORS

Articles to be considered for publication may be on any subject within the field but must not exceed 7,500 words, and should be submitted in a form ready for publication in English, sent as an email attachment to the Editorial Assistant at richard.correll@kcl.ac.uk.

Contributions whose standard of English is inadequate will be returned. Any quotations in Portuguese must be accompanied by an English translation. Submissions in Portuguese may be considered, but publication will be conditional on provision of a satisfactory translation at the author's expense. The Editorial Assistant may undertake translations on request for a reasonable charge.

Text and references should conform precisely to the conventions of the *MHRA Style Guide*, 3rd edn, 2013 (978-1-78188-009-8), £6.50, US $13, €8, obtainable in print or online version from www.style.mhra.org.uk. All articles are subject to independent, anonymous peer review by experts in the field; authors receive written feedback on the editors' decision and guidance on any revisions required. *Portuguese Studies* regrets it must charge contributors for the cost of corrections in proof deemed excessive.

It is a condition of publication in this journal that authors of articles and reviews assign copyright, including electronic copyright, to the MHRA. Inter alia, this allows the General Editor to deal efficiently and consistently with requests from third parties for permission to reproduce material. The journal has been published simultaneously in printed and electronic form since January 2001. Permission, without fee, for authors to use their own material in other publications, after a reasonable period of time has elapsed, is not normally withheld. Authors may make closed-access deposit of accepted manuscripts in their academic institution's digital repository upon acceptance. Full open access to the accepted manuscript is permitted no sooner than 24 months following publication of the Contribution by the MHRA. Contributions may also be republished on authors' personal websites without seeking further permission from the Association, but no earlier than 24 months after publication by the MHRA.

Books for review should be sent to: Reviews Editor, *Portuguese Studies*, Dr Paul Melo e Castro, School of Modern Languages and Cultures, University of Leeds, Leeds LS2 9JT.

Preface

The suggestion of the current volume in honour of Professor Stephen Parkinson was welcomed by *Portuguese Studies* as soon as it was raised by its co-editors, Cláudia Pazos Alonso and Claire Williams. Indeed, it scarcely seems necessary to offer any formal preface to a work that has already been so well prepared, thoroughly revised and clearly introduced by its co-editors. We would, however, wish to highlight three important principles that have emerged from this collaboration. Firstly, *Portuguese Studies* is keen to reinforce its links with the community of researchers in literary and cultural studies, and in the history and social sciences of Portugal, Brazil and Lusophone African countries. Secondly, we are of the opinion that selected papers from well organized symposia or Festschriften in honour of respected colleagues, who have played (and continue to play) a major role in the regeneration and dissemination of the field, are vital for maintaining the high profile of the journal. We endeavour to strike a good balance between accepting individual articles, which are appropriate for publication in a peer-reviewed journal, and collective initiatives, which develop topics of ongoing interest around specific subjects and themes. In both cases the journal plays a crucial role in the development of this substantial field of studies in English, welcoming innovative articles with a major impact as well as opening up new dialogues, implicit or explicit, between researchers from different countries. Thirdly, the history of *Portuguese Studies*, which was founded by Helder Macedo in 1985, has clearly demonstrated that it has different areas of strength and a capacity for growth down three generations of researchers. The present issue is an obvious example of the rejuvenation of Medieval Studies, which has involved scholars from two generations working from different sources and in diverse fields of study, experimenting with new theories and methodologies. The editorial board of *Portuguese Studies* has undergone significant reconfiguration over the past two years and it is very happy to guarantee the future of the journal as both a showcase for the field, and a space for cutting edge intervention.

THE EDITORS

Introduction

Cláudia Pazos Alonso and Claire Williams

University of Oxford

This issue, devoted to medieval and early modern studies, is dedicated to our dear colleague and friend Stephen Parkinson, to mark his retirement in September 2015. The cast of contributors gathered here comprises a range of colleagues in the field of Portuguese studies, many closely linked with Oxford and Stephen himself, including some former and current students. Portugal is one of the countries in Europe with the oldest stable frontiers, dating back to the twelfth century. The present issue takes us from just prior to the formation of the Portuguese nation, formalized in 1143 at the Treaty of Zamora, through to the sixteenth century, a century closely associated with the Age of the Discoveries, but where the medieval legacy remains visibly present in genres such as historiography.[1] The articles are arranged in a broadly chronological order. They showcase a variety of topics, warranting different critical methodologies and approaches: literary and historical analysis, a focus on visual culture, the critical fortunes of medieval manuscripts, and the diachronic development of the Portuguese language across the centuries. Last but not least, they highlight the need for editions of early modern material.

The thirteenth century occupies a significant place in the current volume, in a fitting tribute to Stephen Parkinson, who retained a well-documented predilection for this period throughout his career. Indeed, thanks to Stephen's monumental and ongoing online project on the *Cantigas de Santa Maria*, greater familiarity with this seminal compilation is only one click away, for the uninitiated and experts alike (<http://csm.mml.ox.ac.uk/>). Most recently, he has edited an anthology of *Cantigas de Santa Maria: Alfonso X, the Learned* (MHRA, 2015) which gathers in one volume over forty poems, in a bilingual edition. When it came to choosing a cover image for this themed volume of *Portuguese Studies*, therefore, it made perfect sense to choose a suitable illustration from the vast range in the manuscripts of *Cantigas de Santa Maria*. We hope that the one we settled on,[2] pretty much straightaway, mirrors the

---

[1] Given that the medieval period encompasses several centuries, many treasures of Portuguese literature could not be surveyed in the current issue. For further information about such gems as the secular *cantigas* of various types, the chronicles of Fernão Lopes and, straddling the medieval and Renaissance worlds, the plays of Gil Vicente, we refer our readers to a collaborative volume, spearheaded by Stephen and other colleagues in the sub-faculty of Portuguese at Oxford, the *Companion to Portuguese Literature* (2009, paperback edition 2013).

[2] The illustration belongs to Cantiga 194 in the El Escorial manuscript (Real Biblioteca del Monasterio,

aura that Stephen as a teacher was able to project: that of an experienced tutor, who generated a happy and supportive learning environment and effortlessly captivated the attention of the eager disciples surrounding him, thanks to the magic of the music he produced — seemingly entirely off-the-cuff, for there are no scores in sight!

The volume opens with an article by the Oxford-based historian-cum-administrator **Stephen Lay**, who explores the period immediately preceding the independence of the *condado portucalense* from the kingdoms of Leon and Castile, through an analysis of the *Vita Sancti Geraldi*. Bernard's hagiographic account of the life of his close friend, Gerald, not only provides us with the biography of a holy man but also stands as an important historical source, allowing us to glimpse the cultural changes underway in Portuguese society in the context of the birth of a nation, seen from the perspective of two high-ranking French clerics. Charged with the task of modernizing the Portuguese church hierarchy, this account of their vicissitudes warrants revisiting, for, as Lay argues, it raises complex questions about power and legitimacy.

In the second article, **Kirstin Kennedy**, a former doctoral student of Stephen Parkinson's, and now a Curator at the Victoria & Albert Museum, considers the visual aspect of the *códice rico*. She brings out the significance of the miniatures that illustrate the songs in honour of the Virgin Mary, through an examination of how piety is shaped by sensorial experience. In a further article, **André Penafiel** studies the reception of the *Cancioneiro da Ajuda*, focusing on late medieval and early modern hand annotations, and considers individual responses down the ages. Penafiel (currently undertaking doctoral research under Stephen's supervision) goes beyond existing studies to show that three different hands were involved. He cogently speculates on what this reveals about the various readers concerned and their access to the manuscript, and provides, moreover, in a useful appendix, an accurate transcription of the annotations.

The insights that can be gleaned from the reception of medieval material is complemented by the article that follows, by **Ivo Castro**, an Emeritus Professor from Lisbon University whose multifaceted research, like Stephen's, ranges across medieval studies and linguistics. Castro begins with an overview of the factors involved in the loss and preservation of manuscripts in Old Portuguese, in order to contextualize the significance of one of the largest surviving medieval manuscript traditions: that of the *Regula Benedicti*. He argues convincingly that the Rules' transcription and dissemination over several centuries — with seven manuscripts dating from the fourteenth and fifteenth century alone — allows present-day scholars to gain, from a diachronic perspective, a privileged linguistic insight into the shifts Portuguese has undergone.

MS T.I.1, fol. 255^v). For further information about the *cantiga* and its storyline (about a 'minstrel who sang well', ambushed on the orders of a jealous knight, but rescued thanks to the intervention of the Virgin Mary), please see <http://csm.mml.ox.ac.uk/index.php?p=poemdata_view&rec=194> [accessed 30 June 2015].

Juliet Perkins, recently retired from a lectureship at King's College, London, then brings us into the late medieval period with her article on the *Leal Conselheiro*, a text written by the king, Dom Duarte, in the first half of the fifteenth century. His parents, Dom João I and the English noblewoman, Philippa of Lancaster, produced half a dozen exceptionally accomplished children, known in Portuguese collective memory as the *ínclita geração* [the illustrious generation], after Luís de Camões immortalized them as such in his great epic *Os Lusíadas* (Canto IV, strophe 50). Of those, Dom Henrique (Prince Henry the Navigator) remains the best known internationally today for his instrumental role in the launch of the Age of the Discoveries, closely followed by his sister, Isabella of Portugal, who became Duchess of Burgundy upon her marriage to Duke Philip the Good. Their eldest sibling, Duarte, who went on to become King of Portugal, was a gifted writer, famed for his description of melancholia in *Leal Conselheiro*. Perkins examines here one of the late chapters of this moral treatise, which provides a thought-provoking discussion of father–son relations.

After Perkins' incursion into the first half of the fifteenth century, the volume moves on to the later fifteenth century and into the sixteenth, courtesy of contributions penned by two former colleagues of Stephen at Oxford. Both articles focus on chroniclers who became keepers of the royal archives of the Torre do Tombo and on some of their lesser-known manuscripts. In fact, unlike the other texts considered in the present volume, be it the *Vita Sancti Geraldi*, the *Cantigas de Santa Maria*, the *Cancioneiro da Ajuda*, the *Regula Benedicti* or the *Leal Conselheiro*, the manuscripts under consideration here have yet to be critically edited. The article by **Tom Earle** tackles the *Crónica de D. Afonso V*, by Rui de Pina, composed some time between 1490 and 1504. The eponymous fifteenth-century monarch was the son of Dom Duarte and enjoyed a long reign lasting over forty years (1438–81). The chronicle exists in multiple copies, but Earle offers the first detailed description of a version that will be of particular interest to UK-based readers, having been recently acquired by the Bodleian library.

If writing biographies of individual kings was a well-established medieval historiographic activity, so too was the compilation of books of lineages. The well-known humanist Damião de Góis is one of the notable heirs to this significant tradition, for, as **Catarina Fouto** contends, his unpublished *Livro de Linhagens*, probably composed in the third quarter of the sixteenth century, is a work indebted to that of his predecessors. Unlike the many manuscripts of Rui de Pina's *Crónica de D. Afonso V*, only a few versions of Góis's text are known to exist and, as such, it is perhaps surprising to learn that a critical edition has yet to be attempted, not least given the interest of a work which mirrors what Fouto calls an 'effective centralization of royal power'.

In short, this volume takes us on a revealing tour, from the period immediately preceding the independence of Portugal, through to the aftermath of the Discoveries. Thematically, moral conduct remains one important preoccupation throughout, from an account of the life of the blessed Gerald, via the songs composed in honour of the Virgin Mary, through to the filial devotion exhibited by Dom Duarte. But, even when we are faced with works whose primary purpose was to provide examples of service, piety and/or morality, we gain a fascinating insight not only into the medieval mind but also a society undergoing transformation over several centuries. A second strand that emerges from this volume is the timely reminder that significant material from the pre-modern period remains to be recovered and, indeed, reinterpreted and re-contextualized for a twenty-first-century audience.

The writer Hélia Correia once remarked on how the birth of the Portuguese nation had arisen out of a power struggle between a mother and her son. If there were countless wars to secure kingship in medieval times (and beyond), the gender dimension of this particular power struggle is arresting, for it vividly encapsulates the untimely deposition of the maternal figure in favour of a male-authorized engendering of the nation.[3] On a related note, the present guest editors, two specialists of the modern period with a particular interest in gender studies, could not help noticing the way in which Damião de Góis, too, expediently did away with the female side of lineages. He justified such an omission from official historical accounts as follows: 'nothing else is said of the daughters because they follow the blood line of their husbands, and their children are indicated there' (English translation from Fouto's article). According to books of lineages, then, women were effectively to be regarded as empty reproductive vessels only, whose sole function was to ensure the continuity of the male patrilineal name.

The representation of women in the medieval period, however, is not necessarily non-existent or unidimensional. For instance, one can find an alternative worldview articulated by the *cantigas de amigo*, justly famed for their female voice and perspective. In Rui de Pina's *Crónica de D. Afonso V*, the portrayal of Dona Leonor, Dom Duarte's widow and mother of Dom Afonso V, is far from simplistic. Although Rui de Pina does not hide his disapproval of this Spanish Queen — not least for being a foreigner — he is forced to concede that she was a powerful and effective political operator. And subsequently, on the cusp of the Renaissance, the playwright Gil Vicente is widely known for offering a nuanced portrayal of women, be it through the memorable voice of Inês Pereira, in the eponymous farce showcasing a strong-willed heroine, or that of the inconstant Constança (in *Auto da India*), whose embodied sexual desires take centre-stage. The latter play continues to be successfully taught on the Oxford syllabus up to the present day, wooing new generations of

---

[3] For further details about representations of women in power at the time of the emergence of the Portuguese nation, please see Maria do Rosário Ferreira, 'Urraca e Teresa: o paradigma perdido', in *In marsupiis peregrinorum: circulación de textos e imaxes arredor do Camiño de Santiago na Idade Media*, ed. by Esther Corral (Florence: Galluzzo, 2010), pp. 201–14. Available online at <http://ifilosofia.up.pt/gfm/seminar/docs/URRACA%20E%20TERESA.pdf > [accessed 20 April 2015].

undergraduates to the study of pre-modern Portuguese literature, thanks to its perennial modernity.

Medieval studies and modernity are sometimes perceived as an unlikely pairing, though arguably not in Oxford, at least not since Stephen joined what was then the Sub-faculty of Spanish and Portuguese in 1988. For many years he remained the only Lecturer in Portuguese Language and Linguistics in the UK and, by a stroke of luck for Portuguese studies at Oxford, his arrival coincided with the advent of computers and then the Internet. New technologies have provided a wonderful tool for all of us in the profession, but Stephen fully availed himself of the wealth of opportunities ushered in by the digital revolution, pioneering web-based learning and research long before the term 'digital humanities' had been coined.

His intellectual curiosity and extraordinary capacity for lateral thinking, which over the years have enabled him to make exciting and productive connections between the music, words and images of the *Cantigas de Santa Maria*, remain an inspiration and example to us all. Nor is his original and interdisciplinary approach confined to the research or the teaching of his much loved medieval period of literature. For many years now, his 'Portuguese in Fifteen Minutes' sessions at Open Days, informed by his expertise in linguistics, have become legendary, and rightly so: indeed, they have led many a sixth former to the momentous decision to study Portuguese at university, *ab initio*.

It is our hope that not only Portuguese medieval studies, but equally importantly linguistics and indeed innovative language teaching methodologies, will continue to remain distinctive features of Oxford's Portuguese syllabus well beyond Stephen's retirement. But, needless to say, his astute leadership skills, which led to his appointment first as Chair of the Faculty of Modern Languages and then as Chair of the Faculty of Linguistics (a double first for Portuguese), his congenial ability to see the potential in every person and situation, and, last but not least, his irreverent sense of fun — who else would ever have thought of setting a translation passage in Finals sourced from the comic novel by Alexander McCall Smith entitled *Portuguese Irregular Verbs*? — will be sorely missed by all who had the privilege to work with him. We wish him a long and productive retirement.

Sanctity and Social Alienation in Twelfth-Century Braga as Portrayed in the *Vita Sancti Geraldi*

STEPHEN LAY

University of Oxford

'Even though he stood under strange stars and used the language of another people, he remained steadfast in religious matters and nothing could sway him from the proper observance of correct doctrine.'[1] The man thus celebrated was Gerald of Moissac, a French-born Cluniac monk elected to be Bishop of Braga in the final years of the eleventh century. The *Vita Sancti Geraldi*, an account of his life and deeds, was penned by a fellow Frenchman, Bernard, who accompanied Gerald on his long journey to Portugal. The *vita* adheres to many of the conventions used by hagiographers to describe human sanctity. Bernard recalls Gerald as a pious defender of the beleaguered church and people under his care, a man equally zealous when ministering to the weak as when confronting the powerful. However Bernard's account also reveals his consciousness of a cultural difference between the immigrant Frenchmen and the local Portuguese population. For Gerald and Bernard had another, more controversial agenda: they had come to Braga with a mandate to reform the Portuguese church using the models they were both familiar with in their homeland. These foreign innovations were not universally welcomed by local people, and the reformers faced resistance that ranged from passive inertia to active physical threat. Yet rather than conceal these tensions, Bernard weaves a pervasive sense of social alienation into his overall portrayal of Gerald's sanctity. The result is a poignant and strikingly personal insight into a complex and rapidly changing society.

Bernard's work has survived into modern times via a manuscript no less travelled than the author himself. The *Vita Sancti Geraldi* first emerges into the documentary record in the seventeenth century, among the material gathered from libraries and archives across southern France under the authority of Jean-Baptiste Colbert, chief minister of finance to King Louis XIV. Selections from the library were published by Etienne Baluze in 1680 and reprinted in 1761. A century later the *vita* was included by Alexandre Herculano in the *Portugaliae*

---

[1] *Vita Sancti Geraldi*, in *Portugaliae Monumenta Historica a saeculo octavo post Christum usque at quintumdecimum. Scriptores*, ed. by A. Herculano (Lisbon: Academia das Ciências de Lisboa, 1856), vol. I, p. 54. English translations in this article are by the author.

Monumenta Historica series and so entered the canon of Portuguese historical sources.² There is also extant in Portugal an abbreviated version of the *vita*, preserved in the *Breviário de Soeiro*, a fifteenth-century collection of material pertaining to the cathedral in Braga.³ The identity of the author is clear from the text itself. Bernard speaks of his own first-hand experiences with Gerald and also records information he learned from others. The *vita* appears to have been written shortly after Gerald's death in 1108; however, internal references are somewhat contradictory and commentators have felt more secure seeking fixed points in Bernard's own career as a possible guide. In the *Vita Sancti Geraldi* Bernard refers to himself as Archdeacon of Braga and, since he is known to have become Bishop of Coimbra in 1128, this has been accepted as a likely terminal date of composition.⁴

As a contemporary, first-hand account of medieval Portuguese society the *Vita Sancti Geraldi* has long been recognized as an invaluable, albeit complicated, source. Hagiography is in essence an attempt to portray individual human sanctity and so, by its very nature, seems to promise penetrating insights into a wider society's fundamental beliefs and deepest anxieties. Unfortunately this promise is not easily realized. Hagiographers were not attempting to produce an accurate representation of historical events; rather they were seeking to portray saintliness within the conventions of a specific literary genre, the rules of which cannot always be reproduced or even readily understood by the modern reader. Because their aim was to persuade a potentially sceptical audience of a particular individual's sanctity, these writers might deploy any or

---

² *Vita Sancti Geraldi*, pp. 53–59 [VSG]. An online version of the *Portugaliae Monumenta Historica* is accessible via the website of the Biblioteca Nacional de Portugal. A Portuguese version and commentary was produced by José Cardoso, *Vida de S. Geraldo*, 2nd edn (Braga: Cabido Metropolitano e Primacial, 1995). The manuscript (BN lat. 5296C) is now held at the Bibliothèque Nationale de France, as noted by Jean Dufour *La Bibliothèque et le Scriptorium de Moissac* (Geneva and Paris: Librairie Droz, 1972), p. 8. n. 85. For a description of the manuscript, see Jean Dufour, 'Manuscrits de Moissac antérieurs au milieu du XIIe siècle et nouvellement identifiés: description codicologique et paléographique,' *Scriptorium*, 36 (1982), 147–73 (pp. 164–65).

³ 'Vita' de Saint Geraud, in Pedro Romano Rocha, *L'Office Divin au Moyen Age dans L'Eglise de Braga* (Paris: Fundação Calouste Gulbenkian, 1980), pp. 503–09. The relationship between these two works is considered by Aires A. Nascimento 'Da intenção edificante à lição litúrgica: a rescrita da Vita S. Geraldi de Bernardo, Bispo de Coimbra,' in *Em louvor da linguagem: homenagem a Maria Leonor Carvalhão Buescu* (Lisbon: Edições Colibri, 2003), pp. 323–35.

⁴ José Freire, 'Aspectos literários da *Vita Sancti Geraldi*', *IX Centenário da dedicação da Sé de Braga: congresso internacional: actas*, 3 vols (Braga: Universidade Católica Portuguesa, 1990), I, 575–79; José Mattoso, 'Vida S. Geraldo', in *Dicionário da literatura medieval galega e portuguesa*, ed. by Giulia Lanciani and Giuseppe Tavani (Lisbon: Editorial Caminho, 1993), pp. 666–68. Recent commentators have noted Bernard's use of phrases suggesting geographical distance from Braga, with the implication that the *vita* was written in Coimbra after 1128, as noted by Nascimento, 'Da intenção edificante,' pp. 326–27; and Maria de Lurdes Rosa, 'A santidade no Portugal medieval: narrativas e trajectos de vida', *Lusitania Sacra*, n.s., 13–14 (2001–02), 369–450 (pp. 390–93). However, it seems difficult to reconcile a later date of composition with the absence of any reference to the dramatic events of 1128. In a single year Afonso Henriques ousted his mother Infanta Teresa from power and intervened personally in Coimbra to secure the bishopric for Bernard. Even if humility prevented Bishop Bernard from referring to his own higher office, it seems unlikely that a *vita* written after 1128 would make no mention whatsoever of Afonso Henriques.

all of the literary and rhetorical skills available to them. Yet at the same time the hagiographer's purpose also imposed limitations of its own. 'Representations of the historical reality,' Simon Yarrow has suggested, 'however schematized and topoi-ridden they might be, could not afford to play fast and loose with the expectations of those from whose social practices they garnered their material.'[5] A recourse to historically verifiable facts was also a rhetorical technique — as the hagiographer endeavoured to persuade his audience of the presence of a miraculous sanctity in their midst, so too the descriptions of this sanctity worked most effectively when they had at least some foundation in reality.

Bernard, the author of the *Vita Sancti Geraldi*, was well aware of the rhetorical power of veracity and he attempted to reassure his audience by presenting himself as both an eye-witness and a participant in the events described. This use of the first-person narrator is a literary device sometimes adopted by hagiographers in order to confront the audience with direct, face-to-face testimony. While this practice does create the impression of a closer bond of trust, even complicity, between the author and the reader, such attempts to claim textual authenticity remain problematic, not least because scholars have identified instances in which hagiographical scenes presented as factual (in that the authors cast themselves as participants) could not in reality have taken place.[6] Consequently, rather than accept Bernard's first-person accounts at face value, it is necessary to adopt a more critically nuanced approach to his work. Recent commentators have emphasized the importance of taking account of authorial intention and historical context, along with a sensitivity to the conventions commonly followed by writers composing a work of hagiography.[7] By subjecting the *Vita Sancti Geraldi* to such an examination, the author is revealed as being highly attuned to the historical forces at work around him, while at the same time capable of making skilful use of the commonly accepted conventions of hagiographical writing in the pursuit of his own literary goals.

The *Vita Sancti Geraldi* was composed in the midst of what can only be called a cultural revolution in Portugal. During the eleventh century local traditions came under sustained external pressure as D. Alfonso, king of Leon-Castile and at that time also overlord of Portugal, threw his support behind papal initiatives to reform the Iberian church.[8] D. Alfonso was deeply impressed

---

[5] Simon Yarrow, *Saints and their Communities: Miracle Stories in Twelfth-Century England* (Oxford: Clarendon Press, 2006), pp. 16-17. See also Thomas Heffernan, *Sacred Biography: Saints and their Biographers in the Middle Ages* (Oxford: Oxford University Press, 1988), pp. 3-71.

[6] Heffernan, *Sacred Biography*, pp. 75-79; Aires A. Nascimento, 'Um traço familiar em textos hagiográficos bracarenses medievais: a 1.ª pessoa verbal', *Theologica II*, 35 (2000), 585-98.

[7] See for example Patrick Geary, *Living with the Dead in the Middle Ages* (Ithaca, NY: Cornell University Press, 1994), pp. 22-24.

[8] For an introduction to the complex history of north-western Iberia during this period see Bernard F. Reilly, *The Kingdom of León-Castilla under King Alfonso VI, 1065-1109* (Princeton, NJ: Princeton University Press, 1988) and *The Kingdom of León-Castilla under Queen Urraca* (Princeton, NJ: Princeton University Press, 1982); Richard A. Fletcher, *St James's Catapult: The Life and Times of Diego Gelmírez of Santiago de Compostela* (Oxford: Oxford University Press, 1984); and Stephen Lay, *The Reconquest Kings of Portugal* (London: Palgrave, 2009).

by cultural developments in France and had established strong links with the monastery of Cluny, one of the great spiritual centres of Western Europe. With the encouragement of the reform papacy, the monastery sent the king a steady stream of French clergymen — Gerald of Moissac among them — trained in the newest religious forms approved by Rome. Moreover, D. Alfonso's interest in French culture went beyond religious reform. With the assistance of the monks of Cluny, D. Alfonso negotiated French marriages, first for himself and then subsequently for his daughters, Infanta Urraca and Infanta Teresa. The marriage between Infanta Teresa and a French nobleman, Henry of Burgundy, was to have decisive importance in Portugal, since D. Alfonso had decided that the region would make a suitable dowry for his daughter. By 1096 Count Henry had arrived in the regional capital, Guimarães, to take control of his new lands.

This sudden imposition of foreign leadership and exotic customs was deeply unsettling for many people in Portugal. Bishop Pedro, Gerald's predecessor as Bishop of Braga, was a staunch traditionalist, firmly convinced that the ancient eminence of Braga made him equal in status to any other Iberian churchman.[9] However Archbishop Bernard of Toledo, another Frenchman trained as a Cluniac monk, had been transferred to Spain to spearhead the ecclesiastical reforms. To facilitate his task the archbishop was granted legatine authority over the entire Peninsula and he was determined to enforce this authority in Portugal.[10] When an angry Bishop Pedro sought royal and papal confirmation of his own autonomy, D. Alfonso refused to become involved, while Pope Urban II — who was himself a former monk of Cluny — made clear his support for Archbishop Bernard of Toledo. In frustration, the Bishop of Braga sought and gained the recognition he craved from the Imperial antipope, Clement III. This dangerous gambit proved to be a disastrous misstep: Bishop Pedro was deposed from office in 1091 and forced into monastic retirement, allowing Archbishop Bernard to reorder affairs in Braga to his liking. One of the new arrangements the archbishop instituted was to secure the election of Gerald of Moissac as Bishop Pedro's eventual replacement. Gerald's arrival in Braga could thus be interpreted as a major triumph for French interests in the region and a deliberate snub to the Portuguese traditionalists. It was against this background of social unrest and popular upheaval that the events recorded in the *Vita Sancti Geraldi* subsequently unfolded.

The tense situation in Braga impacted on the final form of the work, as did

---

[9] Avelino de Jesus da Costa, *O Bispo D. Pedro e a organização da diocese de Braga*, 2 vols (Coimbra: Faculdade de Letras, 1959–60), I, 36–42. Bishop Pedro's traditional attitudes are indicated by a letter subsequently sent by Gerald asking if ordinations carried out 'in the Toledan manner' should be allowed to stand. Carl Erdmann, *Papsturkunden in Portugal* (Berlin: Vandenhoeck and Ruprecht, 1927), p. 161, n. 8.

[10] Bernard of Sèdirac, the leading figure in the transmission of French culture in the Peninsula, served as Abbot of Sahagún and subsequently Archbishop of Toledo following the city's capture by Alfonso VI in 1085. Marcelin Defourneaux, *Les Français en Espagne aux XIe et XIIe siècles* (Paris: Presses Universitaires de France, 1949), pp. 32–49.

the author's purpose in writing the *vita*. An aim of all hagiography is to present an image of holiness and this is certainly the case in the *Vita Sancti Geraldi*. In fact Bernard offers the reader an unambiguous statement of his reasons for composing the work:

> Desiring to lead the less instructed to strengthen their faith, we deem it fitting to describe the life of Saint Gerald, Archbishop of Braga, and the miracles which Omnipotent God displayed in his honour to the world of men, in order that, on hearing of the virtues of this one excellent man, they will be inflamed with zeal to imitate him by living a similar life.[11]

This aspiration to celebrate an example of piety that others might follow is frequently cited by hagiographers as their primary motivation. It is also a reminder that Bernard's stated intention was to create a sacred rather than a historical biography. Yet to elevate Gerald as an iconic figure Bernard drew his basic source material from the surrounding society, and his account of the new bishop's interaction with those around him also hints at the possibility of another, slightly different agenda. Gerald's pursuit of ecclesiastical reform is a central theme of the *vita* and Bernard's care to demonstrate that these efforts were supported by both secular and heavenly authority has led modern commentators to suggest that the *Vita Sancti Geraldi* was in part written as a propaganda tool to further the reform agenda.[12] Certainly Bernard was deeply committed to ecclesiastical reform and he presents Gerald's resolve as a major strength in his character. Yet Bernard was also careful to use the conventions of hagiography to weave this more controversial aspect of Gerald's mission back into his overall portrait of sanctity.

Bernard begins his task with a biography that appears to blend a number of elements commonly found in saintly *vitae* with apparently accurate personal information. Gerald, he records, was born in Cahors in southern France to aristocratic parents and was offered as a child to the monastery of Moissac, some sixty kilometres distant from his ancestral lands. Moissac, a venerable and prestigious institution, was at least three hundred years old when it was affiliated with Cluny in the eleventh century.[13] Gerald quickly began to distinguish himself though his virtue and obedience to the monastic rule, so that, despite his youth, the older monks began to imitate his example. Bernard also records that Gerald had a deep love of knowledge and quickly became well-versed in music and grammar. In recognition of his intellectual achievements the monks elected him librarian and he gained a reputation as a skilled teacher. This reputation was soon to set him on the path from Moissac to Braga. Gerald first travelled to Moises to instruct novice monks and it was there that he first

---
[11] *VSG*, v. 1, p. 53.
[12] As Mattoso notes: '[The *vita* confers] um valor quase sagrado à obra de reforma eclesiástica de Geraldo, para assim justificar os clérigos e autoridades eclesiásticas que procuravam executar um programa análogo em Portugal durante as primeiras décadas do século XII.' 'Vida S. Geraldo,' p. 668.
[13] Dufour, *La Bibliothèque et le Scriptorium de Moissac*, ch. 1; Joaquim Bragança, 'Moissac e Braga,' *O Distrito de Braga*, 2 (1964), 189–95.

encountered Archbishop Bernard of Toledo. Unfortunately the author of the *Vita Sancti Geraldi*, Bernard of Coimbra, is imprecise about the date of this meeting between Gerald and his namesake, but it is most likely to have taken place in 1095, when the archbishop was returning to Toledo after attending the Council of Clermont.[14] Initially Gerald served in Toledo as a teacher, assisting Archbishop Bernard in reforming the city's churches; however the deposition of Bishop Pedro left a vacancy in Braga which the Archbishop of Toledo duly filled with his protégé.

The description of Gerald's early career provided in the *Vita Sancti Geraldi* reveals a number of common hagiographical motifs: he is described as being of noble birth, implying both heavenly favour and the right to wield authority over others; similarly his precocious intellect and premature gravity are characteristics commonly attributed to children destined for sainthood.[15] Yet Bernard does not limit himself to these conventional hagiographical elements, rather he uses them as a foundation on which to arrange more distinctive, personalizing details from Gerald's formative years. Specific biographical details play a dual role by strengthening the sense of authenticity while at the same time serving to personalize Gerald and contextualize his sanctity in the real world. A comparable technique is used when Bernard pauses in his narrative to describe the character of the new bishop. Helpfully, Bernard provides the reader with a check-list of attributes widely accepted as forming the basis of conventional sanctity — all of which Gerald is said to have possessed. These include humility, mercy, a great gentleness, a moderate abstinence, splendid modesty, amiability and an ardent love of God. But this depiction of a perfect piety is then humanized through an engaging tableau of Gerald's daily spiritual regime:

> On his knees, with hands clasped, he remained in the *oratio* until daybreak and devoted himself to pious contemplation. Sensibly he never gave thought to falconry, hunting dogs or games of chance. By day he read Holy Scripture and by night dedicated himself to prayer. In celebration of the Mass he always gave his most zealous attention [...] certainly base speech, jesting or other foolish vanity never issued from his mouth.[16]

The image of sanctity Bernard seeks to portray is firmly grounded in the conventions of his chosen genre and the demands of his audience. In addition, Bernard interweaves a number of personal details into this description in order to make Gerald seem both credible and approachable. When Bernard turns

---

[14] Archbishop Bernard of Toledo had witnessed the declaration of the First Crusade at Clermont and, fired with enthusiasm, journeyed to Rome with the intention of joining the expedition to Jerusalem. However Pope Urban intercepted the zealous prelate and ordered him back to his responsibilities in the Peninsula. Rodrigo of Toledo, *Historia de Rebus Hispaniae sive Historia Gothica*, CCCM, 72 (Turnhout: Brepols, 1978), 6, 26, pp. 209–10; Reilly, *Alfonso VI*, p. 269; Costa, 'A vacância da Sé de Braga', p. 106.

[15] André Vauchez, *Sainthood in the Later Middle Ages*, trans. by J. Birrell (Cambridge: Cambridge University Press, 2005), pp. 169–73.

[16] VSG, v. 7, pp. 54–57.

to describing the supernatural dimension to Gerald's life, he adopts the same general method.

To medieval peoples the power to work miracles provided a clear and concrete demonstration of individual human sanctity. Hagiographers were careful to cater to this expectation by including emotive descriptions of miraculous occurrences. The *Vita Sancti Geraldi* presents these miraculous events in two distinct phases, namely before and after his death. Those manifested during Gerald's lifetime are primarily of a type that has been characterized as 'traditional'. These miracles either offer protection to threatened supporters or else punishment to those hostile towards Gerald or his reforming mission. These *ante mortem* miracles also include several instances when Gerald tamed extreme natural forces, particularly storms and dangerous rivers.[17] The miracles attributed to Gerald in the *Vita Sancti Geraldi* fall quite easily into these familiar categories, but what is less conventional are the types of incidental detail Bernard included to enhance these accounts.

In order to give his descriptions of the miraculous a greater verisimilitude Bernard linked them to actual places and real people. He refers to towns and hamlets where events took place and these can be identified in contemporary documents or modern maps. For example, Bernard describes a journey in which Gerald was returning to Braga from the city of Orense. When Gerald's party was caught in a powerful rainstorm at Portela de Homem his companions feared that the nearby chapel at Rio Caldo, where they were hoping to shelter, would be flooded. However, Gerald's prayers protected both the party and their destination and when they arrived they found the chapel not only still standing but also bone dry.[18] So too with the people Bernard described. In addition to his name-dropping of major political figures such as Count Henry, Infanta Teresa and Archbishop Bernard of Toledo, there are also references to local people, many of whom can be traced in other contemporary sources.

One of the miraculous events mentioned involved Archdeacon Mido who, in supporting Gerald's reforming agenda, incurred the wrath of a certain unnamed monk. The monk had gone to the length of hiring two thugs to ambush the unsuspecting archdeacon while he was journeying far from earthly assistance. Although Archdeacon Mido was mounted on a mule and the thugs on fine horses, by commending himself to Gerald the archdeacon was able to outpace his pursuers and escape. A *Midus archidiaconus* certainly existed and is recorded as a signatory in two donations to the cathedral, dated 12 April and 21 October 1099.[19]

---

[17] Benedicta Ward, *Miracles and the Medieval Mind: Theory, Record and Event, 1000–1215* (Philadelphia: University of Pennsylvania Press, 1987), pp. 35–37. For the dangers of crossing rivers, see p. 171.

[18] VSG, v. 14, p. 56. Not only are the locations referred to identifiable, but Gerald's journey to Orense is also mentioned in other documents. In 1100 Gerald ordained Bishop Diogo of Orense (1100–1152) and received from him the obedience of a suffragan. *Liber Fidei Sanctae Bracarensis Ecclesiae*, ed. by Avelino de Jesus da Costa, 3 vols (Braga: Juntal Distrital, 1965–90), doc. 570. See also Costa, 'A vacância da Sé de Braga', p. 21.

[19] VSG, v. 11, pp. 55–56; *Liber Fidei*, docs 149 and 219; Costa, 'A vacância da Sé de Braga', pp. 20–21.

A second miracle testifying to Gerald's spiritual power — and to the lawlessness of Portuguese society at this time — concerned a wealthy woman named Toda who held estates close to Braga. Coveting her wealth, a group of local noblemen banded together with Ordonho, a rascally steward in the house of Count Henry, to kidnap Toda with the aim of forcing her into marriage. On the night before the wedding Toda determined to escape. Calling on Gerald to aid her, she dressed herself as a maid and managed to slip away from Ordonho's castle on the pretext of fetching water. For three days she concealed herself in the forests, eluding the pursuers who hunted her with hounds, until at last she reached the sanctuary of a small church. From there Toda sent a message to Gerald telling of her peril and asking for his protection; he responded immediately, sending his most reliable men to escort her back to the city. Again there is evidence to support this story. On 27 July 1103 one *D. Toda Eitaz* donated her entire lands in and around Braga to the cathedral, saving only a third of the revenues for herself while she lived. Such a grant would not only reward her protector but also remove her from the future attention of unscrupulous suitors.[20]

In the initial sections of the *Vita Sancti Geraldi* Bernard structured his portrayal of Gerald's piety by first using the conventional elements an audience expected to encounter, and then enhancing them with his own knowledge of Gerald's character and the events of his life. In this way Bernard presented an image of sanctity that is both powerful and human, which he then authenticates by describing miraculous events. These miracles were plausibly moderate disruptions of the natural world which could at the same time be accepted by an audience as a divine imprimatur to the model of sanctity being offered to them. Truth, or at least the appearance of truth, was an important element in this strategy and Bernard calls upon his familiarity with the people and places around Braga to reinforce his narrative. However there is one startling exception to this general approach, one aspect of the *vita* in which Bernard was apparently guilty of a basic misrepresentation of actual events.

Although Bernard clearly recognizes the rhetorical value of incorporating factual information into his *vita*, he also takes considerable pains to depict the Braga region prior to Gerald's arrival as a virtual wasteland and the people as having given themselves over to all manner of villainy due to an absence of suitable ecclesiastical leadership. His summary of how this situation had come to pass is direct and damning:

> Over a long period Braga had fallen into ruin and desolation, from the time of St Frutuoso (d. 665?) until the time of the venerable Bishop D. Pedro, who had accepted the *pallium* and privilege from Pope Clement and been deposed by the archbishop of Toledo, legate of the Holy Roman church, and whom — many years later — Gerald succeeded. Consequently Braga,

[20] VSG, v. 12, p. 56; *Liber Fidei*, doc. 173 (see also docs 174 and 204); Costa, 'A vacância da Sé de Braga', pp. 20–21.

which had formerly been metropolitan, was deprived more recently of its ancient dignity.[21]

However this portrayal of desolation and mismanagement was overstated to the point of deliberate distortion. Evidence from documentary sources indicate that the years prior to Gerald's arrival were in fact a time of steady development. The wealth of the diocese was consolidated and Bishop Pedro could call upon sufficient resources to undertake the construction of a new cathedral, which was completed in 1089. Following Bishop Pedro's fall the church was prudently governed by Archdeacon Rodrigo Bermundes who, while unmentioned in the *Vita Sancti Geraldi*, was subsequently elected Bishop, although he did not have this office confirmed in Rome — perhaps because he died before he could undertake the long northward journey.[22] Similarly Bernard's description of the recent past is, at best, partial. Braga did not lose its metropolitan status because of Bishop Pedro's ill-judged approach to Clement III. In fact this metropolitan status had fallen into abeyance generations earlier, in the time of Bishop Paio (d. 1002), and it was frustration at his failure to have this status restored that led Pedro to turn to the antipope.[23] As a long-serving archdeacon Bernard surely knew that the true situation was very different to the image of ruin and neglect he presented; moreover he must also have been aware that many in his audience were cognizant of the truth. Why then this elaborate fiction?

Firstly and most obviously, the creation of an image of devastation allowed Bernard to emphasize Gerald's success by contrasting the supposed chaos and mismanagement of the old regime with the efficiency and effectiveness of the new. At the same time, Gerald's assumption of authority in Braga was a critical point in Bernard's portrayal of a perfect sanctity. Theologians and hagiographers had long sought to grapple with the inherent tension between the monastic ideal of seclusion and a duty to engage with the world outside the cloister.[24] This tension was also a theme Bernard sought to address in the *Vita Sancti Geraldi*. Thus, in the description of Gerald's daily regime, such distractions as hunting dogs, games of chance, or simply idle chatter are acknowledged as just a few of the temptations the secular world presented to a spiritual leader. It is to answer this anticipated question that Bernard manufactures his vignette of Gerald's first sight of their new home:

> When he arrived at the city of Braga and saw the barbarous, depopulated and generally ruinous state of the area, he was astonished, and gave thanks

[21] *VSG*, v. 6, p. 54.
[22] Costa, 'A vacância da Sé de Braga', pp. 110-17; Luís Carlos Amaral, 'A vinda de S. Geraldo para Braga e a nova restauração da diocese,' in *IX Centenário de S. Geraldo (1108-2008). Colóquio de estudos e outros actos comemorativos* (Braga: Universidade Católica Portuguesa, 2011), pp. 156-63; and by the same author 'O património da Sé de Braga entre 1071 e 1108,' in *IX Centenário da dedicação da Sé de Braga: congresso internacional: actas*, I, 513-39.
[23] Costa, *O Bispo D. Pedro*, I, 248-51; Costa, 'A vacância da Sé de Braga', pp. 110-13.
[24] For a discussion of the origins of this tension, see Conrad Leyser, *Authority and Asceticism from Augustine to Gregory the Great* (Oxford: Clarendon Press, 2000).

to God, who had granted him such a place in which he might fully exert himself.[25]

This pious expression of *contemptus mundi* was an important means to emphasize that Gerald was not attracted by the pomp, privilege or status of his office; rather he looked upon the episcopate as an onerous duty he must bear, a means by which he might expiate his own sins in arduous toil. Nor was this to be seen as undue humility or even false modesty; rather it was a crucial issue Bernard had to address directly, since to the pure ascetic any exercise of authority, even when wielded to further a perceived greater good, carried with it the danger of spiritual corruption. This line of thinking clearly had the potential to create doubts in the minds of an audience and made some of Gerald's subsequent actions problematic for the image of sainthood that Bernard sought to create.

By accepting his new position as Bishop, Gerald also shouldered the responsibility for defending the ancient ecclesiastical rights of Braga. Most pressing of these was the cathedral's contested metropolitan status, the same issue that had brought down his predecessor, Bishop Pedro. Undeterred by recent history, Bishop Gerald took up this cause with great energy, which in turn embroiled him in a bitter three-way struggle with his former mentor, Archbishop Bernard of Toledo, and with the formidable Bishop Diego Gelmírez of Compostela.[26] In the face of a prolonged campaign of provocation and intimidation on two fronts, Gerald felt compelled to ignore the established hierarchy in Iberia and instead took his case directly to Rome. This decision represented one of the greatest challenges of his episcopate: failure would surely spell political catastrophe and personal humiliation. Yet while the entire clergy in Braga must have been fully aware what was at stake, Gerald's hagiographer gave very little attention to the bishop's dogged defence of the ancient rights of his cathedral.

In simple, unadorned language the hagiographer recounts that Gerald journeyed to Rome, where he was received with honour by Pope Paschal II. The pope invested Gerald with his *palliam*, the symbolic representation of episcopal authority. His metropolitan dignity was confirmed and the suffragan bishops in Spain were instructed to render to him the proper obedience. The restoration of Braga was subsequently announced to the assembled abbots and prelates of Spain by the papal legate, Cardinal Ricardo.[27] The reader of the *Vita Sancti Geraldi* would look in vain for any hint of the acrimony that had divided Braga from Toledo and Compostela. The Archbishop of Toledo is acknowledged as Gerald's recruiter but their later chilly relationship is overlooked, while the tempestuous Bishop of Compostela is not mentioned in any context whatsoever.

[25] VSG, v. 4, p. 54.
[26] Fletcher, *Saint James's Catapult*, pp. 108–15; Carl Erdmann, *O Papado e Portugal no primeiro século da história portuguesa* (Coimbra: Instituto Alemão da Universidade de Coimbra, 1935), pp. 10–15; Paul Feige, 'La primacía de Toledo y la libertad de las demás metrópolis de España: el ejemplo de Braga', *La introducción del Cister en España y Portugal* (Burgos: La Olmeda, 1991), pp. 74–75.
[27] VSG, v. 6, p. 54; Amaral, 'A vinda de S. Geraldo para Braga,' pp. 175–92.

Details concerning the embassy are strictly rationed and Bernard does not even make clear that Gerald was in fact obliged to make the arduous journey to Rome twice in order to achieve his goals.

It is not lack of ink or parchment that obliged Bernard to be so economical with his words. Instead this reticence seems to be a tacit recognition that Gerald's political success complicated the overall hagiographic narrative. Bernard finds himself in the odd position of creating a false picture of the devastation in Braga to underline Gerald's indifference to worldly acclaim, and then minimizing his great triumph in Rome for exactly the same reason. Significantly, while Bernard acknowledges the papal grant of episcopal authority as a requirement for office, the brief treatment he affords the ceremony suggests that a papal mandate alone could not remove all doubts concerning the moral implications of exercising worldly power. This question becomes still more pressing as Bernard turns to what he clearly believed to be the primary challenge facing Gerald in Braga: the reform of the local church.

During the eleventh century the papacy had taken the lead in a wide-scale programme of ecclesiastical reorganization which had profound social and political implications throughout Christendom. The reforming popes demanded complete independence from secular control and at the same time insisted on imposing their own authority over a more tightly disciplined Church. Under the reform agenda, secular magnates, be they emperors, kings or local nobles, could no longer control church affairs or appointments. Similarly, simony — the common practice of buying church office — was to be eradicated, along with clerical marriage (known as 'Nicholaism'). Moreover, the reformers also sought to modify ecclesiastical doctrines that regulated the personal lives of the laity. In Iberia two of these changes would prove particularly divisive. Firstly, the reformers sought to extend the degrees of kinship between potential marriage partners that were forbidden under ecclesiastical law; in Iberia this meant relationships permitted under traditional practice suddenly fell under the shadow of incest. Secondly, and perhaps most conspicuously to the majority of people, the reform papacy insisted on the replacement of the traditional liturgies, which might have been used in local churches for centuries, with an orthodox liturgy approved by Rome.[28]

This was the reform Gerald sought to bring to Braga and it is apparent from the *Vita Sancti Geraldi* that his efforts prompted widespread discontent. Immediately upon his arrival in the diocese Gerald began to institute changes, instructing the clergy in 'perfect ecclesiastical discipline', raising up those he deemed suitable, and rewarding them with the visible trappings of the new regime. These included ecclesiastical vestments, silver chalices and, most

---

[28] *Santiago, Saint-Denis and Saint Peter: The Reception of the Roman Liturgy in León-Castile in 1080*, ed. by Bernard Reilly (New York: Fordham University Press, 1985); Pierre David, 'Gregoire VII, Cluny et Alphonse VI', in *Études historiques sur la Galice e le Portugal du VIe au XIIe siècle*, ed. by P. David (Lisbon and Paris: Livraria Portugália Editora, 1947), pp. 341–439.

importantly, sacred books originating from his homeland. Behind Bernard's phlegmatic description lies the reality of a concerted bid to replace the traditional Hispanic liturgy with the new imported orthodoxy.[29] Moreover there were also local people who found themselves with specific grievances. Bernard names three knights — Egas Pelagius and two brothers, Paio Pires and Afonso Pires — who fell foul of the new ordinances on affinity and were deemed to have married incestuously. Refusing to accept Gerald's decision they ignored admonition, anathema, and finally excommunication. When Count Henry and Infanta Teresa interceded on Gerald's behalf, this show of secular force, in concert with ominous supernatural portents, brought Egas Pelagius to contrition. The two brothers, however, preferred to leave Portugal and seek sanctuary in Muslim lands. Bernard saw their decision as confirmation of a deep moral turpitude and he records their miserable deaths in exile as a just punishment for their defiance.[30]

Nor were these newly incestuous knights the only aristocratic elements opposed to reform. Secular influence over a local church had been the cause of the feud that culminated with Gerald's supporter, Archdeacon Mido, narrowly escaping the attentions of hired thugs. So too a local nobleman, Soeiro Mendes, sought to keep control of a church and was prepared to publicly debate with Gerald in defence of his customary rights. When the argument ended in an impasse Soeiro challenged his opponent to allow God to choose between them by striking down the one whose position was false. Gerald agreed and, so Bernard records, Soeiro Mendes was dead within the year.[31]

In the pages of Bernard's hagiography Gerald is portrayed as a tireless proponent of the reform agenda. His efforts to overcome the resistance of traditionalist elements in Portuguese society were supported by secular and heavenly authorities; but it was the Archbishop's own readiness to take up this burden which proved decisive. Yet Bernard is also careful to present Gerald's use of power as that of a caring and solicitous authority figure, eager to instruct rather than punish:

> The holy man armed himself with patience, seeking always to turn bad to good, calling on them ceaselessly to mend their ways. But because they were obstinate in their depravity they refused to heed his words [...].[32]

Bernard's image of Gerald is as a teacher confronted by heedless, unruly pupils and his piety is exemplified in his calm resolve to correct their errors. Moreover, in the course of Gerald's confrontation with those opposed to the reform agenda Bernard is able to emphasize another aspect of the burden the

---

[29] VSG, v. 5, p. 54. It is still possible to trace Gerald's hand in the post-reform liturgy. Joaquim Félix de Carvalho, 'S. Geraldo e a liturgia,' in *IX Centenário de S. Geraldo (1108–2008)*, pp. 113–54; Bragança, 'Braga and Moissac', pp. 189–95.
[30] VSG, v. 8–9, p. 55.
[31] VSG, v. 15, p. 56.
[32] VSG, v. 9, p. 55.

archbishop assumed in Braga. Throughout the *Vita Sancti Geraldi*, simmering just below the surface, is the suspicion of a certain cultural dissonance between the French immigrants and the native population, a consciousness of otherness that bursts into view during the confrontations between Gerald and the recalcitrant knights.

From the first sentences of the *Vita Sancti Geraldi* attention is drawn to Gerald's French origins and training. Bernard also describes the future archbishop falling prey to feelings of isolation when he looked up at strange stars or was called upon to communicate in the language of another people.[33] Certainly Bernard himself, who shared these exotic origins, felt an abiding sense of dislocation. When describing himself, the first characteristic Bernard lists is his Gaulish heritage and he refers rather plaintively to his situation as being 'an exile and stranger in a foreign realm'.[34] Furthermore, just as the immigrant Frenchmen sometimes felt excluded from the wider community, so too the local people felt a corresponding sense of distance. A culturally based animosity flares during Gerald's encounter with the two Pires brothers. Overcome with anger, Paio Pires accuses Gerald of being false and hypocritical, and ends his tirade with an enraged shout: 'Your sanctity is not worth a single rooster!'[35] This odd insult seems to be a play on the old Latin pun linking 'gallus' (rooster) with 'Gallus' (resident of Gaul) — a pun which was growing old even in the time of the Caesars.[36] But ultimately the joke, or so Bernard assures his audience, rebounded on Paio Pires: as a result of his obduracy the nobleman lost his lands and his followers. He is left a pathetic figure, departing into exile accompanied only by his infant son and a single faithful dog. The punchline to the story is the small added detail that the loyal dog, last of all Paio's many followers, was a Gallic hound. Bernard seems to relish reversing this insulting play on words — one he had no doubt heard too often — and in doing so reveals a rather ironic sense of humour, tinged perhaps with a residual bitterness.

Yet, when he dwells on these memories, Bernard does not seem to be indulging a desire for retribution. Rather his intention is to weave this additional burden Gerald has borne into the overall portrayal of his sanctity. Throughout the *vita* Bernard returns to a recurring theme of exile. This is the fate, worse even than death, which befalls the most reprehensible of the rogues Gerald encountered. The Pires brothers for example, both came to a miserable end far from their native land. Paio converted to Islam and died 'an exile and virtual prisoner'. His brother Afonso fared even worse. Seeking revenge on those who had driven him out, the embittered nobleman joined in attacking Christian lands alongside the Moors, and shared in their destruction. His body, left unburied in the

---

[33] *VSG*, v. 2, p. 54.
[34] *VSG*, v. 36, p. 59.
[35] *VSG*, v. 9, p. 55.
[36] Gaius Suetonius Tranquillus, 'Life of Vitellius,' in *The Twelve Caesars*, trans. by R. Graves (London: Penguin Classics, 2007), xviii, p. 273.

wastelands, was pecked apart by vultures and crows.[37] So too Soeiro Mendes, who had the temerity to challenge Gerald to a duel of faith, died within the year, a solitary exile, far from his own land.[38] Yet with each iteration of this greatest of all punishments Bernard is also emphasizing that, in taking up the burden of his duties in Braga, Gerald was accepting the same bitter fate. For the good of the community of the faithful, rather than any desire for worldly things, he chose voluntary exile from his own land and people. Bernard is careful to consolidate this point still further in his description of Gerald's final days.

A convention of hagiographical literature is that death marks the apogee of the protagonist's earthly journey and the moment where a mortal human becomes an immortal saint. Hagiographers are therefore careful to arrange the events leading up to the death scene so as to maximize the emotional impact of this point of transition. In the *Vita Sancti Geraldi* Bernard seeks to bring together themes he has developed in earlier sections to create just such a dramatic culmination. He begins by recounting how Gerald, despite feeling the weight of many years upon him, embarked on one last journey:

> He determined to visit the poor, rustic folk who dwelt in the mountains, for these uncultivated people had never before heard learned preaching or received correct instruction in sacred matters.[39]

In the pursuit of this final mission Gerald turns away from the wealth and privilege of his position in the city to pursue his calling among the poorest and — to Gerald's eyes — most alienated in society. He embraces the role of teacher and it is the power of his message, rather than any worldly status, which grants him the authority he needs in this wildest of places. While Bernard seems to be harking back to the great missionary saints, his portrayal also echoes the ideas espoused by another major ecclesiastical figure, Pope Gregory the Great, who had grappled with the apparent incompatibility of the monastic ideal and the duty to take an active role in the world. He had sought to reconcile these positions by arguing that the truly moral life was to perfect oneself through private contemplation and then turn outwards to bring this learning to the wider community.[40] Therefore the true vocation for the righteous man was to instruct others on the paths to sanctity — and this seems to be a proposition Bernard accepted. Certainly Gerald is portrayed as following this path until the end. For the strain of preaching proved too much for his aging body and he succumbed to an illness in the small hamlet of Bornes on 5 December 1108.

Bernard describes Gerald's death as being attended by celestial visions in which his companions were reassured by angels that the archbishop had been accepted into the company of the saints. Bornes lies more than ninety kilometres from Braga and the journey back, which Bernard portrays more as a triumphant

---

[37] *VSG*, v. 9, p. 55.
[38] *VSG*, v. 15, p. 56.
[39] *VSG*, v. 18, p. 56.
[40] Leyser, *Authority and Asceticism*, pp. 131–87.

parade than a funeral march, drew huge crowds of sorrowful and reverent people. Omens and portentous events accompanied the returning cortège and when Gerald was buried in the church of St Nicholas in Braga — a church he had founded himself — miracles were soon reported in the vicinity. Bernard described these miracles in considerable detail and they appear quite different from the supernatural events that had occurred during Gerald's lifetime. The *ante mortem* 'traditional' miracles were most often either protective or punitive, channelling aid to Gerald's supporters or punishments to those who assailed him. The miracles that were witnessed after his death were of the milder type sometimes characterized as 'modern'. These manifestations of saintly power consisted primarily of petitioners afflicted with injury or disease finding healing at his shrine.[41] Bernard recounted these miracles with great artistry in an effort to demonstrate to his audience that Archbishop Gerald had indeed been found worthy of this ultimate honour.

In the final sections of the *Vita Sancti Geraldi* twelve miraculous events are described and Bernard follows his customary method of interleaving the miraculous with details drawn from a more mundane reality.[42] Two of the twelve miracle stories concern supernatural aid given to travellers in distress; the other ten describe healings, and in the majority of cases the symptoms are recorded, along with the names and dwelling places of the people cured. The recipients of these miracles were drawn from all sections of society: priests, monks, noble ladies, burghers from the towns, country-folk and orphans. The illnesses they suffered ranged from complete paralysis to injuries sustained from incautiously swallowing a fish-bone or wounds inflicted by wild pigs. All who petitioned the saint with the necessary penitence received his aid and Bernard recalls with satisfaction that the fortunate pilgrims who benefited at the shrine returned to their towns and families extoling Saint Gerald's holy powers. But the most dramatic witness is held back until the last. Following his litany of the miraculous, Bernard reveals that he too was among those who had been healed by the intervention of the saint. The hagiographer confides that when a tumour in his throat was declared by doctors to be both untreatable and terminal he made a heartfelt plea to Gerald for assistance — and within a day his health had been restored. Thus Bernard presents himself as a direct witness to Saint Gerald's miraculous power and the undeniable fact that he had survived to write the hagiography is submitted to the reader as an ultimate authentication of the portrait of sanctity he had created within its pages.

The *Vita Sancti Geraldi* is a remarkable work of commemoration in which Bernard artfully arranged the events of Gerald's life to construct a compelling case that the French immigrant monk had achieved a perfect sanctity in Portugal. The contemplative life in Moissac provided Gerald with the knowledge and virtue to instruct others; he then perfected the holiness of the

---

[41] Ward, *Miracles and the Medieval Mind*, pp. 35–37.
[42] VSG, v. 24–36, pp. 57–59.

monastery by caring for those dwelling in the hostile regions at the furthest edge of the world. The pious elements of his life fuse together in his death, and his entrance into the company of saints is confirmed by the miraculous cures he grants to the afflicted who visit his tomb. As a hagiographer, Bernard's primary concern was to celebrate Gerald's spiritual journey rather than to record the great political and historical events of his times. Yet his intention was also to influence his audience, and in this lies the great value of Bernard's writing to the modern historian. To sway his readers Bernard found it necessary to provide them with a depiction of an actual world they could at least recognize. Thus the *Vita Sancti Geraldi* presents a plausible picture of a turbulent, varied and complex society, along with a uniquely revealing insight into the cultural tensions convulsing it. For in addition to being a commentator Bernard was a participant, and because he shared Gerald's cultural background his work has a rare poignancy. When Bernard wrote of a saint's exile he also reflected his own sense of social alienation; he describes Gerald's achievements and sacrifices so powerfully because, in a deeply personal way, he had shared in them. Nor did he write in vain: the land which had on occasion seemed so alien now numbers both Bernard and Gerald among its national pantheon of venerated bishops, saints and hagiographers.

Seeing is Believing:
The Miniatures in the *Cantigas de Santa Maria* and Medieval Devotional Practices

KIRSTIN KENNEDY

Victoria and Albert Museum, London

The *Cantigas de Santa Maria* comprise 420 poems which recount the miracles of, and offer praise to, the Virgin Mary. The poems survive in four thirteenth-century manuscripts. Three include music to accompany the poems (in the fourth, the staves remain blank), and two of the manuscripts (known as the 'códice rico' and the 'Florence' codex after their appearance and location respectively) illustrate each poem with panels of miniatures as well.[1] After seven centuries, the miniatures seem to offer a window on a vanished world, and their status as a vivid reflection of medieval life is exhaustively argued in José Guerrero Lovillo's 1949 study of the utensils, furnishings, clothing and buildings represented in the 'códice rico' in the library at El Escorial, which, he found, matched up with the available archaeological evidence.[2] In the years since then, the richly illuminated 'Florence' codex has been subjected to the same scrutiny, colour facsimiles of the 'códice rico' and 'Florence' manuscripts have appeared, and many studies on the working practices of the artists, the relationship between text and image and the significance of a particular use of a visual motif have been published.[3] The importance of the miniatures in the

---

[1] The manuscripts are Madrid, Biblioteca Nacional, MS 10069 (poems set to music, but without miniatures); El Escorial, Real Biblioteca del Monasterio, MS T.I.1 (the 'códice rico', which has poems set to music and illustrated with panels of miniatures) and MS b.I.2 (poems set to music, but only every tenth one accompanied by a single miniature depicting musicians); Florence, Biblioteca Nazionale, MS Banco Rari 20 (the 'Florence' manuscript, with poems accompanied by panels of miniatures, mostly complete, but ruled staves remain blank), and see Stephen Parkinson's overview of the poems in *A Companion to Portuguese Literature*, ed. by Stephen Parkinson, Cláudia Pazos Alonso and T. F. Earle (Woodbridge: Tamesis, 2009), pp. 40–43. For an exhaustive bibliography of studies on Alfonsine poetry, see Joseph T. Snow, *The Poetry of Alfonso X: An Annotated Critical Bibliography (1278–2010)* (Woodbridge: Tamesis, 2012). The searchable database of the texts, metrics and codicology of the manuscripts, established by Parkinson as part of the Centre for the Study of the *Cantigas de Santa Maria* of Oxford University, is available online: <http://csm.mml.ox.ac.uk/> [accessed 20 October 2014].
[2] José Guerrero Lovillo, *Las Cántigas: estudio arqueológico de sus miniaturas* (Madrid: CSIC, 1949).
[3] *El 'Códice rico' de las 'Cantigas' de Alfonso X, el Sabio. Ms T.I.1 de la Biblioteca de El Escorial*, Serie B, Códices artísticos, ediciones facsímiles, 2, 2 vols (Madrid: Edilán, 1979) [henceforth 'Códice rico, facsimile']; Alfonso X el Sabio, *Las Cantigas de Santa María: Códice rico, MS T-I-1, Real Biblioteca del Monasterio de San Lorenzo de El Escorial*, ed. by Laura Fernández Fernández and Carlos Ruiz Sousa, 2 vols (Madrid: Patrimonio Nacional / Testimonio Compañía Editorial / Scriptorium, 2011); '*Cantigas de Santa María': Edición Facsímil del Códice B.R. 20 de la Biblioteca Nazionale Centrale de Florencia*,

overall composition of the manuscripts has also been analysed more critically. The panels structure the sequence of poems in the codices, and the way in which they combine with the text enabled Stephen Parkinson to establish the textual relationship between the four manuscripts and confirm earlier suggestions that the 'códice rico' and the 'Florence' codex were conceived as a two-volume set. Recently he has shown how the emphasis of the expanding collection shifted from the personal to the political.[4]

The miniatures do not simply translate the contents of the poems into visual form, as the illustrations for all the poems, whatever their length, are limited to six or twelve frames;[5] some compression, or even simplification, of the textual narrative is therefore necessary.[6] Another reason for the divergence between text and image lies in the complications of the process of manuscript assembly itself. Parkinson's analysis of text and layout led him to argue that the manuscripts were not copied directly from a stable exemplar, but that compilers and artists worked separately and had access to a range of working materials.[7] Ana Domínguez, meanwhile, argued that some images assembled by the miniaturists display a considerable degree of iconographic innovation, inspired in part by devotional practices advocated by the Franciscan Order, and in part by Alfonso's own political agenda.[8] Layered within the images of miracle

---

siglo XIII, 2 vols (Madrid: Edilán, 1989-91). For the miniatures as a source for social history, see Amparo García Cuadrado, Las 'Cantigas': El códice de Florencia (Murcia: Universidad de Murcia / Real Academia de Alfonso X el Sabio, 1993); John Esten Keller and Annette Grant Cash, Daily Life Depicted in the 'Cantigas de Santa Maria', Studies in Romance Languages, 44 (Lexington: University Press of Kentucky, 1998). For other approaches to the miniatures, see for example Ana Domínguez Rodríguez, 'Texto, imagen y diseño de la página en los códices de Alfonso X el Sabio (1252-1284)', in Imágenes y promotores en el arte medieval: miscelánea en homenaje a Joaquín Yarza Luaces, ed. by María Luisa Melero Moneo and others (Barcelona: Universidad Autònoma, 2001), pp. 313-26; Deirdre Jackson, 'The Influence of the Theophilus Legend: An Overlooked Miniature in Alfonso X's Cantigas de Santa Maria and its Wider Concept', in Under the Influence: The Concept and the Study of Illuminated Manuscripts, ed. by John Lowden and Alixe Bovey (Turnhout: Brepols, 2007), pp. 75-87; Laura Fernández Fernández, 'Imagen e intención: la representación de Santiago Apóstol en los manuscritos de las Cantigas de Santa María', Anales de Historia del Arte, 18 (2008), 73-94.

[4] Stephen Parkinson, 'Layout in the Códices ricos of the Cantigas de Santa Maria', Hispanic Research Journal, 1.2 (October 2000), 243-74 (p. 246); idem, 'Alfonso X, Miracle Collector', in Las Cantigas, ed. by Fernández Fernández and Ruiz Sousa, pp. 80-100.

[5] As noted, for example, by Mihai Iacob, 'A retórica visual no "Códice Rico" das Cantigas de Santa María', Boletín Galego de Literatura, 36-37 (2006-07), 37-59 (p. 45). A lone exception is the miniature that accompanies the first 'loor', or poem of praise, to the Virgin in the 'códice rico', which has eight panels.

[6] For miniatures as a simplification of the text, see Iacob, 'A retórica visual', p. 42, and Ana Domínguez Rodríguez, 'San Bernardo y la religiosidad cisterciense en las Cantigas de Santa María: con unas reflexiones sobre el método iconográfico', in Literatura y cristiandad: homenaje al Profesor Jesús Montoya Martínez (con motivo de su jubilación): (estudios sobre hagiografía, mariología, épica y retórica), ed. by Manuel José Alonso García, María Luisa Dañobeitia Fernández and Antonio Rafael Rubio Flores (Granada: Universidad de Granada, 2001), pp. 289-317 (pp. 296-97).

[7] 'The Evolution of Cantiga 113: Composition, Recomposition, and Emendation in the Cantigas de Santa Maria', La corónica, 35.2 (Spring 2007), 227-72 (pp. 263 and 268). For prose accounts of miracles as an alternative source for the miniaturists, see Vicente Beltrán, 'Texto verbal y texto pictórico: las cantigas 1 y 10 del Códice Rico', Revista Canadiense de Estudios Hispánicos, 9.3 (1984-85), 329-43.

[8] Ana Domínguez Rodríguez, '"Compassio" y "co-redemptio" en las Cantigas de Santa María: Crucifixión y Juício final', Archivo Español de Arte, 281 (1998), 17-35 (p. 35). The influence of a particular Franciscan, Juan Gil de Zamora, on the composition of the Cantigas, is argued by Rocío

narratives or praise to the Virgin are messages about devotional practice, political hierarchy and theological doctrine. In this article I will focus on details in the miniatures that indicate how the artists and their audience understood the world around them and the role of the miraculous therein.[9] My analysis draws on recent studies that highlight the important role played by objects, materials and the senses in thirteenth-century worship.[10]

The splendid appearance of the two richly illuminated manuscripts of the *Cantigas* itself suggests the importance of visual stimuli as well as textual narrative to arouse spiritual devotion;[11] the music which accompanies the poems makes a further appeal to the sense of hearing. Reference to the important role played by the senses in the perception of miracles is constant in the textual narrative of the *Cantigas*. In *cantiga* 152, the Virgin presents a knight with 'hũa branq' escudela | de prata, grand' e fremosa, | chẽa dun manjar mui jalne, | non de vida saborosa, | mas amarga, e sen esto | dava mui maos odores' ['a shining bowl of silver, large and beautiful, full of a dark yellow substance. It was not a tasty food but bitter, and [...] it emitted a foul odor'], which she explains is symbolic of his outer and inner life.[12] In *cantiga* 56, by contrast, the prayers to the Virgin recited by a monk during his lifetime are transformed into five red roses which spring from his mouth when he dies. The five roses, symbolic of the Virgin and the number of letters in her name, also imply the transmutation of the sound of the monk's prayers into a sweet scent that will rise to heaven, just as the Bible explains the perfumed incense of prayer ascends to God.[13] Quite a different sound is made by the tendons of a contorted, crippled

---

Sánchez Ameijeiras, '"Ymagenes Sanctae": Fray Juan Gil de Zamora y la teoría de la imagen sagrada en las *Cantigas de Santa María*', in *Homenaje a José García Oro*, ed. by Miguel Romaní and María Ángeles Novoa Gómez (Santiago de Compostela: Universidad de Santiago de Compostela, 2002), pp. 515–26.

[9] On the different types of information conveyed by texts and images, see the comments in Cynthia Hahn, 'Visio Dei: Changes in Medieval Visuality', in *Visuality before and beyond the Renaissance: Seeing as Others Saw*, ed. by Robert S. Nelson (Cambridge: Cambridge University Press, 2000), pp. 169–96 (p. 170).

[10] The most comprehensive study on the topic is Caroline Walker Bynum, *Christian Materiality: An Essay on Religion in Late Medieval Europe* (New York: Zone Books, 2011), and see the review by Daniel Joslyn-Siemiatkoski in *Anglican and Episcopal History*, 82.1 (March 2013), 119–24 (p. 120). For the application of this approach to a particular object, see Jacqueline E. Jung, 'Crystalline Wombs and Pregnant Hearts: The Exuberant Bodies of the *Katharinenthal* Visitation Group', in *History in the Comic Mode: Medieval Communities and the Matter of Person*, ed. by Rachel Fulton and Bruce W. Holsinger (New York: Columbia University Press, 2007), pp. 223–37.

[11] For the importance of images in medieval discussions of devotion, see Hahn, pp. 183–87.

[12] Alfonso X, *Cantigas de Santa María*, ed. by Walter Mettmann, 3 vols (Madrid: Castalia, 1986–89), II (1988) [henceforth *Cantigas*], 152. 22–24; the English translation can be found in Alfonso X, *Songs of Holy Mary of Alfonso X the Wise: A Translation of the 'Cantigas de Santa Maria'*, trans. by Kathleen Kulp-Hill, Medieval and Renaissance Texts and Studies, 173 (Tempe: Arizona Center for Medieval and Renaissance Texts and Studies, 2000) [henceforth Kulp-Hill], p. 186. Further references to both these editions in abbreviated form are given after quotations in the text. For the evil associations of the colour yellow, see Herman Pleij, *Colors Demonic and Divine: Shades of Meaning in the Middle Ages and After*, trans. by Diane Webb (New York: Columbia University Press, 2004), p. 77.

[13] Revelation 8. 4. For the miniature, see *Códice rico*, Facsimile, I, fol. 83^r, frame five. The miniature is also reproduced in Keller and Grant Cash, plate 31. For the monk as St Bernard, see Domínguez Rodríguez, 'San Bernardo', pp. 314–16.

woman, which creak and crack 'como carr' en pedregal' (*Cantigas*, II, 179. 38) ['like a cart rolling over stones' (Kulp-Hill, p. 215)] at the moment of her cure during Mass by Santa Maria de Salas.

The miniatures also stress the important role played by the senses in people's experience of miracles, and on occasion they supplement the text by depicting the response of the faithful. The conclusion of *cantiga* 11 omits any reference to rituals of praise and thanksgiving at the resurrection of a drowned monk. The final miniature that accompanies the poem, on the other hand, shows how the monks rejoice in the recovery of their drowned treasurer by engaging in different activities that appeal to different senses. They ring the monastery bell, light candles and lamps (also an allusion to the divine light which guides the spiritual vision of Christians), and kneel gratefully to gaze towards the church altar.[14]

The combination of sight, touch, sound, smell, and even taste, was necessary to create an unforgettable mental picture in a person's memory but the senses were not all of equal value in a Christian's journey towards knowledge of God. Twelfth- and thirteenth-century theologians considered sight the most important, because it involved the viewer immediately in an ascending hierarchy of knowledge that could lead to a closer relationship with the divine.[15] There were three levels of vision. Corporeal vision was the lowest, and comprised what the viewer saw with the eyes of his or her body. Intellectual vision occurred in the highest levels of the mind and was the site of the perception of divine truths. Spiritual vision was an intermediate state that involved the recollection of corporeal sight in dreams or in the memory, and which could sometimes reveal divine truth.[16] The mechanics of vision also involved a physical process. The eye emitted a visual ray (or 'species' as medieval scholars such as Juan Gil de Zamora, a Franciscan friar associated with Alfonso, termed the object matter) which, strengthened by the presence of light, darted out to encounter an object. The object that was the focus of this eye-light also emitted rays and the 'species' of viewer and viewed mingled and returned to the viewer's eye, where they arrived eventually in the viewer's memory.[17] The purpose of combining *cantigas* with miniatures, then, was more than decorative or structural. The images were intended to penetrate and influence the viewer's mind, and the importance of sight in this context is emphasized by the artists within the illustrations themselves. They are, moreover, careful to distinguish between corporeal and spiritual vision.

---

[14] *Códice rico*, Facsimile, I, fol. 19ᵛ.

[15] Sarah Lipton, '"The Sweet Lean of His Head": Writing about Looking at the Crucifix in the High Middle Ages', *Speculum*, 80 (2005), 1172–1208 (p. 1179); Hahn, p. 188. For the role of the senses in a pilgrim's experience of Canterbury Cathedral, see Emma J. Wells, 'Making "Sense" of the Pilgrimage Experience of the Medieval Church', *Peregrinations: International Society for the Study of Pilgrimage Art*, 3.2 (Summer 2011), 122–46 (p. 145).

[16] For a summary of these theories, see Hahn, pp. 171–74.

[17] Hahn, pp. 174–75, Michael Camille, *Gothic Art* (London: Weidenfeld and Nicolson, 1996), pp. 21–23; Suzannah Biernoff, *Sight and Embodiment in the Middle Ages* (Basingstoke: Palgrave Macmillan, 2002). For Gil de Zamora, see Sánchez Ameijeiras, p. 519, n. 13.

It is corporeal vision which prompts the kneeling old woman who gazes up at a painted, gilded statue of the Virgin and Child in *cantiga* 38 to repent of her sins.[18] Corporeal vision is also the means by which miraculous events are confirmed. It is not coincidental that the sick cured by the Virgin are people with highly visible conditions, such as leprosy, twisted or crippled limbs, or bodies stabbed by weapons.[19] The closing miniature of many *cantigas* illustrates the textual account of ritualized praise in which the recipient of the miracle and a group of worshippers, lay or ecclesiastical, gaze at an image of the Virgin, the miracle-giver, their presence lending credibility to the events.[20] To be deprived of sight, on the other hand, was potentially a step towards damnation. *Cantiga* 90 praises the Virgin by arguing how her presence confounds the devil. The final miniature includes a detail, not described in the text, that underlines the Virgin's triumph and the connection between physical and spiritual blindness. The devil lies vanquished before an altar between two angels. One holds his head while the other pokes out his eye with his finger.[21]

Spiritual vision, on the other hand, is the result of a closer relationship with the divine and the miniaturists depict it in different ways. In *cantiga* 5 the text explains how St Basil, exhausted after leading his people in prayer and penitence to fend off the Emperor Julian's army, falls asleep before the altar of the Virgin. The miniature shows him prone but with eyes open, gazing up at a vision of her. The blind priest in *cantiga* 92 who, according to the caption to the miniature, sleeps before the altar, is also depicted with his eyes wide open. The Virgin stands before him, looks down and points at him. Similarly, the deaf-mute in *cantiga* 101 stares at the Virgin in a miniature which illustrates the moment when the text explains that he, too, sleeps before the altar.[22] The miniatures, more clearly than the text, are able to highlight the paradox of those who see when they appear to do the opposite. Other recipients of spiritual vision are depicted unambiguously asleep in bed. This is the case of the 'holy man' who is visited by the Virgin in *cantiga* 87, and also the sleeping figure (not mentioned in the text) who lies beneath the Virgin and heavenly host in the

---

[18] *Cantigas*, I, 38. 35–42; *Códice rico* Facsimile, I, fol. 57^v; the miniatures are also reproduced in Ana Domínguez Rodríguez and Pilar Treviño Gajardo, *Las 'Cantigas de Santa María': formas e imágenes* (Madrid: AyN Ediciones, 2007), p. 151. José Guerrero Lovillo, 'Las miniaturas', in *Códice rico*, Facsimile, II, 271–405 (p. 295) cites this poem as an example of sacred splendour as a force for religious conversion.

[19] See for example the panels of miniatures in *Códice rico*, Facsimile, I, which accompany *cantigas* 15 (fol. 27^r, a leper covered with pustules), 61 (fol. 89^v, a man with severely deformed facial features) and 126 (fol. 179^r, a man with an arrow embedded in his cheek). Details of the afflicted from these poems also reproduced in Menéndez Pidal, pp. 162–63. Cf. Esther Cohen, *The Modulated Scream: Pain in Late Medieval Culture* (Chicago, IL: University of Chicago Press, 2009), pp. 133–34.

[20] Deirdre Jackson, 'Saint and Simulacra: Images of the Virgin in the *Cantigas de Santa Maria* of Alfonso X of Castile (1252-1284)' (unpublished doctoral thesis, Courtauld Institute of Art, University of London, 2002), p. 59.

[21] See *Códice rico*, Facsimile, I, fol. 132^r, and in Domínguez Rodríguez and Treviño Gajardo, p. 131.

[22] *Códice rico*, Facsimile, I, fols 11^v–12^r; fol. 134^r; fol. 146^r.

miniatures that accompany *cantiga* 110.[23] Sleep has transported both men to a higher spiritual plane.

Conversely, those who have only corporeal vision are unaware of the presence of the divine and only appreciate this divine intervention when the person who has experienced the vision recounts their experience to them. The blind priest's assistant stands behind him at the moment of the priest's vision, but his eyes are depicted firmly closed. The textual narrative of Basil's miraculous vision explains how he sees St Mercurius slaying Julian and how the Virgin presents him with a written account of these events, bound up in a book. Basil then emerges from his trance-like state and, together with a companion, goes to Mercurius' tomb, where he discovers that the saint's weapons are missing. This confirms to him that his dream was real, and he gives an account of it to his people. The miniature that deals with the immediate aftermath of Basil's vision in *cantiga* 15 emphasizes the importance of sight in the form of images — Basil is not shown reading a book — and highlights the difference between the saint's privileged vision and the limited sight of his companion. When the pair arrive at the tomb, the companion points upwards to the missing arms, while Basil, privileged with divine insight, points to a statue of the Virgin to explain the absence of the weapons.

The gaze of saints upon people was equally important, and in the *Cantigas* this can have political undertones. *Cantiga* 20 praises the Virgin for her tireless defence of mankind from the devil. The fifth miniature is captioned 'Como Santa Maria nos castiga que seiamos boos' ['How Holy Mary instructs us to be good'] and the image depicts two groups of people kneeling either side of an apparition of the Virgin.[24] Those to the Virgin's right are churchmen: led by a bishop, they kneel, clasp their hands and look up at her. Those to her left are laymen. Their position and gestures are identical to those of the ecclesiastics, and they are led by Alfonso (identified as such by the heraldic castles, for the kingdom of Castile, on his robes) who kneels at the same level as the bishop. Although the churchmen occupy the traditionally privileged position to the Virgin's right, in fact it is the king and his followers who are blessed with the sight of her face, as she directs her gaze towards them.[25] In other miniatures a

---

[23] *Cantigas*, I, 87. 20–40 and *Códice rico* Facsimile, fol. 128^r; *Cantigas*, II, 110; *Códice rico* Facsimile, fol. 157^v and see Joseph T. Snow, 'Poetic Self-Awareness in Alfonso's *Cantiga* 110', *Kentucky Romance Quarterly*, 26 (1979), 421–32.

[24] Transcribed in Guerrero Lovillo, *Las Cántigas*, p. 381, and the English translation in Kathleen Kulp-Hill, 'The Captions to the Miniatures of the "Códice Rico" of the *Cantigas de Santa Maria*: A Translation', *Bulletin of the Cantigueiros de Santa Maria*, 7 (1995), 3–64 (p. 12). The miniatures are in *Códice rico*, Facsimile, I, fol. 32^v. For the linguistic and lexicographical information preserved in the miniature rubrics, and a warning about the accuracy of published transcriptions, see José-Martinho Montero Santalha, 'As legendas das miniaturas das "Cantigas de Santa Maria" (códices T e F)', in *Estudos dedicados a Ricardo Carvalho Calero*, ed. by José Luís Rodríguez, 2 vols (Santiago de Compostela: Universidad de Santiago de Compostela, 2000), II, 507–52.

[25] Cf. the commentary in *Las 'Cantigas de Loor' de Alfonso X el Sabio*, ed. and trans. by Luis Beltrán (Madrid: Ediciones Júcar, 1990), pp. 28–35. For the associations of the right side, see for example Acts 2. 33–34.

saint's gaze is the catalyst for moral reform. *Cantiga* 151 describes how a priest devoted to the Virgin but addicted to sex repents and enters holy orders. The priest lives next to a church and can see the interior of the building from his bedroom window. The text refers to the altars in the church and, in an allusion to the importance of the visual, describes how its stained glass windows 'glisten', even though it is night.[26] The miniatures, on the other hand, omit any representation of the windows and instead emphasize the role played by viewer and viewed in the cleric's decision to abandon his sinful ways. The second frame depicts a statue of the Virgin and Child on an altar. Mary looks down at Jesus; the Christ Child looks back to the previous miniature and, specifically, at the priest who, in bed with his concubine, directs his gaze across to the altar. As a result, the priest is physically unable to make love, and leaves his house in remorse.[27]

The power of sight to stir violent emotions is acknowledged in the Alfonsine *Primera Partida*, which condemns excessive mourning of the dead. The law code records that canon law 'defendió que quando touiessen los muertos en la eglesia, que les no touiessen las caras descubiertas [...] porque los omnes en catándolos no se mouiessen a auer piadat' ['forbade that when a corpse was taken into the church it should have its face uncovered; and this was done lest men looking upon it might be so moved to pity as to mourn greatly on its account'].[28] This prohibition is reflected in the depiction of a monk pronounced dead by members of his order in *cantiga* 54: in frame three of the panel his body is shrouded and his whole head is concealed by a brownish-grey cloth.[29] Yet in the context of Christian worship, the visible was essential to stir emotions of pity and compassion for Christ's sacrifice in the hearts of the devout. This is clearly set out in the text of *cantiga* 50, which praises the Virgin for giving birth to Jesus and thereby giving physical form to God. This, the poem explains, is vital, for 'nen amor con doo nunca dos seus feitos seus | ouueramos, se el non foss' [...] | tal que nossos ollos o podessen catar' (*Cantigas*, I, 50. 10–13) ['We would never feel love mixed with pity for his deeds, if he were not such [...] that we could see him with our eyes'].[30] In the third miniature to illustrate this poem, Alfonso kneels before the scene of the Flagellation and covers his face with his robes in a gesture of weeping. His violently emotional response to Christ's torture reflects

---

[26] *Cantigas*, II, 151. 17; Kulp-Hill, p. 185. For stained glass and the medieval religious experience, see Wells, p. 127.
[27] Jackson, 'Saint and Simulacra', pp. 141–44 and *Códice rico*, Facsimile, I, fol. 206[r].
[28] Alfonso X el Sabio, *Primera Partida (manuscrito Add. 20.787 del British Museum)*, ed. by Juan Antonio Arias Bonet (Valladolid: Universidad de Valladolid, 1975), Partida I, título IV, ley xlii (p. 45); English translation in Alfonso X, *Las Siete Partidas*, trans. by Samuel Parsons Scott [first pub. 1931], 5 vols, rev. ed. by Robert I. Burns (Philadelphia: University of Pennsylvania Press, 2001), I: *The Medieval Church: The World of Clerics and Laymen*, Law xliv, p. 36.
[29] *Códice rico*, Facsimile, I, fol. 80[r] and also Domínguez Rodríguez and Treviño Gajardo, p. 44.
[30] My translation; Kulp-Hill, p. 66, is misleading; '*Cantigas de Loor*', ed. by Beltrán, p. 132, has an accurate Spanish version.

the pity aroused in him by what he saw.[31] His retinue observe the scene but make no gestures to betray emotion, which suggests only the king is privileged to receive this intense spiritual experience occasioned by sight.

Other miniatures gloss the text in more subtle ways to demonstrate the presence of the divine in visible and tangible form. Miraculous transformation of living matter is at the centre of the story of the Virgin birth, and the miniatures that accompany *cantiga* 29 suggest that this miracle can be read as an echo of the Immaculate Conception.[32] The narrative records how images of the Virgin and Child appeared miraculously on stones at Gethsemane. The refrain, recalling contemporary theories about the physical impact on the mind of things seen, states that 'nas mentes senpre tēer | devemo-las sas feituras | da Virgen, pois receber | as foron as pedras duras' (*Cantigas*, I, 29. 3-6) ['We should always keep in our minds the features of the Virgin, for the hard stones received their impressions' (Kulp-Hill, p. 40)]. The 'hard stones' of the text are interpreted by the miniaturist as two white columns. This alludes to the specific identification of the stones in the original account of the miracles as columns that supported the baldachin above the Virgin's tomb, and reflects the poem's assertion (also based on earlier sources) that the stones 'shone and glowed' (*Cantigas*, I, 29. 21-22; Kulp-Hill, p. 40).[33] The miraculous image of the Virgin and Child is drawn in outline by the miniaturist, while the text emphasizes that the image is neither painted nor carved (*Cantigas*, I, 29. 10-15).[34] The transformation of the stone columns, therefore, is profound rather than superficial, a fact emphasized in the miniature by the depiction of the devout, who gather round the columns to touch and kiss the images (rather than just gaze upon them).[35] It is also a transformation effected on living matter. Stones, as the prologue to the Alfonsine *Lapidario* acknowledged, were living

---

[31] *Códice rico*, Facsimile, I, fol. 74ᵛ, also in Domínguez Rodríguez and Treviño Gajardo, p. 37. For weeping as an appropriate response to Christ's Passion, see Rachel Fulton, 'Praying to the Crucified Christ', in *From Judgment to Passion: Devotion to Christ and the Virgin Mary, 800-1200* (New York: Columbia University Press, 2002), pp. 66-67; for the iconography of Christ and the Virgin in this poem, see Domínguez Rodríguez, '"Compassio"'.

[32] *Códice rico*, Facsimile, I, fol. 44ʳ, and Domínguez Rodríguez and Treviño Gajardo, p. 112. Cf. Sánchez Ameijeiras, p. 525, for the narrative as a reflection of Franciscan enthusiasm for images that miraculously impress themselves on matter; for the miracle as Alfonso's efforts 'to communicate Mary's real, ubiquitous and detextualized presence to his subjects' see Francisco Prado-Vilar, 'The Parchment of the Sky: *Poiesis* of a Gothic Universe', in *Las Cantigas*, ed. by Fernández Fernández and Ruiz Sousa, II, 474-520 (p. 480).

[33] For an exhaustive account of the textual sources of the miracle, see Richard Kinkade and John Esten Keller, 'Myth and Reality in the Miracle of *Cantiga* 29', *La corónica*, 28.1 (1999-2000), 35-69. In the Latin account by Juan Gil de Zamora, the columns glow green: Sánchez Ameijeiras, p. 522 and n. 18.

[34] On the iconography of the Virgin employed here, and for the depiction of Mary on church columns in medieval Spain, see the observations and bibliography in Rocío Sánchez Ameijeiras, 'Como a Virgen Santa paresceu, paresçia': las empresas marianas alfonsíes y la teoría neoplatónica de la imagen sagrada', in *Alfonso X el Sabio*, ed. by Isidro G. Bango Torviso [exhibition catalogue] (Murcia: Novograf, 2009), pp. 357-65 (p. 363).

[35] Modern art historical attempts to explain the images as veins in the stone are beside the point. See the comments in Domínguez Rodríguez and Treviño Gajardo, p. 111.

things born of the earth (and influenced by celestial bodies).³⁶ The poem text emphasizes that the miracle is God's way of showing that all creatures should honour His mother (*Cantigas*, I, 29. 30–31). While the fifth miniature provides a literal illustration of this,³⁷ the final frame makes clear we are to read the miracle of the Gethsemane columns in the context of an earlier miraculous transformation of a living body, namely that of Mary into Virgin-Mother. Panel six depicts the Annunciation — alluded to, but not mentioned explicitly, in the closing lines of the poem — to suggest how the miracle central to the Christian faith may have come to pass. The iconography reflects a contemporary belief that Mary was impregnated through her ear. Golden rays of matter or 'species' from the chest of God-the-Father beam down to the proper right side of the Virgin's head. Although her ear is not visible in this process, the aural trigger for the transformation is suggested by the figure of the Angel Gabriel, who stands before Mary with a scroll on which are written the words of his greeting to her, 'Aue Maria'.³⁸

The role of human faith in the divine creation of matter is another aspect of devotion highlighted by the miniatures. *Cantiga* 186 of the 'códice rico' narrates the story of a community of Jerusalem monks who fall into poverty.³⁹ Twice they seek assistance from the Virgin and twice she intervenes. Her first response is to fill their stores full of grain, and frame two of the panel of miniatures shows the monks kneeling before two well-filled grain stores, their hands clasped in prayer.⁴⁰ The monks' second appeal is answered with a pile of gold coins, which appear on the altar before the statue of the Virgin and child. The final miniature illustrates the summary final verses which explain how 'o convento deu end' aa Virgen loor, | porque lle atan ben deu quanto mester avia' (*Cantigas*, II, 187. 61–62) ['Then the convent praised the Virgin for it, because she gave them such a gift when they had need of it' (Kulp-Hill, p. 225)].⁴¹ The miniature specifies that their praise takes the form of communion. A bishop celebrates Mass with the congregation of monks, holding the consecrated host aloft for the monks to see. Their faith in the miraculous power of God transforms the unleavened

---

³⁶ Alfonso X, '*Lapidario*' (*según el manuscrito escurialense H.I.15*), ed. by Sagrario Rodríguez M. Montalvo (Madrid: Gredos, 1981), p. 17. See also J. C. Plumpe, 'Vivum Saxum, Vivi Lapides: The Concept of "Living Stone" in Classical and Christian Antiquity', *Traditio*, 1 (1943), 1–14.

³⁷ John Esten Keller, 'The Depiction of Exotic Animals in *Cantiga* XXIX of the *Cantigas de Santa María*', in *Studies in Honor of Tatana Fotitch*, ed. by Josep M. Sola-Solé, Alessandro S. Crisafulli and Siegfried A. Schultz (Washington, DC: Catholic University Press, 1972), pp. 247–53.

³⁸ For medieval theories of Christ's conception, see Leo Steinberg and Samuel Y. Edgerton Jr, '"How Shall This Be?" Reflections on Filippo Lippi's *Annunciation* in London', *Artibus et historiae*, 16 (1987), 25–53.

³⁹ The *cantiga* is number 187 in the published edition (which is based on El Escorial: Real Biblioteca, MS b.I.2, or 'MS E'): *Cantigas*, II, 187.

⁴⁰ *Códice rico*, Facsimile, I, fol. 245ʳ and also '*Cantigas de Santa María*' *de Alfonso X el Sabio, Rey de Castilla*, ed. by Matilde López Serrano (Madrid: Patrimonio Nacional, 1974), plate 16. For the archaeological accuracy of the grain stores, or 'hórreos', see Menéndez Pidal, p. 115.

⁴¹ The miniature rubric is less specific: Guerrero Lovillo, *Las Cántigas*, p. 417, 'Como todo o convento deron loor a Sancta Maria que assi penssou d'eles', and Kulp-Hill, 'Captions', p. 62: 'How all the community gave praise to Holy Mary who cared for them thus'.

wheat flour of the host into the body of Christ, just as the power of their faith had enabled wheat and gold to materialize in their monastery. The miniatures reinforce the fundamental importance of faith in the transformation of spirit to flesh and show how belief in the Sacrament of the Eucharist is central to devotion to the Virgin. This final miniature also illustrates thirteenth-century belief in the transformative power of sight. From the end of the twelfth century, the elevation of the host came to mark the moment of its consecration, and it was sufficient for the congregation to gaze upon the wafer (rather than taste it) in order to receive communion during Mass.[42]

To receive, however, the faithful must also give. The Alfonsine *Primera Partida* unambiguously equates Christian duty, financial generosity and 'praising [God's] name'.[43] The miniatures and text in the *Cantigas* also emphasize this duty, and make clear the relationship between gifts and access to the sacred. They also show how this access is controlled by kings and members of the church. The Portuguese pilgrims in *cantiga* 224 who praise Santa Maria of Terena for the miraculous resurrection of a baby girl also make her 'generous offerings' (*Cantigas*, II, 224. 61; Kulp-Hill, p. 269) according to the text.[44] The final miniature elaborates on this statement, and shows the pilgrims kneeling to kiss the hand of a priest while an acolyte holds out a silver bowl to receive donations. Another acolyte stands behind him, holding a pile of silver coins already donated in the folds of his robes. The miraculous statue of the Virgin is on the altar, behind the group of priests.[45] Kings, by contrast, have unlimited and personal access to the sacred, a point with political resonance given Alfonso's efforts to gain control over local cults of saints as part of a policy to engineer Christian resettlement in the southern, formerly Muslim, areas of his kingdoms.[46] *Cantiga* 2 narrates the miracles performed for St Ildefonsus of Toledo.[47] In one episode, St Leocadia appears during a procession, which the

---

[42] The *Primera Partida* explains that during the consecration of the host, the priest 'must raise the Host that the people may see it': Alfonso X, *Primera Partida*, título IV, ley l (p. 50); Parsons Scott, Law lii, p. 39. On the practice of 'ocular communion', see Biernoff, p. 141 and Miri Rubin, *Corpus Christi: The Eucharist in Late Medieval Culture* (Cambridge: Cambridge University Press, 1991), pp. 148–50. Devotion to the Host in the *Cantigas* is explored by Jesús Montoya Martínez, 'El culto a la eucaristía y sus derivaciones magicas en el siglo XIII', *La corónica*, 36.1 (2007), 189–96, and in the postscript which follows Montoya's article by Alejandro García Avilés, 'Addenda', 197–201. The nutritious and curative powers of the consecrated host are explored in Piero Camporesi, 'The Consecrated Host: A Wondrous Excess', trans. by Anna Cancogne, in *Fragments for a History of the Human Body*, ed. by Michel Feher with Ramona Naddaff and Nadia Tazi, 3 vols (New York: Zone Books, 1989), I, 220–37.

[43] *Primera Partida*, título XX, ley iiii, ed. by Arias Bonet, p. 385 (my translation, Parsons Scott uses a variant text).

[44] On the thematic and structural role of *cantigas* associated with Portugal in the compilations, see Stephen Parkinson, 'Santuarios portugueses en las *Cantigas de Santa María*', *Alcanate*, 1 (1998–99), 43–57.

[45] The panel of miniatures appears in the 'Florence' codex: *Edición facsímil del códice B.R.20*, I, fol. 4^r (*cantiga* 3).

[46] Peter Linehan, *History and the Historians of Medieval Spain* (Oxford: Clarendon Press, 1993), pp. 512–13. See also Connie L. Scarborough, *A Holy Alliance: Alfonso X's Political Use of Marian Poetry* (Newark, DE: Juan de la Cuesta, 2009).

[47] The decision to place this miracle at the start of the collection also had particular significance for Alfonso: see Joseph T. Snow, 'Alfonso X y/en sus *Cantigas*', in *Estudios alfonsies: lexicografía,*

miniature glosses as a solemn procession by high-ranking ecclesiastics and royalty to her tomb, from which she rises.[48] Leocadia addresses Ildefonsus directly and commends him for his praise of the Virgin. While this takes place, the poem describes how King Reccesvinth (reigned 649–72) steps up to the Saint and 'tallou da mortalla' (*Cantigas*, I, 2. 3) ['cut from her shroud'].[49] The miniature shows him cutting a piece of her long, loose sleeve with a sword, a priest beside him holds a golden casket, as though ready to receive this new relic.

Alfonso, too, has unconditional access to relics, though the context is different. *Cantiga* 44 in the 'Florence' codex recounts how relics of the Virgin in Alfonso's large collection of relics remain uncorrupted during his ten-year absence from Seville.[50] The text is accompanied by an incomplete panel of miniatures. Although frame three remains blank, as do the spaces where the faces of the protagonists should be, Alfonso's relationship with his relics is clearly discernible. He is first shown holding a reliquary aloft and kissing it. The cleric who has passed it to him held it wrapped in precious cloth; Alfonso holds the reliquary with his bare hands. The reliquaries, all represented as golden caskets, their lids in a form that recalls a pitched roof, surmounted by a cross, are stored together in a large chest.[51] In his absence, access to them is controlled by royal order: the text states that he locked them away and ordered they not be seen 'often'.[52] On his return to Seville, the text explains that Alfonso found the many of the reliquaries badly damaged and the relics within them decayed, despite the fact they were wrapped in cloth. Only those of the Virgin remained intact. The final three miniatures depict the moment of the king's discovery and his thanksgiving. In frame five, he opens a casket (the details on it are unfinished) to reveal a smaller, pyx-like golden container which we infer from the text contains a pristine relic of the Virgin.[53] Interestingly, despite the account of the text, the artist depicts all the reliquaries intact throughout, a decision which ignores the narrative of the text and shows instead the eternal nature of relics as objects immune to decay.[54]

---

lírica, estética y política de Alfonso X, ed. by José Mondéjar and Jesús Montoya Martínez (Granada: Universidad de Granada, 1985), pp. 71–90.

[48] *Códice rico*, Facsimile, I, fol. 7ʳ and also '*Cantigas*', ed. by López Serrano, plate 2. On the central importance of Leocadia's church for political and ecclesiastical life in Toledo at this date, see Linehan, p. 56.

[49] Kulp-Hill, p. 4, has the misleading 'clutched her shroud'.

[50] In Mettmann's published edition the *cantiga* appears at number 257: see *Cantigas*, II, 366–67.

[51] The panel is reproduced in 'Florence' codex: *Edición facsímil del códice B.R.20*, I, fol. 56ʳ. Smaller colour reproductions in Isidro G. Bango Torviso, 'La Vida del monarca en imágenes', in *Alfonso X*, ed. by Bango Torviso, pp. 194–99 (p. 199) and Domínguez Rodríguez and Treviño Gajardo p. 94, fig. 59.

[52] 'el Rei ensserró-as [...] e nonas mandou catar amyude': *Cantigas*, II, 257. 11–12; Kulp-Hill, p. 313, interprets the line as 'the king [...] did not order that they be closely guarded'.

[53] A detail of frames five and six can be found in María Luisa Martín Ansón, 'El Culto de las reliquias en las *Cantigas de Santa Maria* de Alfonso X el Sabio', *Espacio, Tiempo y Forma, Serie III, Historia Medieval*, 24 (2011), 185–215 (p. 215, fig. 10).

[54] This is an important tenet of Christian faith: see Walker Bynum, pp. 70 and 182–83. Narratives involving repair of holy objects appear in the *Cantigas*, for example no. 211, in which bees miraculously repair a melting Paschal candle, or no. 122, in which first Alfonso VII and then Fernando III of Castile

The non-royal faithful, on the other hand, do not commune with relics on their own, and their access to these holy fragments is carefully controlled by members of the clergy. The relic of the Virgin's shirt at Chartres, enclosed in a large, architectural structure supported by gilded columns and columns of precious red stone, is visited by crowds of pilgrims who kneel together to kiss the columns.[55] Pilgrims arriving at the Holy Sepulchre in Jerusalem (*cantiga* 9) kneel and kiss the sepulchre and the ground beneath it, supervised all the while by a swarthy figure (not mentioned in the text) who oversees them from a window (frame two).[56] In *cantiga* 35, a group of merchants is saved from a pirate attack at sea by strands of the Virgin's hair and a drop of her milk. The text identifies the relics and describes how they are wrapped in fine gauze ('cendal') and placed in a gold casket (*Cantigas*, I, 35. 20–23); the miniatures confine themselves to a representation of the casket. The text explains how the keeper of the relics, canon 'Maestre Bernaldo', holds up the relics for all to see when the ship is threatened by pirates. The passengers rush towards the casket to offer fine cloth, gold and silver in exchange for deliverance from the pirates (*Cantigas*, I, 35. 55–64). The fifth miniature adds other details about the relationship between the frightened faithful and the relics. It shows the reliquary on a pedestal covered with a long, white cloth, closely supervised by 'Maestre Bernaldo', who collects donations from passengers who wish to come into contact with its power. The passenger at the head of the queue kisses the casket while others behind him wait their turn with offerings that will allow them to do likewise.[57]

A miniature that accompanies the brief *loor* 120 also makes explicit the equation between the power of the Virgin Mary, pecuniary donation and controlled access to relics. In the refrain to this poem, Alfonso urges his followers to praise the Virgin 'que nos manten' (*Cantigas*, II, 120. 21) ['who sustains us' (Kulp-Hill, p. 148)]. The fourth miniature represents a scene not specifically described in the text which takes place in a church. A man kneels before a priest, who holds out a thin strip of fringed cloth of gold, set with jewels. The man kisses the cloth and at the same time drops coins into a golden bowl held by the priest's acolyte. Behind the kneeling man is a group of people waiting to take his place; behind the priest is an altar with a statue of the Virgin. The scene has been interpreted as symbolic of Mary's majesty, the strip of cloth the hem of her robe.[58] However, the rich appearance and shape of the cloth suggests we are to identify this as the most precious relic of the Virgin, her

---

repaint a statue of the Virgin, thereby restoring her life-like appearance. For the relationship between relics, reliquaries and precious materials, see also Walker Bynum, p. 20.

[55] *Cantiga* 148, frames 1 and 2. Reproduced in *Códice rico*, Facsimile, I, fol. 204^v. See Teresa Laguna Paúl, 'Reliquias y relicarios', in *Alfonso X el Sabio*, ed. by Bango Torviso, pp. 636–37 (p. 637) for details of the pilgrims kissing the columns and laying lengths of cloth over the reliquary.

[56] *Códice rico*, Facsimile, I, fol. 17^r and also Laguna Paúl, p. 637.

[57] *Códice rico*, Facsimile, I, fol. 52^v–53^r; panel on fol. 52^v reproduced in *Alfonso X*, ed. by Bango Torviso, p. 367.

[58] *Códice rico*, Facsimile, I, fol. 170^v; '*Cantigas de Loor*', ed. by Beltrán, p. 72.

girdle, which she dropped during her ascent to heaven as a gift to the Apostles to remind them of her earthly presence.[59] This interpretation is reinforced by the following miniature, which shows Mary in heaven flanked by two angels. In the context of the poem, this tangible reminder of the Virgin's presence on earth reinforces the message in the opening verse that she was essential in making the spirit flesh so that mankind could know God (*Cantigas*, II, 120. 4).

The representation of the actual relic in the miniature accompanying *cantiga* 120 is prompted by this underlying message, although it runs counter to the dictates of the fourth Lateran Council of 1215, which had forbidden relics to be viewed outside reliquaries. Elsewhere in the *Cantigas* the presence of relics is implied by the caskets of gold which enclose them. The appearance of all these reliquaries owes much to architecture, and in construction they deliberately resemble a church or shrine, sometimes embellished with crockets or surmounted by a cross.[60] Although some scholars have suggested these represent Alfonso's personal collection, the uniform appearance of the caskets depicted throughout the manuscripts would instead seem to reflect the exemplars available to the artists, particularly as the form of these reliquaries recalls twelfth- and early thirteenth-century examples.[61] The exception to these representations is the silver, book-like reliquary depicted in the final two miniatures of *cantiga* 77 in the 'Florence' codex (*Cantigas*, III, 304), which scholars have identified as being owned by Alfonso himself. The reliquary, described in his will as 'la nuestra tabla que fiziemos fazer con las reliquias, a onra de Santa María' ['the panel which we had made with relics, in honour of holy Mary'] survives in the treasury of Seville Cathedral and comprises a silver triptych set with cameos, pearls and fourteen windows of rock crystal, behind which are displayed a total of 372 relics.[62] The design of the 'tablas' reflects later thirteenth-century fashions that allowed viewers to contemplate relics without removing them from their casing (although in the miniatures the 'tablas' are

---

[59] Miri Rubin, *Mother of God: A History of the Virgin Mary* (New Haven, CT: Yale University Press, 2009), pp. 66 and 184.

[60] On reliquaries in the *Cantigas*, see Laguna Paúl, pp. 636–37. On goldsmiths' work in the *Cantigas* more generally, see Marta Poza Yagüe, 'Honra debida a Dios y reflejo del poder del monarca: las artes del metal en el siglo XIII hispano', in *Alfonso X el Sabio*, ed. by Bango Torviso, pp. 310–14, and Menéndez Pidal, p. 194. For reliquaries as miniature churches, see Éric Palazzo, 'Relics, Liturgical Space, and the Theology of the Church', in *Treasures of Heaven: Saints, Relics and Devotion in Medieval Europe*, ed. by Martina Bagnoli and others [exhibition catalogue] (London: British Museum, 2011), pp. 99–109 (p. 99).

[61] Laguna Paúl, p. 638 and Martín Ansón, p. 217 for these reliquaries as royal possessions, and see the comparative examples in García Cuadrado's study of the 'Florence' codex miniatures (pp. 380–83). The consistent representation of casket forms is noted by Mª Luisa Martín Ansón, 'La orfebrería: ajuar cortesano y ajuar litúrgico', in *Las Cantigas*, ed. by Fernández Fernández and Ruiz Sousa, pp. 305–38 (p. 332).

[62] My translation: for Alfonso's will, see *Diplomatario andaluz de Alfonso X*, ed. by Manuel González Jiménez (Seville: El Monte. Caja de Huelva y Sevilla, 1991), doc. no. 521, p. 559. For the miniatures see *Edición facsímil del códice B.R.20*, I, fol. 99^r, and frames five and six reproduced in Martín Ansón, p. 216. On the 'Tablas', see Laguna Paúl, pp. 638–39.

closed).⁶³ Yet the appearance of an identifiable object (albeit represented in simplified form) with personal significance for Alfonso, patron of the *Cantigas*, is arguably not an attempt by the artists to lend greater accuracy to their portrayal of late thirteenth-century Spain. Instead, I suggest that the purpose of including the 'tablas' in the miniatures to this particular *cantiga* is intended to convey a political rather than a theological message to viewers far from the locus of the events described. The poem describes a miracle which took place in Ribela, Galicia (northern Spain). The altar cloth of one of the five altars depicted in all five miniatures (the first panel is blank) is decorated with a design, in gold thread, of heraldic castles enclosed in roundels — the symbol of the kingdom of Castile. In the final two miniatures the 'tablas' appear on this altar, directly above this altar cloth. The text makes no reference to the appearance of this additional reliquary; there are no rubrics to the miniatures. The tacit political point, however, would seem to be that the king's presence, symbolized by an object that stresses his devotion to the Virgin Mary, extends to the farthest reaches of his kingdom. The point is an important one: in 1282, Alfonso's realm slid into civil war and he lost control of all but Seville and some areas of Murcia.⁶⁴ The deliberate depiction of an identifiable reliquary in miniatures accompanying an account about a church in Galicia confirms arguments for the accepted dating of this manuscript to the period 1280–84, and suggests this section at least could date from 1282–84.⁶⁵

The miniatures that accompany the *Cantigas* nuance the texts they illustrate with messages about theological doctrine, social hierarchy and political control. Seductive though it may be to regard them primarily as archaeological evidence of thirteenth-century life in support of the texts, in fact the apparent realism of the images is artfully arranged to convey arguments aimed at the intellect.⁶⁶

---

⁶³ For rock crystal and reliquaries, see Christof L. Diedrichs, *Von Glauben zum Sehen: die Sichtbarkeit der Reliquie im Reliquiar: ein Beitrag zur Geschichte des Sehens* (Berlin: Weiβensee Verlag, 2001), and also Martina Bagnoli, 'The Stuff of Heaven: Materials and Craftsmanship in Medieval Reliquaries', in *Treasures of Heaven*, pp. 137–47 (pp. 141–42); Michael Camille, 'Before the Gaze: The Internal Senses and Late Medieval Practices of Seeing', in *Visuality*, ed. by Nelson, pp. 197–223 (p. 204); Walker Bynum, pp. 28–29.
⁶⁴ Manuel González Jiménez, *Alfonso X el Sabio* (Barcelona: Ariel, 2004), p. 351.
⁶⁵ Laguna Paúl, p. 638; Laura Fernández Fernández, 'Cantigas de Santa María: fortuna de sus manuscritos', *Alcanate*, 6 (2008–09), 323–48 (p. 334).
⁶⁶ The theological implications of miniatures that illustrate architectural construction have yet to be unpacked: see the comments about building and hagiography in Cynthia Hahn, 'Picturing the Text: Narrative in the *Life* of the Saints', *Art History*, 13.1 (March 1990), 1–33 (p. 3). To date, images of architecture in the *Cantigas* have been analysed in terms of contemporary practice or mise-en-page: see most recently Ana Domínguez Rodríguez, 'El arte de la construcción y otras técnicas artísticas en la miniatura de Alfonso X el Sabio', *Alcanate*, 1 (1998–99), 59–83 and Rafael Cómez Ramos, 'La arquitectura en las miniaturas de la corte de Alfonso X el Sabio' *Alcanate*, 6 (2008–09), 207–25.

Early Modern Marginalia in the *Cancioneiro da Ajuda*

ANDRÉ B. PENAFIEL

University of Oxford

Introduction

The *Cancioneiro da Ajuda* features over sixty comments by early modern readers on its pages but they have received almost no studies of their own. In the early twentieth century, Michaëlis transcribed most of the marginalia in her first volume of the *Cancioneiro da Ajuda*, though they were scattered throughout the book, as footnotes to individual poems. In the second volume, after stating that, within the *Cancioneiro*'s marginalia, the later inscriptions are the ones that have 'maior interesse' [greater interest], one finds a four-page study with further transcriptions and corrections to the first volume.[1] A few decades later, Carter, in the second appendix to his edition, includes a list of the marginalia and their locations, with only a few omissions and mistakes.[2] He does not, however, provide any information on the hand of each note, and those added by later readers are not distinguished from those written by medieval revisers working in the original scriptorium, whose correction notes were not erased. Also, a slight inconvenience is the fact that they are referred to by page, rather than folio numbers.

Yet the most important contribution to the study of the *Cancioneiro da Ajuda*'s marginalia came in 2004, with Susana Pedro's *Análise Paleográfica das anotações marginais e finais no Cancioneiro da Ajuda*. Pedro's work has the merit of reproducing diplomatically most of the notes, while systematizing and enhancing both Michaëlis's and Carter's work. That is to say that Michaëlis is comprehensive, but the way in which she presents information makes it difficult to build an overall picture; Carter edits all the marginalia in a single place, but his edition lacks crucial information which would render it more useful. Pedro is comprehensive, structures her edition intelligently and corrects a number of mistakes found in the two previous editions, even if her focus is decisively palaeographical and codicological, and this means that her main concern is not the early modern marginalia or its potential for studies on literary reception.

---

[1] Carolina Michaëlis de Vasconcellos, *Cancioneiro da Ajuda*, 2 vols (Halle: Max Niemeyer, 1904), II, 67; 175-78.
[2] Henry H. Carter, *Cancioneiro da Ajuda: A Diplomatic Edition* (New York: Modern Language Association of America; London: Oxford University Press, 1941).

Finally, Maria Ana Ramos's study *Invoco el rrey Dom Denis* deserves mentioning, even if its relevance for literary reception research is not immediately obvious. Based on two notes, Ramos argued that the manuscript once belonged to Pedro Homem, a fifteenth-century poet connected to the Portuguese royal house. Thus, her theory connects the Galician-Portuguese lyric with the Portuguese aristocracy of the time of the *Cancioneiro Geral*.[3] Its relevance to the present study lies in the suggestion that the marginalia here analysed are contemporary to a specific group of poets, allowing us to see points of contact between thirteenth- and fifteenth-century aesthetics.

This Edition

The present study transcribes, in the Appendix to this article, every piece of late medieval or early modern marginalia in a single place for the first time. Based on the concept of *campo bibliográfico*,[4] a modernizing transcription has been preferred, since Pedro's work is accessible and provides an authoritative diplomatic transcription. By *modernized*, we mean:

(1) special characters, like long-*s* and *r*-rotunda, are standardized, though *i*, *j*, *y*, *u*, *v* and *tils* are employed according to the original spelling;
(2) fragmented words are completed whenever possible;
(3) abbreviated words are expanded;
(4) words are separated and hyphenized according to modern usage.

Due to this article's scope, the earliest marginalia, made at the time of the manuscript production by scribes reviewing and correcting it, have been ignored. Likewise any contemporary inscriptions, like pagination or Michaëlis's pencil annotation on folio 1, have also been disregarded. To facilitate research on literary reception, the data is also grouped under manuscript gathering and poet, as these are crucial details not be found anywhere else.

Even though the manuscript's binding changed over time, the text was edited based on the paper facsimile, which follows the manuscript's state prior to the 1999–2000 restoration. With that sequence in mind, each note is presented in order of appearance and numbered accordingly in the first column.[5] Henceforth, when referring to a specific item in the table, we will adopt the following convention: CA*n*., that is, "Cancioneiro da Ajuda note", followed by the relevant number from the first column of the table.[6]

---

[3] Maria Ana Ramos, 'Inuoco el rrey Dom Denis... Pedro Homem e o *Cancioneiro da Ajuda*', *Actes del VII Congrés de l' Associació Hispànica de Literatura Medieval*, 1 (1999), pp. 127–85.
[4] Ivo Castro and Maria Ana Ramos, 'Estratégia e táctica da transcrição', *Critique textuelle portugaise, Actes du Colloque* (1986), 99–122 (p. 112).
[5] Text edited based on *Cancioneiro da Ajuda: fragmento do nobiliario do conde Dom Pedro: edição fac-similada do códice existente na Biblioteca da Ajuda*, ed. by Manuel Cadafaz de Matos (Lisbon: Edições Távola Redonda, 1994).
[6] This system was devised by the author as a simple method of referring to the notes, and will be used both in this article and in future.

The second and third columns of the table give the CA number and incipit to which the notes refer. The fourth column locates each note within the folio. In order to use this information, one should bear in mind that the manuscript's pages have been numbered more than once and that currently more than one pagination system is used in secondary literature. Here we follow the right bottom-page numbering, which runs from folio 1 to 88. Furthermore, in each manuscript page one finds two columns and it is customary to refer to them as columns A and B, on the recto side, and C and D, on the verso. We simplified this system slightly by referring to columns A and B only.

The fifth column of our table provides each note's hand, that is, to whom the note is attributed. This data was collected both from Michaëlis and Pedro and a few contributions have been added, indicated on footnotes. The final column gives the transcription of each note, followed by any relevant remark, again in footnotes.

The Hands

Hand A, the most prolific — and possibly the oldest — has been described as a fifteenth-century 'gótica cursiva' [gothic cursive].[7] Hand C, the second most frequent, is of a similar type, though 'influenciadas por certas características bastardas' [influenced by certain bastard characteristics].[8] Michaëlis dated it from the end of the fifteenth century, though for Pedro it could have been as early as fourteenth or as late as sixteenth century.[9] More mysterious are a few inscriptions by hand B, so close to the gutter that the text has been trimmed.

Two whole stanzas can be found in the margins. CAn.39, on fol. 33^r, is by a fourth hand, referred as D, being the latest of all: mid-sixteenth century, according to Michaëlis; late sixteenth or early seventeenth, according to Pedro.[10] Michaëlis suggested that it could be by the Portuguese poet António Ferreira, whereas Pedro considered it similar to CAn.59, in which case hand D could safely be assumed to be by a man called Gonçalo Gomes Mirador instead.[11]

The second stanza is on fol. 68 and relates to CA 250. Michaëlis oscillated between attributing it to the medieval scribe or to a sixteenth-century hand.[12] A similar doubt occurred to her when considering the word *vacat*, on fol. 69^r, col. B, l. 11, right, next to CA 253b, presumably to mark that the *cantiga* is a

---

[7] Susana Tavares Pedro, *Análise paleográfica das anotações marginais e finais no Cancioneiro da Ajuda*. Paper presented to the Colóquio Cancioneiro da Ajuda (1904-2004), Lisbon, 11–13 November 2004, Faculdade de Letras, Universidade de Lisboa. Available at: <http://www.fcsh.unl.pt/philologia/Pedro2004_AnalisePaleografica.pdf> [accessed 12 November 2011], p. 18. Michaëlis de Vasconcellos, 1904, II, 176–78, §145, 3°.
[8] Pedro, 2004, p. 20; Michaëlis de Vasconcellos, 1904, II, 175–76, §145, 2°.
[9] Michaëlis de Vasconcellos, 1904, II, 175; Pedro, 2004, p. 20.
[10] Michaëlis de Vasconcellos, 1904, II, 178, §145, 4°; Pedro, 2004, p. 20.
[11] Michaëlis de Vasconcellos, 1904, II, 127.
[12] Michaëlis de Vasconcellos, 1904, I, 488; II, 173.

duplicate of CA 248.[13] Concerning the stanza, Pedro had no doubt in attributing it to a medieval reviser working in the original scriptorium.[14] As for the note, no opinion is expressed by Pedro, though Ramos considered it to be by the same hand of the stanza, which she called reviser 1.[15] Therefore, the stanza on fol. 68 is not included in the table, according to the current consensus, although the word *vacat* is catalogued under CA*n*.51, as there seems to remain some room for doubts about its age.

Michaëlis believed that CA*n*.44 was by a fifth hand, whereas Ramos associates it with CA*n*.58 and CA*n*.60, presumably by a former owner of the manuscript called Pero Homem.[16] Pedro, instead, attributed it to hand A, an opinion which has been adopted here.

This reduces the dated hands to four, though only two of them, A and C, are both readable and prolific enough to render them useful to our purposes here. Finally, there are certain written vestiges less relevant to the study of the manuscript's reception — property marks, *essais de plume* and drawings — included here more for the sake of comprehensiveness.

One case specifically, however, deserves closer attention, namely CA*n*.30, a majuscule *M*, inscribed inside the hat worn by the illuminated picture of a *trovador* representing Pero Garcia Burgalês, on fol. 21^r. This *M* has not been counted so far among the marginalia; rather it was hypothesized by Ramos that it stands for *Magister*, which, combined with the hat, would indicate some special prestige enjoyed by this poet. Although we are inclined to accept her argument concerning the hat, the letter, we would argue, does not stand for *Magister*. The close similarity, so far unnoticed, between this *M* and the one on the inscription *Dona M^a*, CA*n*.52, on fol. 70^r, suggests that they were made by a single reader, situated at a later date, contradicting the idea that the *M* comes from a scribe working in the original scriptorium.

One may contrast those two to other *M*s in the manuscript — for example coloured initial *M*s beginning stanzas on fols 4^v and 5^r. The letter type and the overall shape, with curls at the extremes, are all very similar. Yet the side strokes of the *M*s on fols 21^r and 70^r are wide on top and thinner on the bottom, as it approaches the curls. The *M*s used as initials are normally wide in the middle and thinner on both top and bottom. The middle stroke in particular is quite distinctive in the marginalia, both being slightly bent.

---

[13] Michaëlis de Vasconcellos, 1904, I, 486; II, 174.
[14] Pedro, 2004, p. 12.
[15] Maria Ana Ramos, 'O Cancioneiro da Ajuda: confecção e escrita', 2 vols (unpublished doctoral thesis, Universidade de Lisboa, 2008), available at: <http://repositorio.ul.pt/bitstream/10451/553/1/17066_0_cancioneiro_1.pdf> [accessed 22 August 2014]), p. 344.
[16] Michaëlis de Vasconcellos, 1904, II, 175, §145, 1°; Ramos, 1999, p. 166.

A Short Analysis of Content

As the table and the section above outline, there remains doubt when attributing some notes to one of the main hands. Nevertheless, a few observations can be put forward:

- hand A is present in gatherings one, ten, thirteen and fourteen;
- hand C in gatherings two, three, four, five, six and eleven;
- apparently, hands A and C never occur in the same gathering;
- hand B occurs in isolation (gathering seven), with hand A (gathering one) and with C (gathering four);
- gathering nine is the only one to bear no inscription or drawing of any kind.

Hands A and C are usually abundant in the gatherings in which they appear. It is worth considering why A, writing as many as twenty-three comments in gathering one, for example, would suddenly cease to write on the next, only to return, with a similar intensity, in the tenth. This is particularly significant if we consider point three above. It would appear that these two hands date from a time when the manuscript was not yet bound, that the readers were not reading the gatherings in the sequence we know today and, more disconcertingly, that whatever hand A possessed was not available to C and vice-versa. Gatherings seven, eight, nine and twelve might constitute yet a third group of gatherings not available to or at least not handled by either hand A or C.

This confirms the palaeographical hypothesis that hands A and C are roughly contemporary to one another and suggests that, at this stage, the manuscript was in a considerably dissembled state. Somewhat later, it would appear, is hand B, testifying to a new period for the manuscript, one in which the two or three groups of gatherings are all reassembled. This, however, still pre-dates the binding: hand B is the one to have written close to the margins which were later trimmed, presumably by the time of its first binding, in the sixteenth century.

If Pedro is right and CA*n*.44 is indeed by hand A, we can circumscribe these three hands to the period ranging from the second quarter of the fifteenth century, roughly when Juan de Mena was active, up to the sixteenth century, when the manuscript was bound. This partly confirms and partly restricts the dating advanced by Michaëlis based on palaeography, mentioned above. Incidentally, this period overlaps with that covered by Garcia de Resende's *Cancioneiro Geral* and, since the language employed by these three hands is Portuguese, rather than Castilian, we can say that the marginalia connect the earliest Iberian courtly lyric with late medieval and early modern Portuguese courtly poetry.[17]

It is also worth noting that the Évora folios — the eleven loose folios found around 1840 in the Biblioteca Pública de Évora — do not form any pattern here.

---

[17] Ramos first advanced this conclusion, though based almost exclusively on CA*n*.58 and CA*n*.60.

They include folios annotated by hands A, B, C and even non-annotated ones, as the table below reveals:

Évora folios	Marginalia's hand
fol. 4 (gathering I)	A
fol. 16 (gathering III)	C
fol. 17 (gathering III)	Ø
fol. 29 (gathering V)	Ø
fol. 36 (gathering VI)	Ø
fols 40–45 (gathering VII)	B

This is because these eleven folios were torn out from the manuscript after it was bound, further confirming that the marginalia's period was already over by then.[18]

A final aspect to consider is what hands A and C express in terms of literary taste. Michaëlis contrasted marginalia expressing approval, all of which she attributes to C, to those written by A, mainly jocose in tone. Pedro, however, disagrees in some attributions, and she seems to be right. Hand C is remarkably consistent: it is larger than A, appearing exclusively by the first line of each annotated poem. When in column A of a manuscript page, hand C can be found close to the majuscule that initiates a poem; in column B, by the end of the first line, that is to say that hand C normally occurs in the inner or outer margins. Therefore, CA*n*.5 and CA*n*.19 are clearly not from C: the former is in a small letter, written between columns A and B, towards the end of the third stanza, whereas the latter, also in a small letter, was written by the fourth line of manuscript. CA*n*.4, however, casts some doubts.

In total, there are twenty notes expressing approval, including CA*n*.1 and the slightly ambiguous CA*n*.23 and CA*n*.43. Of those, fifteen are by hand C, meaning that approval is the single emotion expressed by this hand. Conversely, hand A expresses a full range of emotions: sometimes approving of the poet, at others jesting, it is difficult to determine whether he also expressed disapproval, as he seems to engage in a written dialogue with the poems he comments on. He also included some interjections, carefully marked as 'Latin' the occurrences of the word *ergo* and gave paraphrases or summaries of a poem's predominant idea, all in a thin letter, close to the text, with no place preference.

The most annotated poet by far is João Soares Somesso, receiving as much as twenty-three comments, mostly by hand A, ranging from irony to approval. Concerning praise, João Soares Somesso, Martim Soares, Airas Carpancho, Rui Queimado, João Garcia de Guilhade, Pai Gomes Charinho and Fernão Velho all received one favourable comment each; Vasco Praga de Sandim, three; Nuno Fernandes Torneol and Pero Garcia Burgalês received five each.

---

[18] We would argue that there can be no doubt that this was the order of events, that is, the binding precedes the plundering of the Évora folios. Michaëlis refers five stubs related to the first five folios and cut stitching where the last six folios were inserted. *Vide* Michaëlis de Vasconcellos, 1904, II, 136; 148.

The above list shows no specific pattern. It spans the whole period covered by the *Cancioneiro da Ajuda*: Sandim and Somesso are among the earliest poets, whereas Charinho is one of the latest. The poems that are praised do not reveal, on the readers' part, any specific preference concerning versification or content. A poem marked by intricate formal features like Martim Soares's CA 45 is not annotated. It is found in gathering two and was presumably accessible to hand C. Yet an equally sophisticated and very similar poem by Burgalês, CA 87, was considered good by hand C. This same hand approved of CA 104, one out of four poems in which Burgalês plays with the secrecy *topos* by declaring that his lady has one out of three ordinary names (Joana, Sancha and Maria). Hand C, therefore, was probably aware of the conventions which established that the beloved's name must be kept secret and enjoyed the humorous twist by Burgalês. But the other three poems in this cycle — CA 89, CA 105, CA 106 — all of which employ the same joke, were ignored.

To say that these expressions of taste are unsystematic does not mean that they are useless, though. They reveal something, fragmentary as it may be, about the literary taste of fifteenth-century Portuguese audiences. Above all, they testify to a special, possibly renewed, interest in Galician-Portuguese lyric, which was regarded both as poetry worthy of private reading and as a possible source for new compositions, as revealed by CA*n*.44. In the future, it would be worth considering whether the annotated poems can be linked in some way to poems or preferences detected in fifteenth-century *lírica palaciana*. As for Galician-Portuguese lyric, these marginalia, as well as some rare statements to be found elsewhere — like the *Livros de Linhagens* and a few rubrics accompanying *cantigas* — add to the meagre ranks of quasi-contemporary expressions of taste, which may complement studies on Galician-Portuguese aesthetics.

Appendix: Late medieval and early modern marginalia to the *Cancioneiro da Ajuda*

First gathering

— Vasco Praga de Sandim

1.	CA 1	Deus, meu Senhor, se vos prouguer	f. 1ʳ, col. A, ll. 18/19, left	A	*diz u[er]dade*¹
2.	CA 2	Senhor fremosa, grand'enveja hei	f. 1ʳ, col. A, ll. 21/22, left	A	*este avia ēveia aos que via morrer*
3.			f. 1ʳ, col. B, bottom centre	A	*esta tijnha ssua alma mall pensada*²
4.	CA 3	Senhor fremosa, par Deus, gran razon	f. 1ᵛ, col. A, l. 1	A?³	*boa*
5.	CA 10	Que sem conselho que vós, mia senhor	f. 3ʳ, col. B, l. 17, left	A	*boa*
6.	CA 13	Par Deus, senhor, sei eu mui bem	f. 3ᵛ, col. B, ll. 15/16, left	A	*fazia-lhe pesar este ē na muito amar*

— João Soares Somesso

7.	CA 15	De quant'eu sempre desejei	f. 4ᵛ, col. A, ll. 5/6, left	A	*ora pois faze-lho*
8.	CA 16	Muitas vezes em meu cuidar	f. 4ᵛ, col. A, ll. 9/10, left	A	*beber sobre o cheiro*
9.			f. 4ᵛ, col. A, ll. 21/22, left	A	*muito pode alla fe*
10.	CA 17	Nom me poss'eu, senhor, salvar	f. 4ᵛ, col. B, ll. 9/10, right	A	*estaa bem satesfeito*
11.			f. 4ᵛ, col. B, l. 24, right	A	*bo fe [***]*⁴
12.	CA 18	Agora m'hei eu a partir	f. 5ʳ, col. A, ll. 14/15, left	A	*mas muito*
13.			f. 5ʳ, col. A, bottom	A	*mata-llo*
14.	CA 20	Nom tenh'eu que coitados som	f. 5ᵛ, col. A, l. 26, right	A	*este leixa os feitos⁵ a deos*
15.	CA 21	Punhei eu muit'em me guardar	f. 5ᵛ, col. B, l. 9, right	A	*calar*

---

¹ Following Michaëlis de Vasconcellos, 1904, I, 6; 1904, II, 76, who glossed it as *verdade*.

² This is the most diplomatic reading, also found in Pedro. Michaëlis de Vasconcellos offers two alternative readings: *empensada* (1904, I, 8) and *empregada* (1904, II, 176).

³ Very difficult to determine, though A might be the best hypothesis here. Although it is placed in C's preferred position (outer margin, first line), the b-shape and size suggest a different hand. Furthermore, there is not any note consensually attributed to C in this gathering, which, again, reinforces a preference for hand A. Finally, the b-shape is similar to that of note 5 and the general outline to that of note 19, both attributed by Pedro to hand A. However, Michaëlis de Vasconcellos, 1904, II, 176, believed that the three of them were by hand C.

⁴ Although there are clearly some letters after the *e*, Michaëlis de Vasconcellos, 1904, II, 176 transcribes it as *bofe*. Pedro, 2004, p.17 suggests *bofe ssy*.

⁵ Michaëlis de Vasconcellos, 1904, II, 176 does not attempt to transcribe this word.

Early Modern Marginalia in the *Cancioneiro da Ajuda* 191

16.	CA 22	Já m'eu, senhor, houve sazon	f. 5ᵛ, col. B, l. 20, right	B?[1]	[***][2]
17.	CA 22			A	*outro dia te vera*
18.	CA 23	Se eu a mia senhor ousasse	f. 6ʳ, col. A, ll. 14/15, left	A	*mylhor he muito dize-llo logo**
19.	CA 24	Senhor fremosa, fui buscar	f. 6ʳ, col. B, l. 3, right	A	*boa*
20.	CA 27	Desejand'eu vós, mia senhor	f. 6ᵛ, col. A, l. 1, left	A	*ergo*
21.	CA 28	Já foi sazom que eu cuidei	f. 7ʳ, col. B, l. 23, left	A	*guar-te e cala-te*
22.	CA 29	Ben'o faria, se nembrar	f. 7ᵛ, col. A, l. 11, left	A	*latim*

Second gathering
— Martim Soares

23.	CA 59	Por Deus, senhor, nom me desamparedes	f. 14ʳ, col. B, ll. 17/18, left	C?[3]	*fjna*[4]

Third gathering
— Airas Carpancho

24.	CA 64	Quisera-m'ir — tal conselho prendi	f. 16ʳ, col. A, l. 1, left	C	*Muito boa*

— Nuno Fernandes Torneol

25.	CA 70	Ir-vos queredes, mia senhor	f. 18ʳ, col. B, l. 9, right	C	*muj boa*[5]
26.	CA 78	Ai eu! e de mim que será?	f. 19ᵛ, col. B, l. 1, right	C	[sign] *boa*[6]
27.	CA 79	Ai mia senhor! U nom jaz al	f. 19ᵛ, col. B, l. 18, left	C	[sign] *boa*

Fourth gathering

28.	CA 80	Pois naci nunca vi Amor	f. 20ʳ, col. A, l. 13, left	C	[sign] *boa*
29.	CA 81	Preguntam-me por que ando sandeu	f. 20ʳ, col. A, l. 8, right	C	[sign] *boa*

[1] Difficult to determine the hand, though, based on its place on the margin, size and the *q*-shape, it is clearly not A.
[2] Michaëlis de Vasconcellos, 1904, II, 76 considers this as 'ilegível' [illegible] but, on p. 178, states that 'se parece a *porquê*' [looks like *porquê*]. Pedro ignores it. There also seems to be a blurred majuscule *m* two lines above it.
[3] A larger, bolder hand. Could this be C? The position, between two columns, would be unusual, though not unique. Yet, it is consistent with other notes by C as it is placed right at the first line of the *cantiga*.
[4] That is the interpretation of Michaëlis de Vasconcellos, 1904, I, 124 and 202 who contrasts the hand with the scribe's similar word *fiida*. Pedro is silent about it.
[5] Michaëlis de Vasconcellos neglected this note.
[6] This, like the next six notes and number 46, have an ornamental mark before and, sometimes, after the text. Michaëlis de Vasconcellos, 1904, I and Carter, 1941 interpreted them as large Cs, abbreviating *cantiga*, whereas Pedro, 2004, p. 19, more accurately, transcribes them as Xs.

		— Pero Garcia Burgalês			
30.	CA 86	Senhor, per vós sôo maravilhado	f. 21^r, col. A, illumination	?	M
31.	CA 87	Ai eu coitad'! e por que vi	f. 22^r, col. A, l. 17, left	C	[sign] *boa*
32.	CA 88	Se eu soubesse, u eu primeiro vi	f. 22^r, col. B, l. 16, right	C	[sign] *boa* [sign]
33.	CA 88	Se eu soubesse, u eu primeiro vi	f. 22^v, col. A, l. 13, left	C	[sign] *boa* [sign]
34.	CA 92	Se Deus me valha, mia senhor	f. 23^r, col. B, l. 22, right	B	*boo diz dajá*[1]
35.			f. 23^v, col. A, ll. 5/6, left	?	*cartuxo*
36.	CA 93	Pola verdade que digo, senhor	f. 23^v, col. A, l. 26, left	C^2	*boa*
Fifth gathering					
37.	CA 104	Joana, dix'eu, Sancha e Maria	f. 26r, col. B, l. 19, right	C^3	*mujto boa*
Sixth gathering		— Rui Queimado			
38.	CA 129	Nostro Senhor Deus! e por que neguei	f. 33^r, col. A, by the picture, left	C^4	*mujto boa*
39.	CA 130	Deste mund'outro bem nom querria	f. 33^r, col. B, ll. 16/17, right	D	an illegible stanza[5]
Seventh gathering		— João Soares Coelho			
40.	CA 165	Nunca coitas de tantas guisas vi	f. 42^v, col. A, l. 5, left	B	[Este quer] *mal a quen quer bem a sua amiga* [e m]*al a quen a mal quer*[6]

---

[1] This is probably the most obscure note, partly because the text was trimmed on the right margin. No consensus has been reached: Michaëlis de Vasconcellos, 1904, I, 263 transcribes as: Outro ben d'este mundo non querria | pol[as] coitas qu' amor me faz sofrer | que mia sen[h]or meu mal todo sabia | e que soubes)' eu sempre atender. |Se esse ben ouvesse, averia | o mais do ben que ja querri' aver | ella o sabe ben lho dizer (riscado e substituído pelo verso seguinte: soubera o ela ben sen lho dizer) | e o sen posera en min como d … | nunca lho ous …. dizer. In 1904, II, p.178, an alternative readings by Britto-Rebello is provided: que mia senhor meu mal todo entender | e que soubesse eu bem ġ o entendia (ll. 3–4); and como dizia | Nunca lhe … d' alma dizer. (ll. 8–9).
[2] Pedro, 2004, p. 19 attempts *bôo diz' da fa* and Pedro, 2004, p. 55 attempts *bôo diz' daran*; Carter, 1941, p. 178 offers *bôo dizer daran*; Pedro, 2004, p. 19 suggests *R° boo diz dasá*.
[3] Pedro, 2004, p. 19 does not attempt to attribute it to any hand. Because of the *b*-shape and its position by the majuscule, C is the best guess, following Michaëlis de Vasconcellos, 1904, II, 176.
[4] Pedro, 2004, p. 19 has doubts in attributing it to C. Again, because of its position by the first line of the poem, C is the safest hypothesis.
[5] Pedro, 2004, p. 19 has doubts in attributing it to C. The position is unusual, by the picture, rather than by the majuscule.
[6] This is the reconstruction of another trimmed note by Michaëlis de Vasconcellos, 1904, I, 331. Pedro, 2004, p. 19 gives a slightly different reading.

EARLY MODERN MARGINALIA IN THE *CANCIONEIRO DA AJUDA* 193

Eighth gathering				
41.	Blank page		?	a drawing
Tenth gathering				
	— João Garcia de Guilhade	f. 47ᵛ, centre		
42.	CA 230 Senhor, veedes-me morrer	f. 62ʳ, col. B, l. 4, right	A	rrespondeo-lhe
43.	CA 231 U m'eu parti d'u m'eu parti	f. 62ᵛ, col. A, l. 6, left	A	fina¹
44.	CA 232 A bõa dona por que eu trobava	f. 62ᵛ, col. A, l. 21, left	A²	e deste aprendeo joam de mena
45.		f. 62ᵛ, col. B, l. 7, right	A	trobasses tu bem e nõ lhe pesara
46.		f. 62ᵛ, col. B, l. 16, right	A	gabarse-nos quer³
47.	CA 233 Amigos, quero-vos dizer	f. 63ʳ, col. A, l. 7, left	A	andae ẽ era m[**]o vades⁴
	— Pai Gomes Charinho			
48.	CA 246 A dona que home 'senhor' devia	f.67ʳ, col. B, ll. 17/18, right	?	se a nõ visse p[...] perdia o ssem [...] e [**] [...] amigos al e dix[...]⁵
Eleventh gathering				
49.	CA 250 Coidava-m'eu, quand'amor nom havia	f. 68ʳ, col. A, l. 18, left	C	[sign] Mujto boa
50.	CA 252 Senhor fremosa, pois que Deus non quer	f. 68ᵛ, col. B, bottom	?	a grotesque
51.	CA 253b Oí eu sempre, mia senhor, dizer	f. 69ʳ, col. B, l. 11, right	?⁶	vacat
52.	CA 256 De quantas cousas eno mundo son,	f. 70ʳ, col. B, bottom	?	Dona Mᵃ

¹ Following Michaëlis de Vasconcellos, 1904, I, 451. Pedro, 2004, p. 18 reads *fino*.
² Pedro, 2004, p. 18: 'Maria Ana Ramos, no estudo em que debate a identificação do "Pêro Homem", provável possuidor do Cancioneiro, sugere que a ele se poderia atribuir a autoria (apenas) da nota marginal do fl. 62ᵛ' [Maria Ana Ramos, in the study in which she discusses the identity of 'Pêro Homen', who probably owned the Cancioneiro, suggests that we can attribute to him only the authorship of the marginal note on fol. 62ᵛ]. The quotation, however, was not found in Ramos's article. Michaëlis de Vasconcellos, 1904, II, 175 believed that this and note 40 were the only inscriptions by a fifth hand, older than all the others. Pedro, 2004, p. 18, conversely, argues that this is hand A.
³ Michaëlis de Vasconcellos, 1904, I, 453 offers *gabar-sse-me quer*.
⁴ Michaëlis de Vasconcellos, 1904, II, 177 final reading is *andae ẽ era maa u vades*. Pedro, 2004, p. 18 sees *andae ẽ era maao vades*. However, there might be more letters between *m* and *o* than either of them believed.
⁵ Michaëlis de Vasconcellos, 1904, I, 331 gives a partial transcription and believes it to be by hand A. Given the ink colour and position in the margin, this is very unlikely. Pedro attributes it to the reviser.
⁶ Michaëlis de Vasconcellos, 1904, I, 331 initially dates it from the sixteenth century. Later, in Michaëlis de Vasconcellos, 1904, II, 174, she expresses sheer indecision: 'copista, revedor, leitor ou collacionador'. Ramos, 2008, p. 344 attributes it to reviser 1. Pedro ignores it.

	— Fernão Velho			
53.	CA 259 Senhor que eu por meu mal vi	f. 71ᵛ, col. A, l. 3, left	C	*muj mujto boa*
54.		f. 71ᵛ, col. A, ll. 4/6, left	?	*several y*
55.		f. 71ᵛ, col. A, l. 7, left	?	*a johā de [***]*
Twelfth gathering				
56.	Blank page	f. 77ʳ, full page	?	various drawings and inscriptions
Thirteenth gathering				
	— Pero da Ponte			
57.	CA 288 Tam muito vos am'eu, senhor	f. 81ᵛ, col. B, l. 15, right	A	*e por este sse dise guardando he quē deos guarda*
Fourteenth gathering				
58.	Blank page	f. 86ᵛ, top	?	[sign or E] *p° hom*[*]
59.		f. 86ᵛ, centre/left	?	*guonçalo guomez mirador guonçalo guomez mirador guonçalo g*[***]*m*
	— Rui Fernandes de Santiago			
60.		f. 88ᵛ, top	?	[sign or E] *p° hom*[*][1]
61.	CA 309 Ora começa o meu mal	f. 88ᵛ, col. A, ll. 18/19, left	A	*ao demo ao demo o amor*
62.	Blank page	f. 87ʳ, full page	?	various inscriptions and drawings[2]

---

[1] Michaëlis de Vasconcellos, 1904, II, 178 offers *P. Gomes dasinhaga*.
[2] Michaëlis de Vasconcellos, 1904, II, 179 transcribes six fragmentary inscriptions.

The Manuscript Tradition of the *Regula Benedicti* in Portuguese

IVO CASTRO

Lisbon University

All the known manuscripts written in Old Portuguese would fit comfortably on the shelves of one, not very large, bookcase.[1] This scarcity can be explained in a number of ways. Many books that once existed have been lost, destroyed by either human or natural causes, while the production of manuscripts, both of originals and of transcriptions and translations, was almost certainly not intensive. Scriptorial centres and libraries, usually located under the same roof (at monasteries such as Alcobaça, Santa Cruz de Coimbra, Arouca, Lorvão and a few others), were scarce. Private book-collections, whose contents can be glimpsed in the wills and legacies of their owners, look small by modern standards, but were probably average for the period. For example, king Dom Duarte, himself a writer, owned sixty-four books 'em linguagem', i.e. in Portuguese, in what appears to be a substantial library;[2] his brother Fernando, who died young, possessed only eleven books in Portuguese. Their nephew, Condestabre Pedro de Portugal, also a writer, kept a large library of ninety-six books, but only four of them were in Portuguese, perhaps because he lived abroad most of his life.[3] Over the course of two centuries (1090 to 1299), Coimbra Cathedral was bequeathed a total of twenty-two legacies of books, only one of which exceeded thirty items. We do not know which languages those books were written in, but it is likely that they were mainly in Latin, since their former owners were men of the church — bishops, canons, scholars.[4] Exceptional in

---

[1] All the references made below to individual works, when no specific mention is made otherwise, come from these sources: *Bibliografia de textos antigos galegos e portugueses (BITAGAP)* database <http://bancroft.berkeley.edu/philobiblon/bitagap_en.html>; Isabel Vilares Cepeda, *Bibliografia da prosa medieval em língua portuguesa* (Lisbon: Ministério da Cultura, Instituto da Biblioteca Nacional e do Livro, 1995); Ivo Castro, *Introdução à história do português*, 2nd edn (Lisbon: Colibri, 2006), pp. 92–94; M. A. Valle Cintra, *Bibliografia de textos medievais portugueses* (Lisbon: Centro de Estudos Filológicos, 1980).

[2] In comparison, Richard II of England owned twenty books and his uncle Gloucester 120; this was 'by far the largest collection of which evidence remains from the reign of Richard II' (V. J. Scattergood, 'Literary Culture at the Court of Richard II', in *English Court Culture in the Later Middle Ages*, ed. by V. J. Scattergood and J. W. Sherborne (London: Gerald Duckworth & Co., 1983), pp. 29–44 (pp. 32–33), quoted in Ana Isabel Buescu, 'Livros e livrarias de reis e de príncipes entre os séculos XV e XVI: algumas notas', *eHumanista*, 8 (2007), 143–70 (p. 144)).

[3] S. Silva Neto, *Textos medievais portugueses e seus problemas* (Rio de Janeiro: Casa de Rui Barbosa, 1956), pp. 117–25.

[4] Aires A. Nascimento, 'Circulação do livro manuscrito', in *Dicionário da literatura medieval galega e portuguesa*, ed. by Giulia Lanciani and Giuseppe Tavani (Lisbon: Caminho, 1993), pp. 155–59.

this respect, and many others, is the wealth of the library at Alcobaça, well preserved to this day. With the exception of three books now at the British Library, its contents are almost entirely kept at the Biblioteca Nacional de Portugal (BNP): 464 manuscripts, of which 350 date from before the sixteenth century.[5] Among the latter, a considerable number are in Portuguese, thanks to the intensive production of translations that was a prominent part of this monastery's activity in the mid-fifteenth century.[6]

Serafim da Silva Neto, a Brazilian scholar personally responsible for the retrieval of some important manuscripts now held in the library of Brasília University (including a fourteenth-century *Livro das Aves*, by Hugo de Folieto, and a fifteenth-century copy of *Diálogos de São Gregório Magno*, among others), once wrote a melancholy essay about 'Algumas perdas da literatura medieval portuguesa' [some losses from medieval Portuguese literature].[7] He worried about books whose existence could be taken for granted, but could not actually be found. For example, the *Livro de Merlim* in Dom Duarte's library might be the missing companion to *Livro de José de Arimateia* and *Demanda do Santo Graal*, the two extant Portuguese survivors of the Arthurian trilogy known as the Post-Vulgate *Roman du Graal*; Karl Pietsch conjectured that one *Livro do Amante*, from the same library, could be the necessary link between John Gower's *Confessio Amantis* and a Spanish translation (through the Portuguese), the *Confision del Amante*.[8]

Many more could be added to this list. For instance, it is safe to assume that a full Portuguese translation of the *Siete Partidas* by D. Alfonso X of Leon and Castile was completed fairly early: a fifteenth-century copy of *Primeira Partida* is kept at the BNP in Lisbon, and fragments of the other *Partidas* can be found in various libraries and archives,[9] with the sole exception of the *Quarta Partida*. The existence at some point of a translation of the full text can thus be treated as a safe bet. Not a guess, but a certainty, is the former existence of *Crónica do Mouro Rasis*, an early translation by Gil Peres of a work by the Andalusian historian Ahmad al-Razi, an acknowledged source of both André de Resende's *História da antiguidade da cidade de Évora*, and of the *Crónica Geral de Espanha de 1344*. Also missing is a set of *Letters* by Lopo de Almeida, Conde de Abrantes, once reported to be at the IANTT (Instituto dos Arquivos Nacionais–Torre do Tombo), in Lisbon.

---

[5] Henceforth the following initials will be used in the text: BNP (*Biblioteca Nacional de Portugal*, Lisbon); IANTT (*Instituto dos Arquivos Nacionais–Torre do Tombo*, Lisbon); BNF (*Bibliothèque Nationale de France*, Paris); ÖNB (*Österreiches National Bibliothek*, Vienna); ACL (*Academia das Ciências de Lisboa*); RAH (*Real Academia de la Historia*, Madrid); BN (*Biblioteca Nacional*, Rio de Janeiro).
[6] A. A. Nascimento, 'Alcobaça', in *Dicionário da literatura medieval galega e portuguesa*, pp. 32–35.
[7] S. Silva Neto, *Textos medievais portugueses*, pp. 111–16.
[8] K. Pietsch, 'Zum Text der *Confision del Amante* por Joan Goer', *Zeitschrift für romanische Philologie*, 46 (1926), 428–44.
[9] Those fragments are: *Primeira Partida* (fourteenth century), in Lisbon; *Segunda Partida* (fourteenth century), in Lisbon, Braga and Coimbra; *Terceira Partida* (fourteenth century), in Lisbon, Braga and Coimbra; *Quinta Partida* (fourteenth century), in Lisbon; *Sexta Partida* (fourteenth century), in Lisbon; *Setima Partida* (fourteenth century), in Évora and Lisbon.

Some works had more luck. Their existence in the Middle Ages cannot be doubted, since they are quoted in texts or library inventories but, although the original manuscripts have been lost, they are now known through later copies. According to Silva Neto, the *Livro da Reynha Dona Elisabethe*, of which a 1572 edition is now the earliest version, suffered the misfortune of disappearing twice: not only the fourteenth-century original, mentioned in the inventory of Prince Fernando's library, but also a fifteenth-century copy, seen and described in modern times. Not dissimilar is the case of the *Livro de Montaria* by Dom João I of Portugal, nowadays represented by only one fairly modern copy, made from a seventeenth-century copy considerably later than the date of its composition in the early fifteenth century. Recently, however, press reports have revealed that some older fragments have been surfacing in several places in Galicia, so there is hope of a partial recovery of the work in its original shape.

Other cases of the same nature — the manuscripts of two of the oldest genealogical treatises, known as *Livro do Deão*, c. 1340, and *Livro Velho de Linhagens*, c. 1343 — have been lost, but the texts exist in the form of no less than seven and nine modern manuscripts, respectively, all produced after 1700. A similar type of manuscript tradition can be seen with the *Crónicas* of Fernão Lopes (*D. Pedro*, *D. Fernando*, *D. João I*), because they were used, along with the genealogies, for the legitimization of aristocratic families; plenty of modern sequential copies exist, but there are practically no medieval ones of archetypal value.

The loss of written documents, through outright destruction or just from going astray in the long corridors of an archive, is a natural, perhaps unavoidable, setback. Nevertheless, texts are being recovered here and there. Old manuscripts, when they could no longer be read with ease or when a fresh copy had been made, were treated unceremoniously as recyclable material. They were cut up and used to reinforce the bindings of new books that were more appealing to the reading public. Sometimes, leaves of parchment became the external material used in the binding process, making them quite easy to spot and rescue. Piece by piece, these neglected documents are now being rediscovered and are highly valued as textual relics, quite rightly more appreciated than the younger books to which they were once sacrificed.

Not many of these recoveries were known to Silva Neto. The *Rolo Vindel*, a thirteenth-century parchment folio with seven *cantigas de amigo* by Martin Codax, with musical notation, was found by a Spanish bookseller, Pedro Vindel, reinforcing the covers of a fifteenth-century *De Officiis*. Silva Neto was unable to locate this precious manuscript,[10] but it is presently known to be safely in New York (Pierpont Morgan Library, M. 979). Another relevant discovery of a similar nature was made by Harvey L. Sharrer in Lisbon at the IANTT: the *Pergaminho Sharrer* is a leaf of parchment (once part of some as yet unknown codex), written in the thirteenth century, with seven *cantigas de amor*, also with music, by Dom Denis of Portugal (IANTT, Fragms. Caixa 20, n. 2, Casa Forte).

---

[10] S. Silva Neto, *Textos medievais portugueses*, p. 114.

Yet another rescue: four fragments of a fourteenth-century *Merlin* were found inside the covers of a book in the Biblioteca de Cataluña, Barcelona (Ms. 2434). They most likely belonged to a book that Silva Neto longed to locate.[11]

Undoubtedly, many books were simply lost. It is possible, however, for book archaeologists to extricate lost or previously unknown texts from their hiding places. After all, the *Livro do Amante* was not lost, as Silva Neto feared, but simply stored in a library outside Portugal (Madrid, Biblioteca de Palacio II-3088). Nonetheless, vanishing manuscripts are not the sole reason for this state of affairs.

Surviving Manuscripts in Old Portuguese

Even if all lost manuscripts were, by some miracle, to be recovered, the hard fact remains that the literature originally produced, copied or translated in medieval Portugal did not amount to a large body of work. Eluding any cultural or, in literary terms, canonical implications of this fact — since neither the number of texts or of authors, nor their qualities, are in question here — let us merely register that this period shows a limited capacity in the generation of prose textual traditions.[12] In general, Old Portuguese texts gave rise to small traditions, composed of no more than a few manuscripts; nothing to compare with the opulent traditions we are used to finding in Old French literature, where it was common for there to be large numbers of manuscripts of any particular work. About sixty manuscripts of the *Estoire del Saint Graal* can be found in libraries around the world, but they are a mere shadow of an even wider manuscript tradition that developed between the thirteenth and fifteenth centuries in northern France, south-east England and a few peripheral places. This is not an isolated case, but one quite typical of medieval French literary output.[13]

Against this wider background, let us now concentrate on Old Portuguese prose texts — still extant and identified by major bibliographies — originally composed, or translated, or transcribed before 1500. Smaller texts, fragments, and letters will be excluded from our corpus, as will any copies dating from the sixteenth century onwards, whether in manuscript or printed form.

For this, it is almost mandatory to use the BITAGAP database (with some

---

[11] Ivo Castro, 'Merlim', in *Dicionário da literatura medieval galega e portuguesa*, pp. 456–58. See, for more details on fragments, the Coimbra University database *Fragmed. Corpus Portugaliae Fragmentorum* <http://fragmed.net/>.
[12] The same could be said of the poetic output in Galician-Portuguese: three *cancioneiros* of lay songs (two in Lisbon, *Ajuda* and *Biblioteca Nacional*; one at the Vatican), the Vindel and Sharrer fragments, and four manuscripts of the *Cantigas de Santa Maria* (two at the Escorial, one in Toledo and one in Florence).
[13] Ivo Castro, 'Remarques sur la tradition manuscrite de l'*Estoire del Saint Graal*', in *Homenagem a Joseph M. Piel*, ed. by Dieter Kremer (Tübingen: Niemeyer, 1988), pp. 197–99. For more, consult Brian Woledge, *Bibliographie des romans et nouvelles en prose française antérieurs à 1500* (Geneva: Droz, 1954); Françoise Vielliard, *Manuscrits français du Moyen Âge* (Geneva: Fondation Martin Bodmer, 1975).

help from the not updated, but more user-friendly, *Bibliografia* by Isabel Cepeda): both sources record not only manuscripts and editions that actually exist, but also those to which there is some kind of reference. In other words, they provide us with a reasonably reliable view not only of each text's recension (the sum of its textual witnesses, its manuscripts, which one can actually locate, read and use for editorial purposes), but also, at a second level, of all the available knowledge about other copies that we are only aware of through historical or intertextual references, but, since they no longer exist, we are not allowed to consider as witnesses.

Of course, this presents risks of two kinds: firstly, two references may point to the same manuscript and not to different ones; secondly, absent manuscripts, however important, may elude our radar if no mention has ever been made of them. It is at this second level that a manuscript tradition is reconstructed, as a tentative way of establishing the relationship formed by actual textual witnesses and by conjectured liaisons required to trace the upper stages of a *stemma codicum*. For practical reasons, since not many Portuguese texts have been thus philologically scrutinized, I have tended, in the grouping of the lists below, to favour the first and stricter level as a criterion, thus only including manuscripts that actually exist and can be read. Further research and new manuscript findings will, without doubt, result in a more extensive panorama than what follows.

Only a few texts exist in the form of *three or more* manuscripts in Old Portuguese written before 1500:

(1). *Regra de São Agostinho* — three medieval MSS in Porto, Aveiro and Lisbon BNP; several from the sixteenth century onwards
(2). *Regra de S. Bento* (fourteenth–fifteenth century) — seven MSS in Lisbon BNP and IANTT, Braga and Porto, together with six more MSS from the sixteenth century onwards
(3). *Colações dos Santos Padres do Egipto*, by João Cassiano (fifteenth century) — four MSS in Lisbon BNP, one in Paris BNF
(4). *Livro do Desprezo do Mundo, de Isaac de Ninive* (fifteenth century) — three MSS: Lisbon BNP, Évora, Rio de Janeiro BN
(5). *Livro da Virtuosa Benfeitoria*, by Pedro Duke of Coimbra (fifteenth century) — three MSS in Viseu, Madrid RAH and Oxford Bodleian
(6). *Diálogos de Gregório Magno* (fourteenth–fifteenth century) — two MSS in Lisbon BNP, plus one in Lisbon IANTT and one in Brasília

About the same number of texts are now represented by two medieval manuscripts:

(1). *Vita Christi*, trans. (in spite of the title) from Ludolphus of Saxony (fifteenth century) — four volumes in Lisbon BNP and fragments in Évora
(2). *Espelho da Cruz*, by Domenico Cavalca (fifteenth century) — two MSS in Lisbon BNP

(3). *Crónica Geral de Espanha de 1344* (fifteenth century) — two MSS in Paris BNF and Lisbon ACL
(4). *Horto do Esposo* (fifteenth century) — two MSS in Lisbon BNP
(5). *Castelo Perigoso*, trans. of Fr. Robertus, *Chastel Périlleux* (fifteenth century) — two MSS in Lisbon BNP

Finally, the great majority of the texts are supported by only one medieval manuscript:

(1). *Primeira Partida*, trans. of Alfonso X, *Siete Partidas* (fifteenth century) — one MS in Lisbon BNP
(2). *Soliloquios do Pseudo Agostinho* (fifteenth century) — one MS in Lisbon BNP
(3). *Livro das tres crenças*, trans. of Alonso de Valladolid, *Libro de las tres creencias* (fourteenth century) — one MS in Lisbon BNP
(4). *Crónica do Infante Dom Fernando*, by Fr. João Álvares (fifteenth century) — one MS in Madrid BN
(5). *Crónica dos Gerais da Ordem dos Frades Menores*, together with *Martírio dos Cinco Mártires de Marrocos* both by Fr. Arnaldo de Sarano (fifteenth century) — one MS in Lisbon BNP
(6). *Lenda de Barlaão e Josafate* (fifteenth century) — one MS in Lisbon BNP
(7). *Meditações e pensamentos*, by Pseudo-Bernardo (fifteenth century) — one MS in Lisbon BNP
(8). *Contemplação das sete horas canónicas*, by the same Pseudo-Bernardo (fifteenth century) — one MS in Lisbon BNP
(9). *Actos dos Apóstolos*, by Bernardo de Brihuega (fifteenth century) — one MS and fragments in Lisbon BNP
(10). *Catecismo da Doutrina Cristã* (fifteenth century) — one MS in Lisbon BNP
(11). *Livro dos Ofícios*, trans. by D. Pedro Duke of Coimbra of Cicero, *De Oficiis* (fifteenth century) — one MS at Madrid BN and fragments in Paris BNF
(12). *Livro da Ordem dos Cónegos Regrantes e Crasteiros* (fifteenth century) — one MS in Porto
(13). *Crónica da Conquista do Algarve* (fifteenth century) — one MS in Tavira
(14). *Crónica da Fundação do Mosteiro de S. Vicente e da Tomada de Lisboa aos Mouros* (fourteenth century) — one MS at Lisbon BNP
(15). *Demanda do Santo Graal*, trans. of *Queste del Saint Graal* and *Mort Artu* (fifteenth century) — one MS in Vienna ÖNB
(16). *Diálogo de Robim e do Teólogo* (fifteenth century) — one MS in Lisbon BNP
(17). *Dicionário de Verbos Latim-Português* (fourteenth century) — one MS in Lisbon BNP
(18). *Leal Conselheiro*, by D. Duarte King of Portugal (fifteenth century) — one MS in Paris BNF

(19). *Livro da Ensinança de Bem Cavalgar Toda Sela*, by D. Duarte, King of Portugal (fifteenth century) — one MS in Paris BNF
(20). *Livro de Esopo* (fourteenth century) — one MS in Vienna ÖNB
(21). *Livro de Alveitaria, de mestre Giraldo* (fourteenth century) — one MS in Lisbon BNP
(22). *Livro de Naturas, de Frei Gil de Santarém* (fifteenth century) — one MS in Évora
(23). *Livro do Amante*, trans. by Robert Payn of John Gower, *Confessio Amantis* (fifteenth century) — one MS in Madrid
(24). *Vida de São Bernardo*, trans. of G. de Saint-Thierry, *Vita Sanctis Bernardi* (fifteenth century) — one MS in Lisbon BNP
(25). *Livro das Aves, de Hugo de Folieto* (fourteenth century) — one MS in Brasília
(26). *Vergel de Consolação*, by Jacobo de Benavente (fifteenth century) — one MS in Lisbon BNP
(27). *Flores de Direito*, trans. of Jacobo de las Leyes, *Flores de Derecho* (thirteenth century) — one MS in Lisbon IANTT
(28). *Escada Celestial*, trans. of Johannes Climacus, *Scala Paradisi* (fifteenth century) — one MS in Lisbon BNP
(29). *Espelho dos Monges*, trans. of *Speculum Monachorum*, by the same author (fifteenth century) — one MS in Lisbon BNP
(30). *Livro dos Milagres de Nossa Senhora das Virtudes*, by Fr. João da Póvoa (fifteenth century) — one MS in Lisbon BNP
(31). *Livro da Corte Imperial* (fifteenth century) — one MS in Porto
(32). *Livro dos Milagres dos Santos Mártires de Marrocos* (fifteenth century) — one MS in Porto
(33). *Livro de Falcoaria*, by Pero Menino (fifteenth century) — one MS in Lisbon BNP
(34). *Livro das Três Virtudes*, trans. of Christine de Pisan, *Livre des Trois Vertus pour l'Enseignement des Princesses* (fifteenth century) — one MS in Madrid BN
(35). *Regras para informarmos os meninos em latim* (fourteenth century) — one MS in Oxford Bodleian
(36). *Disciplina dos Monges*, trans. of Hugo de S. Vitor, *De Institutione Novitiorum* (fifteenth century) — one MS in Lisbon BNP
(37). *Segredo dos Segredos*, trans. of Pseudo-Aristoteles, *Secretum Secretorum* (fifteenth century) — one MS in Lisbon BN
(38). *Imitação de Cristo*, trans. by Fr. João Álvares of Thomas a Kempis, *Immitatio Christi* (fifteenth century) — one MS in Porto
(39). *Vida e Feitos de Júlio César*, trans. by Vasco de Lucena of *Li Faits des Romains* (fifteenth century) — one MS at the Escorial and one fragment in Lisbon BNP

More texts could be added to this list,[14] but they would not really help us to reach any conclusion other than this: a large portion of the literary-historical output in Old (and Middle) Portuguese produced small manuscript traditions that have been reduced to one item, indeed almost to the brink of disappearance. Efforts to find and classify new or lost manuscripts, albeit in fragmentary condition, are therefore of the greatest utility. Only more discoveries like these can help us improve on that conclusion, in cases where it becomes apparent that newly found manuscripts descend from ancestors other than those we already know, meaning that their textual tradition had more residents than previously thought. That seems, by the way, to be the case of the Madrid *Livro do Amante*, which has been identified not as the manuscript belonging to Dom Duarte's library, but as a second copy of that text.[15]

Our knowledge of the real conditions of production, existence and transmission of each of the individual texts in the lists above is so scarce that it is prudent not to draw any firmer conclusions. We can, however, cautiously make some further comments: a few of these texts were the object of plural transmission in the Middle Ages in Portugal, but the majority of them were not. A few more texts have had wider and later transmissions; a textual collation of these might help to infer whether or not they can be traced back to older manuscripts that are now mislaid or destroyed, thus enhancing their value, or whether they descend from already known manuscripts, thus falling into the class of *codices recepti* (i.e. of little textual interest). It is possible, if not certain, that the medieval traditions of many texts were larger than what we now possess. Nothing prevents us from assuming that these traditions have lost manuscripts in line with their dimensions: large traditions have lost more manuscripts, small ones fewer. In order to conclude otherwise, we need much more information.

The *Regula Benedicti*

All this brings us to the realization that the seven medieval manuscripts of the *Regra de S. Bento*, together with its six copies from the sixteenth century onwards, form a manuscript tradition of considerable size, probably the largest in Old Portuguese, not to mention several old printed versions. The structure and development of this tradition of exceptional dimensions therefore deserves closer attention.

The *Regula Benedicti* reached the Iberian Peninsula relatively late: the *Marca Hispanica* (roughly modern Catalonia) in the early ninth century, Castile in

---

[14] A brief mention should be made of three composite manuscripts from Alcobaça, now at Lisbon BNP, each containing a number of short hagiographies, some in dual version: Alcobaça 181 (*Diálogos de S. Gregório, Aleixo, Cativo Monge Confesso*), Alcobaça 461 (*Isaac, Duque Antíoco, Egipcíaca, Pelágia*, etc.), Alcobaça 462 (*Barlaão e Josafate, Eufrosina, Egipcíaca, Tarsis, Aleixo, Pelágia, Amaro, Túndalo*, etc.).

[15] Buescu, 'Livros e livrarias de reis e de príncipes', pp. 154–55.

the tenth, and later still in the western kingdoms.[16] By the end of the eleventh century, it had spread to the territory soon to become Portugal, mainly through the initiative of the order of Cluny. In fact, the *Regula* was followed not only by Benedictines, but also by Cistercians, whose main House was Alcobaça. Indeed, it was the Cistercians who would form the majority of its readership, and Alcobaça scriptorium would be responsible in large measure for the *Regula* translations into Portuguese *Regra*, and furthermore Alcobaça library would house most of its manuscripts.

In 1993, José Mattoso summarized the *status quaestionis* thus:

> Mencionemos, antes de mais, as duas versões alcobacenses da *Regra de S. Bento* (que, como se sabe, rege não só os beneditinos mas também os cistercienses), contidas nos BNL Alc. 14 e 231, e publicadas primeiro separadamente por Fr. Fortunato de S. Boaventura e por J. Burnam, e depois em edição conjunta, e comparada ainda com uma outra versão originária de Lorvão, por J. J. Nunes. Existe, porém, outra versão alcobacense publicada igualmente por J. J. Nunes, a do BNL Alc. 44, e ainda a feita por Fr. João Álvares para uso dos beneditinos [...][17]

> [First and foremost, we must mention the two Alcobaça versions of the *Regra de S. Bento* (which, as we know, governed not only the Benedictines but also the Cistercians), held in the BNL Alc. 14 and 231, first published separately by Fr. Fortunato de S. Boaventura and J. Burnam, and then brought together in an edition by J. J. Nunes which compared them with a further version originating from Lorvão. There is, however, a further Alcobaça version, also published by J. J. Nunes, at the BNL Alc. 44, and yet another: that made by Fr. Joao Alvares for the use of the Benedictines [...].]

Mattoso only mentions five manuscripts, those that had been published before 1993. The oldest one (Lisbon BNP Alcobaça 14) is a long fragment which was first edited and published by Fr. Fortunato de S. Boaventura in 1829,[18] and then by José Joaquim Nunes in 1926.[19] The second manuscript is Alcobaça 231, also at Lisbon BNP. It was first edited and published by John M. Burnam,[20] then by Nunes,[21] and most recently by Sara Figueiredo Costa.[22]

---

[16] José Mattoso, 'A introdução da Regra de S. Bento na Península Ibérica', in *Religião e cultura na idade média portuguesa*, 2nd edn (Lisbon: IN-CM, 1997), pp. 55-90 (pp. 73-74).
[17] José Mattoso, 'Regras Monásticas', in *Dicionário da literatura medieval galega e portuguesa*, p. 572.
[18] 'Fragmentos de uma versão antiga da Regra de S. Bento', in *Collecção de inéditos portuguezes dos seculos XIV e XV*, 3 vols (Coimbra: Real imprensa da Universidade, 1829), I, 243-91.
[19] 'Evolução da língua portuguesa, exemplificada em duas lições principalmente da mesma versão da Regra de S. Bento e ainda nos fragmentos da mais antiga que se conhece', *Boletim da Classe de Letras da Academia das Ciências de Lisboa*, 15 (1922), 928-72; 16 (1926), 588-637.
[20] *An Old Portuguese Version of the Rule of Benedict: Palaeographical edition from the Alcobaça MS N° 300 in the Bibliotheca Publica of Lisbon*, ed. by John M. Burnam (Cincinnati, OH: Cincinnati University, 1911), pp. 11-78. Burnam quotes the old shelfmark of this manuscript.
[21] 'Evolução...', *Boletim da Classe de Letras*, 14 (1922), 222-313; 15 (1922), 224-62.
[22] *A Regra de S. Bento em português: estudo e edição de dois manuscritos*, ed. by Sara Figueiredo Costa (Lisbon: Colibri, 2007).

The third manuscript is the former Lorvão 32, now Lisbon IANTT, Casa Forte 99, published partially by Nunes,[23] and fully by Sara Costa in the work cited previously.

The fourth manuscript is Alcobaça 44 (Lisbon BNP), edited and published by Nunes.[24]

The last manuscript is Porto BPMP, Fundo Azevedo 18, and it was edited and published by Adelino de Almeida Calado.[25] It is a translation made in 1477 by the Benedictine abbot João Álvares for the benefit of the monks of his monastery of Paço de Sousa, as he declares in the incipit: 'Me pareçeo que se*gundo* o q*ue* perteeçe a meu oficio eu deueria de fazer poer en nosso linguajem a forma e oreginal da d*i*cta regra' [I think it fits my office to have the form and original of this rule rendered into our common language] (fol. 2^v). The formula *fazer poer* [to have rendered] does not, in my opinion, rule out Álvares himself as being the translator of the text.

Of the hitherto unpublished manuscripts of the *Regra* (not mentioned by Mattoso), three can be dated from the fifteenth century: Braga 132, Lisbon BNP Alcobaça 73 and Iluminado 70. Also, five from the sixteenth: Lisbon IANTT Semide 3, BNP Alcobaça 223 and Iluminado 209, Lorvão Monastery 18. Coimbra 636. The following table shows the entire collection of *Regra* manuscripts of which we have knowledge:

Lisbon	BNP	Alc. 14	c. 1350	trans. 1
Lisbon	BNP	Alc. 231	1414–1427	group 1
Lisbon	BNP	Alc. 44	c. 1430	group 2
Braga	ADBP	Mss 132	1451–1500	group 1
Lisbon	BNP	Alc. 73	1461–1475	group 1
Porto	BPMP	Azevedo 18	1477	trans. 2
Lisbon	BNPI	l. 70	1495–1515	group 2
Lisbon	IANTT	Semide 3	1535	group 2
Lisbon	BNP	Alc. 223	1501–1550	group 1
Lorvão	Monastery	18	1546?	
Lisbon	IANTT	Casa Forte 99	1565 (ex Lorvão 32)?	
Lisbon	BNP	Il. 209	1576–1600	trans. 3
Coimbra	BGUC	636	c. 1791	trans. 2bis

In the last few years, with the exception of Lorvão 18 and Coimbra 636, all of these manuscripts have been edited in separate diplomatic editions and six of them are available at the site of Centro de Linguística da Universidade de Lisboa <http://oficinamssbento.wordpress.com/edicoes/>; the others will follow shortly.

These editions prepared the ground for an extensive critical examination of texts, individually and in collated form. There is much to be done in that sense,

---

[23] 'Evolução...', *Boletim da Classe de Letras*, 14 (1922), 222–313; 15 (1922), 224–62 (only variant readings).
[24] 'Textos antigos portugueses. VII', *Revista Lusitana*, 21 (1918), 91–145.
[25] Published in Fr. João Álvares, *Obras*, ed. by Adelino de Almeida Calado, 2 vols (Coimbra: Atlântida, 1959), II, 6–90.

but the collation of their variants and the description of each manuscript have given fairly clear comprehensive answers to issues that, in some cases, had been difficult to formulate.

The first issue was easy to resolve. In fact, Mattoso and Nunes, while somewhat disagreeing (with Nunes speaking of 'two readings of the same version', while Mattoso says there were 'two versions'), had both already tackled it. The question was: do all known manuscripts descend from the same translation? If so, the history of monastic orders in Portugal would have to deal with the idea of a central institution, both doctrinal and scriptorial, prevailing over every congregation that owned copies of the *Regra* in their libraries. Even Alcobaça, which owns copies of several translations, would hardly qualify for such a central role.

There are, in fact, several independent translations, some are individual manuscripts, others are groups. These groups, coming from the same sub-archetype (the original of their translation), offer the added interest of linguistic updates by each copyist, thus highlighting which forms and structures were falling out of use and in need of replacement at the time of each step. As José Joaquim Nunes was quick to notice (in the title he gave to his edition: *The Evolution of the Portuguese Language* [...]), the *Regra* is the perfect text for describing the evolution from Old to Classical Portuguese. There was a crucially short and sharp period of change, called Middle Portuguese, that took place in the mid-fifteenth century, precisely when several of the translations and their copies were made. The oldest manuscript, Alcobaça 14, dating from c. 1350, is a good representative of Old Portuguese; six manuscripts from the fifteenth century show evidence, stage by stage, of the progression of Middle Portuguese; five others date from the sixteenth century; the latest, dated 1791, is a copy made by the palaeographer João Pedro Ribeiro from João Álvares' translation (although critically it is a mere *receptus*, linguistically it is not without value).[26]

Next, it is important to analyse the individual translations, of which there are three: Alcobaça 14, Porto Azevedo 18, BNP Iluminado 209. Alcobaça 14 is linguistically peculiar, even for its time, and seems to be the work of an extremely conservative translator. He uses archaisms such as *seenço* (instead of *silencio*, as the other manuscripts do), *mha* (*minha*), *dixi, pugy* (*disse, puse*), *paravras* (*palavras* was already very common in Galaico-Portuguese poetry).

---

[26] With individual editions now available, it is possible to improve on the collection of linguistic data that Nunes and myself (Castro, *Introdução à história do português*, pp. 172–84) have had at our disposal to trace the changes the language went through in the late Middle Ages. A sample of such improvements can be found in S. A. Toledo Neto, 'Indícios de parentesco entre dois testemunhos da *Regra de São Bento*: colação entre Alc. 44 e Il. 70', *Caligrama* (Belo Horizonte), 15.2 (2010), 67–88, and in two forthcoming essays: P. Carvalho, J. Serafim and João Paulo Silvestre, '*The Rule of Saint Benedict* — Portuguese Versions: Building a Diachronic Lexicon', in *Planning Non-Existent Dictionaries*, ed. by João Paulo Silvestre and Alina Villalva, *Dicionarística*. IV (Lisbon: Centro de Linguística — University of Lisbon); and Joana Serafim, 'A tradição manuscrita portuguesa da *Regula Benedicti*: tentativa de enquadramento na família europeia', *Dedalus*, 17–18.

His translation is shorter and closer to the Latin original, sometimes to the point of obscurity: he renders *propter taciturnitatem* literally as *espões o ceenço*, while other translations prefer *por o silençio* or *por amor e guarda do silençio*; he omits the verb in *A morte e vida nas mãos da lingua*, faithful to the original *Mors et vita in manibus linguae*. Finally, his text abounds in present participles (*parauras ociosas e riso mouentes*), while other translators leave behind this stern latinism for more modern choices: *palauras ociosas e que mouam a rijso*. No other known text follows this translation.

The second individual translation (Porto Azevedo 18) is the work of Fr. João Álvares, dated 1477. The author was a prolific and influential humanist, close to Prince Fernando, and this translation can be considered almost a personal work, certainly deserving of scrutiny.

The third translation (Lisbon BNP Iluminado 209) is a rather modern manuscript, from the late sixteenth century, after all the other translations had been done. Why not reproduce one of those? Possibly because they were unknown or not accessible to the translator (he probably experienced the same difficulties Álvares encountered at Paço de Sousa). As a result, we have a different work, with many individual readings of a separative nature, that mark out this manuscript in opposition to all the others: *primeiro dia* (not *calendas*), *sanctissima trindade* (not *sancta trindade*), *em cima* (not *de suso*), *Ouve filha* (not *Filho/Filha ascuita*), *irmãos* (not *freires/frades*).

In addition to these autonomous translations, another two have propagated and have given rise to at least seven manuscripts, probably a few more. They can thus be assembled in two groups, ordered chronologically and setting both translations in the first half of the fifteenth century:

First group of MSS:
BNP Alcobaça 231
Braga 132
BNP Alcobaça 73
BNP Alcobaça 223

Second group:
BNP Alcobaça 44
BNP Iluminado 70
IANTT Semide 3

A few more manuscripts, as well as editions printed in the sixteenth and seventeenth centuries, are yet to find their place in this framework.

Variants collated between translations are of a separative nature; in fact, they are the basis for the identification of any independent translation. But, at the same time, they act as conjunctive variants within one group, the identity of its members coming from one common ancestor, the original of that translation. In any short segment of text, it is possible to find a number of different lexical and syntactic options that have been made in quick succession by the two translators, while keeping practically intact the general flow and meaning of the text. The very first lines of the *Regra* are a good example of this, as is shown by the oldest members of the two groups (Alcobaça 231 and 44):[27]

Alcobaça 231
Começa se o prologo da Regla de san beento abbade
   Filho ascuyta os preceptos e **mandamentos** do meestre. e inclina e abaixa a orelha do teu coraçõ. e recibe **de boamente** e toma o amoestamento e cõselho do padre piadoso. e **aficadamente o comple** e ponhe en obra. **porque te tornes** per trabalho de obediencia. aaquel **do qual te partiste e arredaste** per priguiça e peccado de desobediencia. **Poys** por esto. **a ty hora eu digo** o meu sermon e as minhas palauras. **quen quer** que tu es que queres renunciar e **fugir** aos proprios deleytos e **plazeres da carne** e deste mundo. *e* tomas armas de obediencia muy fortes *e* muy claras *e* nobres p*er*a seruir a jh*es*u *christ*o. senhor *e* uerdadeyro Rey:...

Alcobaça 44
Começa sse o prologo da Regla de ssam beento abbade
   FJlho ascuyta os preçeptos e **encomendamentos** do meestre. e inclina e abaixa a horelha do teu coraçõ. e **cõ boa uoontade** reçibe e toma ho amoestamento do padre piadoso. e **cõ gramde eficaçia o cõpre. pera te tornares** a el. per trabalho d obediençia. **do qual tu eras departido e alonguado** per priguiça e pecado de desobediençia. E **porende eu digo a ti** qualquer que tu es que queres renunçiar e **desprezar** os propios dileitos e **pecados e uãa gloria** deste mundo *e q*ueres batalhar *e* lidar *com* o diaboo. *e s*eruir a ih*es*u *christ*o senhor *e* u*er*dadeiro rey.

[Listen carefully, my child, to your master's precepts, and incline the ear of your heart. Receive willingly and carry out effectively your loving father's advice, that by the labor of obedience you may return to Him from whom you had departed by the sloth of disobedience. To you, therefore, my words are now addressed, whoever you may be, who are renouncing your own will to do battle under the Lord Christ, the true King, and are taking up the strong, bright weapons of obedience.]

The readings in bold type are the relevant variants, both separative and conjunctive:[28] while keeping the two translations apart, they are common to all manuscripts of each. Here, side by side, are the most important examples in the *Prologo*, together with a small sample from later chapters:

Prologo	
Mandamentos	encomendamentos
de boamente	cõ boa uoontade
aficadamente o comple	cõ gramde eficaçia o cõpre
porque te tornes	pera te tornares

---

[27] The transcription of the Portuguese segments is slightly simplified, with the loss of graphical variants. The English translation quoted here is a modern one, by Leonard Doyle <http://www.osb.org/rb/text/rbejms1.html#pro>.
[28] The terms 'conjunctive' and 'separative' are used in the critical sense attributed to them by Paul Maas (*Textkritik*, 1927; ital. trans. *Critica del Testo* (Florence: Le Monnier, 1975), pp. 54 ff.); also D'Arco Silvio Avalle (*Principî di Critica Testuale* (Padova: Antenore, 1972), p. 45), but it should be noted that here they do not concern copy errors (Fehler), but traces of intentional decisions made by translators.

te partiste e arredaste	tu eras departido e alonguado
Poys	porende
a ty hora eu digo	eu digo a ti
quen quer	qualquer
fugir	desprezar
plazeres da carne	pecados e uãa gloria

Ch. 7

que se cavidava	castigando si mesmo
reigno de deus	gloria do paraiso

Chs 8–12

conuem a ssaber	scilicet
vigilias	matinas
seedas	cadeiras
muy nomeados doutores	muy grandes doutores

Ch. 28

Enton o abbade use de ferro que corte e talhe tal monge do mosteyro lançando o fora del	Estonçe o abbade use do exenplo da sancta scriptura

In conclusion, all the medieval (and classical) manuscripts of at least five separate translations of the *Regra de São Bento* have been edited and are easily accessible, or on the way to being so. They offer ample new material for the description of the evolution of the language in its transition from Old to Modern Portuguese. They also suggest that the *Regra* had a considerable reading public, requiring not only the production of several translations, but also copies of several of those translations. The quantities involved, not matched by another medieval text in Portuguese, give food for thought. The same could be said of the fact that, in spite of the monastic nature of the text, some of its readers seem not to have been able to use its Latin versions, of which there must have been plenty. In Portugal's archives, there are still at least six Latin manuscripts: one from Lorvão at Lisbon IANTT, two from Alcobaça at Lisbon BNP, two in Évora and one in Porto. The relationship between Latin and Portuguese manuscripts is yet to be fully determined and therefore there is plenty of work to be done.

Service, not Subservience: Chapter 98 of Dom Duarte's *Leal Conselheiro*

JULIET PERKINS

King's College London

Stephen Parkinson has referred to the 'unexpected modernity' of D. Duarte's personal reflections in his *Leal Conselheiro* [Loyal Counsellor].[1] Indeed, it is the personal voice of the monarch that is the undeniable attraction of this moralizing work. The present-day reader feels a shock of recognition at the king's psychological perception, his unflinching self-analysis, and the unsentimental way he dissects his own and others' motives and deeds. I would also suggest that modernity is found in D. Duarte's awareness of 'reception theory' and 'reader response', for he is equally astute about how his eventual audience might best find its way into his treatise and take its lessons. What is not so modern is the way his indomitable Christian faith imbues his thoughts and actions, but that is our problem, not his.

This article will focus on one of the best-known passages of *Leal Conselheiro*, Ch. 98 'Da pratica que tinhamos com El Rei, meu Senhor e Padre, cuja alma Deos haja' [Concerning our conduct towards the King, my Lord and Father, may God rest his soul]. Paradoxically, despite its being based purely on personal recollections, it comes over as one of the least 'modern'. Its portrayal of the ultra-harmonious relationship between D. Duarte, his brothers, and their father, D. João I, is founded on the old-fashioned virtues of obedience and humility. I will first contextualize the chapter in the treatise as a whole, and then look at how D. Duarte practised the reconciliation of the will with the virtues demanded by Christian and Classical teaching to achieve family harmony, given the particular influence of the fifth-century monk, John Cassian, on his thought. I hope that the dedicatee of this article excuses my going over information about the *Leal Conselheiro* that is already familiar to him, on the grounds that it is barely known outside Portugal and Brazil.[2]

---

[1] Stephen Parkinson, 'Fernão Lopes and Portuguese Prose Writing of the Middle Ages', in *A Companion to Portuguese Literature*, ed. by Stephen Parkinson, Cláudia Pazos Alonso and T. F. Earle (Woodbridge: Tamesis, 2009), p. 54. His remark includes the *Livro dos Conselhos* [Book of Good Counsel] and I would also apply it to D. Duarte's *Livro da Ensinança de Bem Cavalgar Toda Sela* [A Guide to Riding with Every Type of Saddle].

[2] The *Livro da Ensinança* has fared slightly better. Extracts translated by Amélia Hutchinson were included in Richard Barber's *The Knight and Chivalry*, rev. edn (Woodbridge: The Boydell Press, 1995), pp. 212–14. Complete translations are: *Etude du premier traité d'équitation portugais: livro da ensinança de bem cavalgar toda sela*, trans. by Carlos Henriques Pereira (Paris: L'Harmattan, 2001);

The *Leal Conselheiro* was prepared by Dom Duarte in the last year, perhaps in the last few months, of his reign (1433–38).[3] As we learn from the prologue, its compilation was prompted by a request from his queen, Leonor of Aragon, for him to gather together his own writings for the good discipline of the conscience and will that he had amassed over the years.[4] Acknowledging that his virtuous queen does not herself need guidance in this respect, he has decided the best way to respond to her request is to make a treatise of the material, together with some additional items. By so doing, not only will he please her, but also gain some measure of respite from his own cares and obligations. Through the discipline in pondering on and writing about wisdom and virtue, he will guard against acting contrary to such values. Since all conditions of men should follow a virtuous path, he hopes that others may profit from his treatise, especially those who learn best from what is expressed briefly and simply rather than from subtle arguments. Also lying behind his intentions is St James's teaching: 'he which converteth the sinner from the error of his way shall save a soul from death, and shall hide a multitude of sins.'[5] He suggests that D. Leonor call it 'loyal counsellor' and that she take it as an ABC of loyalty: A stands for the ability and passions in each of us; B for the great good that comes to those who follow virtue and goodness; C for the ways in which our evil and sins may be corrected. Since his treatise is destined for lords and their people who, regarding the issues raised therein, are as children compared with learned men (and D. Duarte includes himself in the former), they need to be instructed appropriately (p. 9).

As for the source of his writing, he says: 'mais screvo por que sinto e vejo na maneira de nosso viver, que per studo de livros nem ensino de leterados' [I write out of what I experience and observe in the way we live our lives rather than from book learning or the teaching of scholars] (p. 9). He recommends reading it slowly and in small doses; his readers should be like bees that, hovering over branches and leaves, usually alight on the flowers, from which they take part of their nourishment. As he tells the Queen, he thinks his treatise should principally be destined for a select group of the Portuguese court, those who wish to lead virtuous lives. Recognizing the diversity of men and their receptiveness, he uses an analogy from horsemanship: just as there are bits of various kinds, some of which fail to curb one horse whilst successfully

---

The Royal Book of Jousting, Horsemanship and Knightly Combat: A Translation of King Dom Duarte's 1438 Treatise 'Livro da Ensinança de Bem Cavalgar Toda Sela', trans. by António Franco Preto, ed. by Steven Muhlberger (Highland Village, TX: Chivalry Bookshelf, 2005).

[3] *Leal Conselheiro, o qual fez Dom Eduarte Rey de Portugal e do Algarve e Senhor de Cepta*, ed. by Joseph M. Piel (Lisbon: Livraria Bertrand, 1942), pp. ix–x. Piel speculates that D. Duarte may have been aware of his impending death, which impelled him to give an account of his deeds and leave a work behind him (p. x).

[4] Dom Duarte. *Leal Conselheiro*, ed. by Maria Helena Lopes de Castro (Lisbon: IN–CM, 1998), p. 7. Unless otherwise stated, further page references in the text are to this edition. English translations are my own.

[5] The General Epistle of James, 5. 20 (Authorized Version).

controlling another, so with moral teaching. He hopes that some readers will take his counsel, refrain from doing ill, and be guided to live righteously. On the other hand, he acknowledges that there are those who will scorn such teaching, and he would be relieved if they did not read his treatise. Finally, he says that he translates and copies other people's writings, as support for what he writes. Taking the example of John Gower's instruction through moral tales in the *Confessio Amantis* — while admitting his own insufficiency of invention to emulate it — he has no hesitation in quoting others, not in order to cover up his poor writing but to benefit those who read the matter within.

In the course of his treatise, D. Duarte does indeed carry out what his prologue promises. He cites, paraphrases, copies or translates, from Scripture, the Fathers and Doctors of the Church, classical philosophers of antiquity, and medieval figures such as Giles of Rome, Ramon Lull, the Pseudo-Aristotle, Gower, St Gregory and Andrea de Pace. He marshals in ninety chapters his thoughts and reading notes about understanding, memory, will, the sins, vices and virtues (in all their shades and from many perspectives), with a further eleven on a variety of other topics. Given the unequal treatment of the material in terms of length, focus or polish, the repetition of points, the somewhat obscure rationale for the ordering of chapters, and the eleven heterogeneous texts which seem to have little bearing on the principal aim of loyal counsel, it is inevitable that *Leal Conselheiro* has occasioned much consideration of its coherence and structure.[6]

If we can safely reject Oliveira Martins' hasty judgement of it as 'a confused compilation',[7] it is not so easy to place it within one genre (a moral treatise, a study in moral philosophy, a manual of right conduct and spiritual education, a work of political philosophy, being some of the possibilities). As João Dionísio points out, the diversity of genres corresponds to that of the authors cited by D. Duarte, and the range of literary forms works against the single attribution of moral treatise.[8] Latterly, Márcio Muniz has studied *Leal Conselheiro* from a political perspective and, following Ana Isabel Buescu, examined its affinity

---

[6] Apart from Piel's 1942 Preface, important studies are: Rodrigues Lapa, 'D. Duarte e a prosa didáctica', in *Lições de literatura portuguesa: época medieval*, 10th edn, rev. (Coimbra: Coimbra Editora, 1981); António José Saraiva, 'O *Leal Conselheiro*', in *O crepúsculo da Idade Média em Portugal*, Part III (Lisbon: Público/Gradiva, 1996), pp. 226-35; Robert Ricard, 'Le *Leal Conselheiro* du roi D. Duarte de Portugal', in *Études sur l'histoire morale et religieuse du Portugal* (Paris: Fundação Calouste Gulbenkian–Centro Cultural Português, 1970), pp. 62-86; Rogério Fernandes, 'D. Duarte e a educação senhorial', *Vértice*, 37 (1977), 387-405; José Gama, *A Filosofia da Cultura Portuguesa no 'Leal Conselheiro' de D. Duarte* (Lisbon: Fundação Calouste Gulbenkian–Junta Nacional de Investigação Científica e Tecnológica, 1995); João Dionísio, 'D. Duarte, leitor de Cassiano' (unpublished doctoral dissertation, Faculdade de Letras da Universidade de Lisboa, 2000); Márcio Ricardo Coelho Muniz, 'Os leais e prudentes *conselhos* de El-Rei D. Duarte', in *A literatura doutrinária na Corte de Avis*, ed. by Lênia Márcia Mongelli (São Paulo: Martins Fontes, 2001), pp. 245-305. The last-mentioned has a valuable section on the critical fortune of *Leal Conselheiro*.

[7] J. P. Oliveira Martins, Ch. VI 'O Leal Conselheiro', *Os filhos de D. João I* (Lisbon: Imprensa Nacional, 1891), pp. 153-80 (p. 167).

[8] João Dionísio, 'Literatura Franciscana no Leal Conselheiro, de D. Duarte', *Lusitania Sacra*, 2nd series, 13-14 (2001-02), 491-515 (p. 509 and n. 37).

with the 'mirror of princes' genre, in particular Giles of Rome's *De regimine principum* and the *Secretum secretorum* of Pseudo-Aristotle; he suggests it is a variant form, the mirror of the counsellor.[9] For the purposes of the present article, though, one will not go too far astray with the ABC-of-loyalty label.

Within the two-part framework (the treatise proper, and the additions), the material can obviously be grouped into smaller clusters. Not wishing to repeat the details given by Piel, Ricard and Muniz,[10] each of whom gives greater or lesser emphasis to the structure and content of various chapters according to their focus of interest, I give here a brief summary to help orientation. After the Prologue, Chs 1–9 treat of man's psychology, of understanding, will and memory, and their constituent parts. Chs 10–33 deal with the seven capital sins, and other associated passions, with some (such as sadness) receiving more extensive treatment than others.[11] Chs 34–62 then turn to the virtues, theological and cardinal, in which Prudence is particularly highlighted. Within this group are chapters on Charity and the four manners of love (of which friendship is the most virtuous and perfect), and on love between married couples (43–45). Although the title of Ch. 46 is off-putting (advice on how good women should fear their husbands), it is a subtle disquisition on virtue and friendship which follows on logically from the previous chapter.[12] Chs 63–80 return to and amplify analysis of the vices and virtues, with D. Duarte drawing heavily on his theological and philosophical sources. He expands upon the relation of the sins with human passions, and the theme of contentment or spiritual satisfaction. When discussing the virtues, he demonstrates the perils of both a lack and an excess in exercising them. Chs 81 and 82 develop a metaphor of the five 'houses of the heart': each room in the house has a correlation of ends or purposes,

---

[9] Márcio Ricardo Coelho Muniz, 'O *Leal Conselheiro* e a tradição do Espelho de Príncipe: considerações sobre o gênero', in *Actas del IX Congreso Internacional de la Asociación Hispánica de Literatura Medieval (A Coruña 18–22 de setiembre de 2001)*, ed. by Carmen Parrilla and Mercedes Pampín, 3 vols (Noia: Toxosoutos, 2005), II, 89–103; also his unpublished doctoral dissertation, 'O *Leal Conselheiro* de D. Duarte, e a tradição dos espelhos de príncipes' (Faculdade de Filosofia, Letras e Ciências Humanas da Universidade de S. Paulo, 2003), which I have not had the opportunity of consulting; Ana Isabel Buescu, *Imagens do Príncipe: discurso normativo e representação (1525-49)* (Lisbon: Cosmos, 1996).

[10] See n. 6.

[11] This group contains D. Duarte's personal account of his melancholia and cure (Ch. 19). As such, it is not so much a digression as an intense illustration of the causes of sadness, which begins in Ch. 17. Here, he considers the opinion that six passions (one of them sadness) are associated with anger; he decides this is not the case, because they may arise in the absence of anger. In Ch. 18, he nuances John Cassian's definition of sadness as the gravest of sins with reference to St Paul, to distinguish between the type that leads to death, and the type that leads to penitence and the desire for perfection, and which bears the hallmarks of obedience, humility and patience. These virtues are much in evidence in his own case study, and are naturally relevant to his counsel to his brother, the Infante D. Pedro, written in September 1425 upon the latter's departure for Hungary (Ch. 23). He cautions him to temper his feelings, exercise self-control, guard against anger, trust in the Lord's grace to guard him from sadness and draw upon man's innate powers to govern himself, his feelings and his understanding.

[12] It is not easy to render 'temor' without negative connotations. Even less amenable nowadays is the following chapter, 47, a translation of Thomas Aquinas' opuscule on the perils of intimate discourse with spiritual women.

leading from the outer to the innermost chamber, from pleasure, benefit, physical health, honourable actions, to God's service and the path of virtue. Chs 83 and 84 are concerned with right conduct as a knight (using material from the *Livro de Ensinança*) and in administrative affairs; and with self-discipline (citing Ludolphus of Saxony's *Vita Christi* on maintaining equanimity in the face of troubles, using experience to achieve virtue). Ch. 88 is an *exemplum* (a rarity in this work) concerning a mirror, cloak and tambourine. In Chs 89 and 90, D. Duarte turns to the spiritual guidance of Gregory the Great on liberality, stressing a rational approach to giving, one that aims neither to incur poverty deliberately nor to fall into avarice — as elsewhere, the influence of the Aristotelian mean is evident. A transitional chapter, 91, functions as an index for the next eleven chapters. This varied group covers, for example: reading the Gospels; an *exemplum* in which the choice between a virtuous and a sinful life is likened to choosing either a sound or a rotten boat in which to cross a turbulent river; rules for the royal chapel and choristers; rules for the royal household; health and diet; hours of the offices in the chapel; the familial relationship with D. João I; translating into the vernacular; and methods for calculating the hours of the day. Ch. 103 is the epilogue, in praise of loyalty for the good ordering of the body and soul, the household and the kingdom.

Chapter 98 has a clear lineage. It began life as a letter from D. Duarte to his Aragonese brothers-in-law, dated 25 January 1435, in response to a request from their ambassador. The letter was copied into his *Livro dos Conselhos*, and then transcribed into the *Leal Conselheiro*.[13] It is the longest text in the work, occupying fols 89^r to 93^r in a manuscript of ninety-four folios. D. Duarte was at pains to state his authorship of the letter at many opportunities, thus demonstrating its special value and privileged place in the treatise.[14]

Although the tone set by the letter format and the lack of explicit citation of favoured sources (the Bible, Aristotle, Cicero and Cassian) make the chapter unusual, it still has to be read in the context of those sources as regards obedience, charity, friendship and love. D. Duarte prepares for this contextualization, so to speak, referring in earlier chapters to his parents' role, from different perspectives.

In Ch. 39, on the ways in which man can be conditioned and altered, he acknowledges the vital role played by heredity and parents in man's nature, understanding and virtue. Another determining factor is 'conversaçom' ('familiarity', or 'social intercourse'), through which positive influences come from one's superiors and friends. With his parents providing a good example

---

[13] Later, it would make a fourth appearance as the basis of Fernão Lopes's account, 'Que maneyra tinhão em goardar obydiencia a seu padre estes jfantes', *Cronica del Rei Dom Joham*, Part 2, ch. 144, ed. by William J. Entwistle (Lisbon: IN-CM, 1968; repr. 1977), pp. 308–11.

[14] This is argued convincingly by João Dionísio who points out that its special status is signalled in the manuscript by a larger and more artistic initial capital letter, 'D. Duarte *mise-en-abîme*: sobre uma redundância no capítulo LRVIII do *Leal Conselheiro*', *Românica. Revista de Literatura*, 5 (1996), 129–40. Piel (p. 357, n. 1).

to their subjects, the nation as a whole improved in morals and virtue. Furthermore,

> as molheres de sua criaçom quanta lealdade guardarom todas a seus maridos, donde as mais dos reinos filharom tal exempro que antre todalas do mundo, do que enformaçom havemos, em geeral merecem grande louvor. E se ũu moesteiro é bem regido em dereita devaçom quantos a el veem de custumes desvairados, todos se tornam pouco mais ou menos a ũa maneira de vida e custumes. E nom é maravilha, porque tres cousas, principalmente, nos enduzem a bem viver, scilicet Temor, Sperança e Amor. (p. 153)

> [to such an extent were the women under their protection ever loyal to their husbands, an example that others in the kingdom followed more than anywhere else in the world, as far as we know, that they are deserving of great praise. If a monastery is well ordered in true devotion, all those who enter it, however varied their usage, gradually come to a common way of life and usage. This is not surprising, since three things, in the main, guide us to live well, namely Fear, Hope and Love.]

It is within the context of Ch. 43 on Charity, that D. Duarte specifically mentions the Fifth Commandment — and indeed it is the only mention of the Commandments — explaining that it applies not just to parents but to all with whom a temporal and spiritual bond requires honour and obedience. Charity is a virtue that cannot dwell in those who are self-centred, greedy, proud or disdainful. In support of this, he draws on his sources and his own experience:

> Ca se leerdes ũa colaçom que fala d'amizade e o livro que Tulio dela fez, e Epistolas de Seneca, o Trautado de Joham de Linhano, e certos capitolos da prática que guardavamos ao mui virtuoso Rei nosso senhor e padre cuja alma Deos haja, que adiante serom scriptos, verees bem que taes persoas nom podem alguem, dereitamente, per virtude, amar nem guardar dereita caridade. (p. 168)

> [If you read one of the Conferences that speaks of friendship, Tully's book on it, Seneca's Epistles, and John of Legnano's treatise, as well as certain chapters about the conduct we maintained with the most virtuous King, our lord and father, God rest his soul, to be found further on, you will clearly see that no one, of uprightness and virtue, can love or keep true charity with such people.]

In Ch. 44, it is friendship (rather than obedience), that is stressed as vital to the good relations with his parents and siblings. There is more than a touch of pride in acknowledging that his later reading of Cicero only confirmed what their upbringing had already taught them:

> Consiirando como Nosso Senhor me outorgou viver sempre sem falicimento em amizade mui special com os mui virtuosos Rei e Rainha [...] e com todos meus irmãos, nom simprezmente como servidor ou per obrigaçom de dívido, mas em aquela mais perfeita maneira que outros achar se podessem, firmados em grande amor e boas voontades de toda parte [...] nom me

pareceo, quando vi o livro de Tulio e outros que dela falam, que achava cousa nova nem contraira de que usavamos. (p. 171)

[When I consider that Our Lord permitted me to live always and unfailingly in very special amity with the most virtuous King and Queen [...] and with all my brothers, not just in serving them or through the obligation of blood ties but in that more perfect manner that others may find if they can, founded on great love and good will on both sides [...] it did not seem to me, when I read Tully's book, and others that speak of it, that I found anything new or contrary to our customary behaviour.]

In Ch. 48, D. Duarte gives the first hint of how we should understand his account of his father's character, when he warns against expecting perfection in others, and recommends overlooking small faults in someone who is basically good; the same applies to people we love. He continues:

E nom filhemos que milhor ama quem mais sente, como fazem os namorados, mas aqueles que mais realmente mantem e guardam as boas lex d'amizade, o que se nom pode bem conhecer sem per longa conversaçom em feitos desvairados, por os quaes se diz que se convem comer com algũa, ante que o bem conheçam, ũu moio de sal. (p. 197)

[Let us not accept that the one who loves most is the one who feels most, as lovers do, but those who truly maintain and keep the good laws of friendship, which cannot be truly known without long discourse about many things; for which reason it is said that one must eat a peck of salt with someone before one can know him properly.]

Lastly, in the index chapter, Ch. 91, he recommends his account of the conduct maintained with his father to those who wish to be on good terms with their lords and other people whose friendship they wish to keep; without a reasonable amount of virtue, which both sides must possess, their conduct will fall short.

Ch. 98 begins by D. Duarte referring to the counsel he had given his brothers-in-law when they were together in Abrantes about maintaining concord with their monarch (drawing upon his family experience), and to the subsequent request from their ambassador to have it in writing. He states how he and his brothers early on received their grounding in good conduct, not through reading but by the grace of God; and when reason awoke in them, they brought this to bear on their intention to live rightly. He explains that they were all guided by what was pleasing to God. In order to be in harmony with their father, they first had to direct themselves in accordance with His will, since that was the uniting force for them all. The other driving force was the love and fear that they had for their father; above all they feared behaving in any dishonourable or disreputable way that would bring shame upon them (p. 350). Then begins a comprehensive account of their behaviour and conduct.[15] The

---

[15] A. H. de Oliveira Marques, 'Introdução', in *A literatura doutrinária na Corte de Avis*, ed. by Lênia Márcia Mongelli (São Paulo: Martins Fontes, 2001), pp. xxiii–xxiv, points out that the princes' conduct would appear to be more appropriate to children than to adolescents, though the letter apparently related to the period after Philippa of Lancaster's death in 1415.

sheer detail, although at times repetitive and cumbersome, is important, not only as the centrepiece of the mechanics of loyalty, and because it gives a rich portrait of D. João I, but also as a social document. However, since space here precludes enumerating the fifty or so aspects, I give just a sample.

If the princes were in doubt about whether something was displeasing to their father they held off doing it until they found out what he wished, so that they could not excuse themselves by saying they were in ignorance. Curbing their anger and their own wishes, and disregarding the voices of others, they did what was to his service and pleasure, so as not to be 'fair weather friends' and fail him in bad times. They were always assured of the king's love and esteem and certain it would never change; however, because they set such value on this certainty, they were cautious in everything that touched on his service and pleasure, as if he might not be so utterly steadfast. Their hearts took on the function of a proctor, whose role was to interpret the king's actions in the best possible light; even when the latter were manifestly wrong, they reminded themselves that only God was perfect and that they should bear their father's imperfections as they would wish he bore theirs.

They did not promote their interests above his but offered unreservedly to follow his opinion, believing that God would give their deeds a better outcome than they could foresee. They did not speak ill of him either in public or in private but, whenever occasion arose, praised him as far as they reasonably could. They accepted his commands and rule even if they felt them mistaken, because their duty was solely to obey him. They provided him with whatever feasts, games and seemly entertainment would give him pleasure, rather than thinking of their own preferences. If, for his relaxation, he wished to speak to them at length, they listened patiently without interruption or signs of boredom. They acted as mediators, if people were aggrieved at the king because he refused them something. On the other hand, if some notable person was likely to irritate the king, they returned him to the latter's good graces. In tasks they undertook for him, they took care not to go beyond his brief, even when others asked it of them, or they wished to. They maintained confidentiality in all that he charged them with. They guarded against irritating or crossing him, against sulking, or criticizing him. When their father replaced them with someone else in a certain office, duty or role, they endeavoured not to be upset. They neither listened to, nor agreed with, those who criticized the king. They changed the subject, if their conversation displeased him. If he was ill, they went to him immediately.

In all these aspects and more, D. Duarte claims that he and his brothers maintained this conduct; that there was neither jealousy, greed, avarice, wilfulness nor pride between them. They put up with each other's individual traits and wishes even if they disagreed, as if they were all of one mind, letting bygones be bygones. He describes their conduct as reaching out to the king through the three powers of the soul — vegetative, sensitive, and rational. They served and obeyed him through things that gave physical pleasure; they sought to do his will and, in their persons, to appear orderly and well dressed, thus giving aesthetic pleasure; and they conducted themselves as virtuously as they could, in order to please his rational soul. Always truthful, however, D. Duarte has to confess that these norms were not always maintained to the same degree by everyone, depending on the character qualities that God had endowed them with. But:

> a voontade, proposito e desejo de todos ũu era, e assi boo, mercees a Deos, em que falimento nom sentiamos, nem na maneira que cada ũu em todas estas partes guardava que fosse digno de reprehensom. (p. 360)
>
> [our will, intention and desire was the same in all of us and hence good, thanks to God, in that we did not have a sense of failure, nor that the manner each of us bore in all these matters might merit reprehension.]

He relates that their good and honourable conduct towards the king was maintained to the end, at his death and burial, in the protection of his servants, and the execution of his testament and other good works for the unburdening of D. João's conscience. Recognizing that such conduct is not possible with all lords, nor within all friendships, D. Duarte turns once more to his guiding lights, Cicero and Cassian:

> Ca scripto é amizade perfeita nom pode seer senom antre persoas virtuosas, de ũu proposito e querer e nom querer nas cousas principaes, que hajam entendimentos humildosos e voontades concordavees, fundadas em muita lealdade de grandes, largos e boos corações, pera fazerem e dizerem e soportarem por seu senhor ou amigo quanto dereitamente fazer se deve, e lhes obedecerem nas determinações de todas cousas dereitas e honestas; porque ũa das mais principaes lex de taes amizades é nunca requerer cousas injustas ou torpes, nem as fazer, posto que requeridas sejam. (p. 361)[16]
>
> [It is written that perfect friendship can only exist between virtuous people, of one purpose, likes and dislikes in the principal things, who possess humble understanding and reconcilable wills, based on the strong loyalty of great, large and good hearts, to do, say, and bear on behalf of one's lord or friend what rightly should be done, and to obey them in decisions in all true and honest things, because one of the principal laws of such friendships is never to request unjust or vile things, nor do them, even if they are requested.]

It is not surprising that D. Duarte's chapter has evoked a variety of reactions. For Piel, it is 'spontaneous and admirably sincere', one of the most beautiful passages in the book.[17] Robert Ricard, however, regrets the fact that D. Duarte was obliged to exercise reserve and discretion in relating such matters, thus reducing the historical significance.[18]

---

[16] Identified by Dionísio, *D. Duarte, leitor de Cassiano* (p. 362) as Cicero, *De amicitia*, V.18 and XII.40, and John Cassian, *Conferences*, XVI ['The First Conference of Abbot Joseph on Friendship'] Ch.3 ['How friendship is indissoluble'].
[17] Piel, p. 357, n. 1.
[18] Ricard, p. 69.

Mário Martins stresses that there can be no love without admiration, and that D. Duarte's fear of his father had nothing servile about it; rather, it was equivalent to respect. He also qualifies the princes' obedience, in that they would always obey their father unless it were contrary to God's will. Obviously, he finds exaggeration in the account, especially given the precarious nature of relations between D. João I and the Infante D. Pedro:

> No entanto, este pequeno tratado refere-se ao *dever ser*, embora afirme que *era*, para honrar a memória do pai e dar mais força à sua doutrina, apresentando-a como praticada na vida real.[19]
>
> [However, this little treatise relates to what *should be*, although it states it *was*, in order to honour his father's memory and give greater force to his doctrine, presenting it as practised in real life.]

For Paulette Demerson, D. Duarte's humble admission of sometimes falling short of perfection does not diminish the fact that we are confronted with a range of remarkable qualities — purity of heart, courtesy, exquisite delicacy, deference, devotion, filial piety and generosity — only encountered in exceptional human beings.[20]

José Gama notes that the theme of friendship is analysed perhaps more deeply and sympathetically than that of loyalty. The whole account in Ch. 98 is contained within the parameters of friendship, its exercise being the sure sign of loyalty.[21] In the same vein is the perceptive study by Maria de Lurdes Correia Fernandes, who first notes that the chapter describes the princes' relation with their father in terms of both lord and friend, and indeed exemplifies behaviour between friends. She then shows how D. Duarte's attitude is one of constant obedience, desiring to please the king, to know his mind, based on humility and abdication of his will. The father as public figure is the focus of much of D. Duarte's account; hence, the conduct described has a parallel in the ideal conduct of subjects with their lord.[22]

From a more practical perspective, Oliveira Marques asks: 'Realidade objetiva de uma família modelar? Neblina de recordações? Ou antes hipocrisia necessária para morigeração dos súditos, para "dar o exemplo" de que a época tanto carecia?' [The objective reality of a model family? A haze of memories? Or, rather, the necessary hypocrisy for improving the morals of one's subjects, to 'set the example' that the age so lacked?].[23]

---

[19] Mário Martins, 'Pais e filhos no "Leal Conselheiro"', in *Estudos de cultura medieval*, vol. III (Lisbon: Edições Brotéria, 1983), pp. 199–206 (p. 204). Original emphasis.
[20] Paulette Demerson, 'L'Amour dans *O Leal Conselheiro* de Dom Duarte', in *Arquivos do Centro Cultural Português*, 9 (Paris: Fundação Calouste Gulbenkian, 1983), 483–500 (p. 486).
[21] Gama, pp. 99 and 105.
[22] Maria de Lurdes Correia Fernandes, 'Da doutrina à vivência: amor, amizade e casamento no "Leal Conselheiro" do Rei D. Duarte', *Revista da Faculdade de Letras. Línguas e Literaturas*, II série, I (Porto, 1984), 133–94 (pp. 180–81).
[23] A. H. de Oliveira Marques, 'Introdução', p. xxiv.

Luís Miguel Duarte, the most recent biographer of D. Duarte, approaches the chapter in two ways: from the perspective of political propaganda, D. Duarte was composing the foundational text of the Avis family mythification; from the human perspective, he finds the portrait is too good to be true. Like Mário Martins, he refers to the dissensions in the family, but suspends scepticism to conclude:

> talvez a imagem da família perfeita tivesse fragmentos de verdade, como devem ter todas as boas imagens para serem eficazes. Talvez estes tópicos, de tão repetidos, acabassem por fazer parcialmente o seu caminho na cabeça dos infantes — e, se o *Leal Conselheiro* cumprisse o seu papel, nas de outros nobres. Estou certo de que entre os irmãos houve longos períodos em que a amizade e a fraternidade prevaleceram genuinamente sobre a inveja e o despeito.[24]
>
> [perhaps there was a grain of truth in the picture of the perfect family, as there must be in all good pictures if they are to be effective. Perhaps these topics, repeated so often, ended up by being partly accepted in the princes' minds — and, if the *Loyal Counsellor* fulfilled its mission, in those of other nobles. I am sure that, among the siblings, there were long periods during which friendship and brotherliness genuinely prevailed over jealousy and resentment.]

For all the validity of Luís Miguel Duarte's comment, I think he undervalues D. Duarte's intention, how things should be on a spiritual and moral level. If one can accept the obvious sincerity and truthfulness, one must also tackle the tensions between feelings and conduct, between love, obedience and friendship. Although, as Mário Martins and José Gama showed, loyalty and friendship go hand in hand, there is not an automatic link with obedience. Paulette Demerson is content to leave D. Duarte's obedience as abdication of will, but that does not sit easily with the evidence of his active and positive life. It is interesting, if not indicative, that D. Duarte does not devote a chapter in *Leal Conselheiro* to obedience *per se*. As mentioned above, he explicitly refers to the Fifth Commandment only once (Ch. 43), and it is worth remembering that the operative word there is 'honour', not 'obey'. Is it that he takes obedience as implicit in all his actions? Or is there a more questioning attitude to the exhortation? Certainly, obeying God took priority over obeying his father, as he says in Ch. 98. To my mind, this demonstrates not unthinking filial subservience but a determined effort to conquer self-will and to put himself at the service of others. To explore this further, I will make a brief excursion into the teachings of John Cassian, whose *Institutes* and *Conferences* are both used in the majority of sections of the *Leal Conselheiro*.[25] In Owen Chadwick's definition, 'the *Institutes* were written for those in the active life, the *Conferences* for those who were reaching "higher". Yet the *Conferences*, more often than not, are as

---

[24] L. M. Duarte, pp. 295–96.
[25] Dionísio, *D. Duarte, leitor de Cassiano* (p. 2) gives evidence for Portuguese translations being undertaken before D. Duarte came to the throne, allowing the possibility that it was at his initiative.

engaged with the "life of virtue" as the *Institutes*.²⁶ The overlap between the two works has a certain relevance to D. Duarte's active–contemplative binary.

It is a truism that obedience is of prime importance for the monk. For Cassian, it was one of the 'core monastic virtues' and it had to be 'genuine, immediate, unhesitating, and complete'.²⁷ This is certainly shown in the *Institutes*, Book IV (Of the Institutes of the Renunciants), where the obedience is often extreme and, to our eyes, nonsensical and irrational. One example (Ch. 24) concerns the Abbot John who, at the command of his senior, laboured for a whole year to water a stick in the desert to see if it would grow. Another (Ch. 27) tells of the Abbot Patermucius, throwing his young son into the river at the command of his senior, to emulate Abraham.²⁸ One might see this kind of obedience as a physical acting out of a stage on the mystic path towards total eradication of the will and submission to God. However, D. Duarte's will to serve God and his father, though perhaps it has its measure of mysticism, never forsakes reason.

The other topic of the *Institutes* that links to D. Duarte is the journey from fighting against the sins to the habit of virtue. (From that stage, the monk goes on to a life of contemplation.) The bottom rung of the ladder is the fear of the Lord, which leads to compunction, renunciation, humility, mortification, driving out the vices, flowering of virtue, purity of heart, on to perfect charity.²⁹ Seen in this light, the freedom with which D. Duarte refers to fear of his father loses some of its negative connotation. *Conference* 11, 'The First Conference of Abbot Chaeremon on Perfection', Ch. 13 'Of the fear which is the outcome of the greatest love', helps us to understand what D. Duarte meant by those terms:

> Whoever then has been established in this perfect love is sure to mount by a higher stage to that still more sublime fear belonging to love, which is the outcome of no dread of punishment or greed or reward, but of the greatest love; whereby a sons fears with earnest affection a most indulgent father [...] while there is no dread of his blows or reproaches, but only of a slight injury to his love [...].³⁰

And, quoting 1 John 4. 18, 'there is no fear in love, but perfect love casteth out fear', Cassian makes the distinction between the beginners, 'those who are still subject to the yoke and to servile terror', and those who 'pass on from that penal fear to the fullest freedom of love, and the confidence of the friends and sons of God.'³¹

---

²⁶ Owen Chadwick, *John Cassian*, 2nd edn (Cambridge: Cambridge University Press, 1968), p. 93.
²⁷ Jonathan Morgan, 'Obedience in Egyptian Monasticism according to John Cassian', *St Vladimir's Theological Quarterly*, 55.3 (2011), 271–91 (pp. 271 and 276).
²⁸ *The Twelve Books of John Cassian on the Institutes of the Coenobia*, trans. and notes by Edgar C. S. Gibson, A Select Library of Nicene and Post-Nicene Fathers of the Christian Church, 2nd series, vol. 11, ed. by Philip Schaff and Henry Wace (New York: The Christian Literature Company; Oxford and London: Parker & Company, 1894); <http://www.osb.org/lectio/cassian/inst/instpref.html> [accessed February 2013].
²⁹ Chadwick, p. 93.
³⁰ *John Cassian. The Conferences*, trans. and notes by Edgar C. S. Gibson, A Select Library of Nicene and Post-Nicene Fathers of the Christian Church (New York, 1894), p. 357; electronic version: Christian Classics Ethereal Library <http://www.ccel.org/ccel/cassian/conferences.html> [accessed March 2013].
³¹ *John Cassian. The Conferences*, pp. 357–58.

Making all due allowance for the chasm between Cassian's rules for the contemplative life and the active life of a monarch, I suggest that D. Duarte brings into play not only obedience but also Cassian's purity of heart (that acme of virtue for the monk) since he has discussed in previous chapters of *Leal Conselheiro* all the other virtues under their own names. So what looks like an unnaturally humble approach in relation to his father's will may actually be the fruit of all the virtues. As Jonathan Morgan points out, the virtues

> share a kind of relationship best described as mutual inherence with one another, making up a beautiful mosaic where each virtue has distinct identity and place while interrelating with the others. [...] Cassian ascribes a virtue-like obedience a place of greater prominence when compared to most of the other virtues. Nevertheless, when we understand this relationship of reciprocity shared among the virtues we are able to make better sense of the seemingly contradictory statements he makes concerning their hierarchy. Even the prominent virtues of obedience, humility, renunciation and discernment require the presence of all other virtues in order to attain the ideal of perfection.[32]

From this perspective, Duarte's examination of all the virtues in the chapters preceding Ch. 98 emerges as the theoretical platform for the practice of right conduct. Clearly, in his meditations on Cassian's teachings he brought his reason to bear in the extent and scale of his service and self-denial. His loyal insistence on the good relations he and his brothers enjoyed leaves unstated the battle that went on in their hearts and minds to achieve them, but his reading of Cassian leaves us in no doubt that the path to obedience was long and hard.

His portrait of family relations was created out of the pure intention of love and service, supported by God's grace. His advice regarding friendship, loyalty and the exercise of virtue is directed towards unity of mind and purpose, which can obviously be extended beyond the personal level to a desire for concord in his kingdom. Despite his pride in the harmonious relationship with his father, he was too modest to be vainglorious about it. As for wider recognition of his qualities, it would be for Fernão Lopes to harp explicitly upon the theme of filial obedience, with examples drawn from the Bible and Classical history, to eulogize the princes of Avis.[33] To D. Duarte's personal reticence about his own good qualities, Lopes would respond with a group panegyric, so we can only wish that he had been a little more forthcoming about his notable and unique patron.

This is a revised version of a paper given at the 2013 Oxford conference of the Association of Hispanists of Great Britain and Ireland. I am grateful for the many comments and suggestions from the attendees, especially Jane Whetnall and Barry Taylor.

---

[32] Morgan, pp. 281–82.
[33] See n. 13.

Rui de Pina, *Crónica de D. Afonso V* and Bodleian MS Don. c. 230

T. F. EARLE

Oxford University

The present article is concerned with a manuscript of a chronicle in Portuguese, acquired by the Bodleian Library, Oxford, in 2013 from Bloomsbury Auctions, London. The *Crónica de D. Afonso V* was written between 1490 and 1504 by Rui de Pina, royal chronicler and archivist, who was born probably in the 1440s and died, at a great age, in 1522. This is the first attempt to describe the codex and to establish its place in the rich manuscript tradition of Rui de Pina's work. For the moment, it must be regarded as a provisional account only, a preliminary step towards the understanding of the relationship of the many manuscripts to each other and the eventual production of a critical edition.

Description of the MS

The Oxford MS (to be referred to henceforward as OB, i.e., Oxford Bodleian) is a paper folio, 294mm by 203mm. It is the responsibility of a single copyist, writing in what appears to be an early sixteenth-century cursive hand. There are two foliations, the earlier in ink using Arabic numerals, the second in pencil, also in Arabic numerals, and noting 181 leaves. More recently, the final free endpaper has been numbered 182. There are, however, unfoliated leaves between fols 98 and 99, and 137 and 138, so the total should be 183, or 184 if the endpaper is included. The earlier foliation in ink is faint throughout and in some places invisible. It appears to run from 63 to 246, so that OB must formerly have been part of a longer codex. For the moment, what that codex contained must be pure speculation. It is not impossible, however, that it was Rui de Pina's own *Crónica de D. Duarte*, which in some of the MSS listed on BITAGAP is a text of around 60 folios. There is a MS in the Biblioteca Nacional de Portugal in which the *Crónica de D. Duarte* precedes the *Crónica de D. Afonso V*,[1] and the first edition of 1790 also prints the two chronicles in that order. Perhaps, then, one of the MSS which the eighteenth-century editor used also contained the two chronicles.

The *Crónica de D. Duarte*, who was D. Afonso's father, would naturally be copied before the one about his son, but it seems to have been composed after

---

[1] It is Códice 896, which begins with a truncated version of the *Crónica de D. Duarte*, placed before the *Crónica de D. Afonso V*.

the *Crónica de D. Afonso V*. Martins de Carvalho thinks that Pina finished it after 1514, for in Ch. 7 there is a reference to the *Ordenações Manuelinas*, a compilation of legal texts made 1512–14.² That date would also be a *terminus a quo* for the copying of OB, if it originally included the *Crónica de D. Duarte*.

Quires are unnumbered and unmarked; there are verso catchwords on every leaf but no signatures. Based on the assumption that the modern sewing preserves the position of the original quire centrefolds (at fols 5/6, 15/16, 25/26 etc.), the MS appears to collate as eighteen ten-leaf quires plus a final, damaged quire now of three leaves but formerly of more. Fol. 182^v ends abruptly with the words 'mandou lançar polla cleresia', from Ch. 211, while fol. 183^r begins with some words from the final chapter, 'mercê e requerer justiça'. The break, which is evidence of physical damage to the MS after its completion, is equivalent to the quantity that would occupy two leaves, calculated by reference to other MS copies.

A single watermark occurs throughout the MS, in both correct and inverted orientation. It does not appear to be associated with any countermark. Since the mark appears once per bifolium, in each quire there are five folios without any mark and five with it. The mark itself, consisting of a heart with three flowers, may be tentatively identified as related to Briquet no. 4291, dated 1518 from a document produced in the region of Toulouse. However, as the modern editor of Briquet points out, the information provided is not sufficient to allow us to know when the paper was produced, except that it was before 1518.³ French marks of this kind are sometimes found in sixteenth-century Portuguese books.⁴ This is another indication — though, it must be admitted, an entirely speculative one — as to the date of OB, 1514–18.

The modern binding in brown calf has a device of a knight in armour with a sword and plumed helmet, framed by two columns with a scroll on each.⁵

The Bodleian manuscript has never been described in detail before, but it is not unknown. In May 2012 it was sold at Swann's Auction Galleries, New York, and a comparison with the photograph of the title page made on that occasion reveals that it is the same MS which is now in Oxford. After the sale it was rebound.⁶ The American auctioneers, incidentally, counted the number of folios correctly. At some point prior to the sale it was in the possession of Afonso Cassuto, a Lisbon bookseller and auctioneer, who died in 1990.

Earlier owners or users have left their mark on the MS in the form of marginalia. Names and dates are sometimes repeated in the margins, additional

---

² See Rui de Pina, *Crónica de D. João II*, ed. by Alberto Martins de Carvalho (Coimbra: Atlântida, 1950), Introdução, p. xxvi. The *Crónica de D. Afonso V* was probably written over a long period, 1490–1504; see below.
³ C. M. Briquet, *Les Filigranes*, ed. by Allan Stevenson, 4 vols (Amsterdam: Paper Publications Society, 1968), I, 19.
⁴ Information kindly supplied by Prof. Artur Anselmo.
⁵ I am indebted to Prof. David Hook for his generous assistance in the description of the Oxford MS.
⁶ See BITAGAP (manid 5509).

historical information is provided on fols 135, 137 and 161, and attention is drawn to lacunae in the text, fols 100^v and 128^v. The comments about matter missing from the text are in a faint hand, perhaps of the seventeenth century. They indicate that the annotator had available what he regarded as a more complete copy of the chronicle, though it was almost certainly not the printed text, which did not appear until 1790.

On fol. 100^v the reader is warned that more than half of Ch. 125 is missing. This long chapter contains Rui de Pina's 'Exclamação' at the death at the battle of Alfarrobeira of Prince Pedro, the regent who is the undoubted hero of the first half of the chronicle. The reason for the omission is not damage to the MS — only the final quire shows evidence of that, as already explained — but rather the copyist's lack of appreciation for the historian's rhetorical effusion, for he comments: 'E porque isso é mui comprido o deixo e venho ao caso' [And because this is very long I leave it here and return to the matter in hand].[7] It may be the case also that the copyist felt he could intervene in this way in Pina's text because it had not yet reached a definitive form.

Further marginalia on fols 128^v and 130^r note that whole chapters are missing, Chs 146, about the death of the Duke of Bragança in 1461, and 149, about the storm which severely damaged the royal fleet on its way to attack Tangiers in 1463. In addition, the brief Ch. 147, which records the death in 1463 of D. Catarina, Afonso V's sister, who had been promised in marriage to Edward IV of England, is taken out of chronological sequence and placed on fol. 147^v, before Ch. 169.[8] If Prince Pedro is the hero of Rui de Pina's chronicle, Afonso, Duke of Bragança, is certainly one of the chief villains, but the omission and transposition of these chapters are unlikely to have been made on ideological grounds, for they have nothing in common.

Importance of the Chronicle and the Need for a Critical Edition

Rui de Pina's *Crónica de D. Afonso V* is the most important narrative source that exists for that king's long reign (1438–81). Pina's rather negative view of his subject has strongly influenced subsequent historians, from the sixteenth century to the present day, not least because, as is now generally recognized, he was a very accomplished writer. His clear narrative, with its dramatic contrasts between right and wrong, wisdom and folly, reads well. Although always respectful towards royalty, the higher nobility and the church he is not afraid to be critical, either openly or by implication. His critical attitude is most obvious in his accounts of the behaviour of members of the powerful clan of

---

[7] All the translations are mine. Throughout this article the orthography of quotations in Portuguese has been modernized, except where modernization might interfere with the phonetic characteristics of the language in the early sixteenth century.

[8] Pina is ambiguous about the date of D. Catarina's death, saying only that it happened after 1461. Saul António Gomes, *D. Afonso V, o Africano* (Lisbon: Círculo de Leitores, 2009), p. 235, gives it as 1463.

the Braganças, an attitude he must have acquired during his many years in the service of D. João II, whose hatred of the clan was notorious. However, Pina normally succeeds in writing as a plain man who has made his own judgements of men and events, and that makes his account extremely persuasive. Writing in 1950, Alberto Martins de Carvalho saw in him 'alguma ingénua verdura do homem da idade-média, patenteando em muitos pontos a natural sinceridade que as palavras hão-de exprimir simplesmente' [Some of the ingenuousness and immaturity of medieval man, revealing in many places a natural sincerity which his simple words express].[9] Nearly seventy years later it may seem that the ingenuousness is not necessarily all on Pina's side, but there is no doubt that he knew how to give the impression of truthfulness and fair dealing.

In his time, and for at least a century after his death in 1522, Rui de Pina was a highly regarded writer, whose chronicles were copied many times. Around forty manuscripts of the *Crónica de D. Afonso V* survive, although it was not published until 1790. However, modern scholars almost invariably cite it by reference to the first edition, or to one or other of the two twentieth-century reprints.[10] The need for a critical edition, first called for by Madahil in 1935, is obvious, for the printed text is very defective, and no effort has ever been made to improve it.[11] Its value as a reliable witness must be called into question from the very start, since it incorporates readings from two different manuscripts, as the editor explains. One of these may perhaps be identified with a MS now in the Biblioteca Nacional, but the whereabouts and consequently the usefulness of the other is for the present unknown.[12] The twentieth-century reprints do not correct even the most obvious errors of the first edition, one of which is to have numbered Ch. 22 as Ch. 21, so that the true numeration of Chs 22–214 is one ahead of that given in the printed versions.[13]

Madahil compared the first edition to a MS now held in the Arquivo Municipal of Coimbra, and was able to show that the MS, though relatively late — it was copied in 1563–64 — contains a number of readings which are clearly superior to those of the printed text. OB is likely to be older than the Coimbra MS, and in many instances coincides with it. Perhaps the most striking of Madahil's discoveries was of a whole paragraph in Ch. 19 omitted by the first edition. The missing lines are present in OB, as well as in the Coimbra MS, and in the other MSS consulted for this study. The first edition's meaningless

---

[9] Rui de Pina, *Crónica de D. João II*, ed. by Alberto Martins de Carvalho (Coimbra: Atlântida, 1950), p. xxxi.
[10] The first edition, by the Abade José Correa da Serra, was published in his *Collecção de livros ineditos da historia portugueza*, vol. I. Subsequent reprints are by G. Pereira (Lisbon: Bibliotheca de Classicos Portuguezes, 1901–02) and M. Lopes de Almeida (Porto: Lello, 1977).
[11] António Gomes da Rocha Madahil, 'Subsídios para uma edição crítica da crónica de D. Afonso V, de Rui de Pina: variantes apresentadas pelo códice pertencente à Biblioteca Municipal de Coimbra', *Ethos*, 1 (1935), 49–67 (p. 67).
[12] For Correa da Serra's editorial practice, see his edition of the chronicle, p. 197, and Madahil, p. 50. Further information about the relationship of the printed text to BNP Cod. 395 can be found below.
[13] In this article the chapters are referred to by the correct number, not those of the printed text.

'segundo juízo comum e especiais' [in common judgement and experience],[14] in Ch. 40, p. 260, also appears in its correct form 'segundo juízo comum e experiências' in OB, fol. 26^r, and in Ch. 47 it supplies the line which the first edition omits after 'tais dois reis' [two such kings], p. 273.

These and many other errors throw doubts on the value of the first edition as a witness of Pina's text. Some of them are the responsibility of the eighteenth-century printers, but enough of them coincide with Cód. 395 of the Biblioteca Nacional to suggest that Correa da Serra used that MS, or one with a close family relationship to it, when preparing his edition. Cód. 395 reads 'juízo comum e especiais', while in Ch. 195 MS and printed text, p. 568, give the French town of Perpignan an extra syllable, 'Peropinhão'. Most MSS give a phonetically correct rendering: 'Perpinhão'. In Ch. 55 an undoubted error of the first edition may derive from the MS's version of the death on board ship of D. Fernando de Castro. The MS says of him: 'Acabou sua vida nele de uma bombardada', which is an acceptable reading, but with words in a different order from OB and a number of other witnesses: 'acabou nele de uma bombardada sua vida' [His life ended there from a cannon-shot]. The first edition follows the order of Cód. 395, closely if not exactly, but has an error all its own: 'Acabou nele sua vida de uma bombarda', p. 293.

Plagiarism, Recycling and the Construction of a Chronicle Narrative

To understand the likely place of OB among the manuscripts of the chronicle it is necessary to have some idea of how medieval chroniclers in Portugal went about their work. Rui de Pina and his predecessors, Fernão Lopes and Gomes Eanes de Zurara, are the three great chroniclers of late medieval Portugal. As part of their role in the royal service they were expected to concern themselves with the history of their country from its earliest days, but they are best known for their work on the period from the accession of D. Pedro (1357) to the death of D. João II (1495) — roughly speaking, the history of their own times. Exactly what the contribution of each is was still a matter for debate, for all three made use of the work of those who went before them, usually without acknowledging that they had done so. The modern historian Joaquim Veríssimo Serrão says that what Rui de Pina did, or did not, copy from Zurara is a question which has left deep marks on the whole of Portuguese literary history: 'Nenhum outro caso de originalidade textual deixou marcas tão profundas na cultura portuguesa' [No other dispute over textual originality left such deep marks on Portuguese culture].[15]

This is probably an exaggeration, for the practice did not cease on Pina's death in 1522. The humanistic historian Damião de Góis, who is critical of Pina,

---

[14] 'Especiais', the plural form of the adjective 'especial' [special] means nothing in the context.
[15] Joaquim Veríssimo Serrão, *Cronistas do Século XVI posteriores a Fernão Lopes* (Lisbon: Biblioteca Breve, 1977), p. 55.

nevertheless used his *Crónica de D. Afonso V* when writing his own *Crónica do Príncipe D. João*,[16] and Garcia de Resende used another of Pina's works, the *Crónica de D. João II*, when writing his own history of the reign of the same king.

Plagiarism can take different forms. In the case of the medieval chroniclers it is difficult to make the accusation of wholesale copying stick because, if this is what they did, they were careful to destroy the evidence. Reworking material assembled or drafted by others, however, is quite a different issue, and it is likely that this was Pina's practice when writing his *Crónica de D. Afonso V*, which in the view of those who knew Pina, as well as later commentators, owes a good deal to Zurara.[17] In his *Crónica da tomada de Ceuta* Zurara himself at least gives the impression that he had covered the events of Afonso's reign as far as the death of D. Pedro: 'Mas do que se depois seguiu acerca da morte do Infante Dom Pedro, fica um grande processo para se contar ao diante, onde perfeitamente podereis saber [...]' [But as to what happened afterwards, regarding the death of Prince D. Pedro, there is much matter to be told, by which you will learn perfectly [...]].[18]

The present article, which is largely devoted to a single manuscript of the chronicle, does not hope to resolve the issue of plagiarism. However, it is helpful to bear in mind the image of the chronicler not as an original creator, but rather as the reworker and reshaper of material written by others and, indeed, sometimes by himself. The texts of an author of this kind will be fluid, subject to reconsideration and rewriting, and will be represented by a wide variety of witnesses, including witnesses of various stages of the chronicle's composition.

The Date of the Chronicle

It is likely that the chronicle was composed over a long period, during which it would have been revised more than once. It seems certain that by 1504 Pina had finished both it and the *Crónica de D. João II*, because in that year he was allowed to use half the *tença* (payment from the king) that he had received as a reward for his labours on both chronicles as a dowry for his daughter.[19] A problem which has exercised modern scholars is deciding which of the two chronicles

---

[16] Damião de Góis, *Crónica do Príncipe D. João*, ed. by Graça Almeida Rodrigues (Lisbon: Universidade Nova de Lisboa, 1977) p. lix.

[17] See, for a contemporary view, João de Barros, *Ásia: Primeira Década*, ed. by António Baião (Coimbra: Imprensa da Universidade, 1932; facsimile reprint, Lisbon: Imprensa Nacional, 1988), p. 69, and also the eighteenth-century bibliographer Barbosa Machado, *Biblioteca Lusitana*, s.v. Ruy de Pina.

[18] Gomes Eanes de Zurara, *Crónica da tomada de Ceuta*, ed. by Reis Brasil (Mem Martins: Europa-América, 1992), Ch. 43, p. 159.

[19] José Corrêa da Serra, *Collecção de livros inéditos*, I, 64–65. Serra's statements are supported by references to chancery documents in the Torre do Tombo, and their accuracy is confirmed by Francisco Leite de Faria, *Uma relação de Rui de Pina sobre o Congo escrita em 1492* (Lisbon: Junto de Investigações do Ultramar, 1966).

was written first. Alberto Martins de Carvalho believes that it was the *Crónica de D. João II*, despite the fact that it deals with a chronologically later period (1481–95), while Joaquim Veríssimo Serrão affirms the opposite.[20] A solution to the conundrum may be found in the document issued by D. João's chancery, dated 16 February 1490, which makes provision for a *tença* of 9560 reis to Pina: 'esguardando ao trabalho e à ocupação grande que Ruy de Pina escrivão da nossa câmara tem com o carego que lhe demos de escrever e assentar os feitos famosos assi nossos como do nossos reinos que em nossos dias são passados, e ao diante se fizeram [*sic*] em que recebemos muito serviço' [Regarding the work and the great occupation which Rui de Pina, secretary of our chamber, has in the task which we set him of writing and recording our famous deeds, and those which in our kingdoms have been performed in our time, or will be in the future, by which we receive much service].[21] D. João would not have considered that his 'feitos famosos' were confined to those occurring while he was on the throne, for he had been very active politically and militarily in the latter years of his father's reign, though still a mere prince.

Pina devotes a number of chapters of the *Crónica de D. Afonso V* to the role of the prince in the Spanish war and its diplomatic aftermath (1475–79), so perhaps he was writing the two chronicles at the same time. One might therefore expect to see cross-references between them, but there are very few, perhaps only one in each of the chronicles to the other. At the start of the *Crónica de D. João II* Pina mentions D. Afonso's interment at Batalha, 'como em sua crónica é mais declarado' [As in his chronicle is set forth at greater length],[22] while in the *Crónica de D. Afonso V* Pina, fast forwarding to the execution of the Duke of Bragança in 1484 on a charge of treason against the by now king, D. João, tells the reader that this event 'em seus tempos e lugares está mais declarado' [Is further set forth in its time and place] (Ch. 125). The same, slightly ambiguous phrase is repeated with reference to the unfinished *Crónica de D. Manuel* (Ch. 145) and must refer to chronicle writing.

References to events in D. Manuel's reign occur in both the earlier chronicles, which is further indication that Pina had them in hand simultaneously. In Ch. 145 of the *Crónica de D. Afonso V*, in which Pina reviews the achievements of D. Henrique (Prince Henry the Navigator), he brings the history of the overseas expansion down to the time of writing and mentions the discovery of the sea route to India. The exalted religious expectations which Pina derived from this event suggest that he was indeed writing in the very early years of the sixteenth century. Much more prosaically, Martins de Carvalho notes a reference, in the *Crónica de D. João II*, to the marriage of D. Dinis de Bragança in 1501.[23]

---

[20] See Rui de Pina, *Crónica de D. João II*, ed. by Alberto Martins de Carvalho, Introdução, p. xxvi and Joaquim Veríssimo Serrão, *Cronistas do Século XVI posteriores a Fernão Lopes*, p. 50.
[21] Quoted by Corrêa da Serra, *Colecção de livros inéditos*, I, 62. As Leite de Faria points out (p. 11), 'fizeram' is presumably an error for 'fezerem' or 'fizerem'.
[22] *Crónica de D. João II*, ed. by Alberto Martins de Carvalho, p. 5.
[23] *Crónica de D. João II*, ed. by Alberto Martins de Carvalho, Introdução, p. xxv.

Evidence of Pina's habit of revising not just other people's work, but also his own, is provided in Francisco Leite de Faria's important study of a text by Pina about the Congo, written in 1492 and translated into Italian in the same year. Only the translation survives, but that shows quite plainly that when Pina came to write up the *Crónica de D. João II* he made very considerable changes to what he had written earlier.[24]

The Omissions of OB and a Possible Hypothesis Regarding Them

It is time now to return to OB and to some of the problems specific to it. As noted above, some chapters are missing or misplaced in the undamaged quires of the MS. Although the copyist certainly intervened on at least one occasion — when he cut short Pina's rhetorical lamentations over the death of D. Pedro — it is difficult to ascribe the other alterations to a conscious aesthetic or ideological decision. A better hypothesis might be that the copyist of the Oxford MS did not have before him a definitive version of the chronicle. It is possible to speak of a definitive version, even though it would be a mistake to identify that with the *textus receptus*, the printed text, whose defects have already been noted. However, there is, in the Torre do Tombo, a MS of the chronicle which looks as though it had Rui de Pina's approval for, besides being richly decorated and carefully copied in a book hand, it contains a picture of the historian presenting his work to D. Manuel, the king who commissioned it. It also contains a 'Tabuada', a table of contents, unlike the majority of copies of the chronicle, including the OB. It is certainly possible that the MS in the Torre do Tombo, CRN/17, may not be the only one with a claim to be considered definitive, but in the present state of our knowledge it looks as though it provides the best indication of how Rui de Pina wished his work to be read by posterity. This royal manuscript contains 214 chapters — the same total, as it happens, as the printed edition, though, as previously explained, there they are incorrectly numbered.

The omissions of the OB need not necessarily be ascribed to scribal error. This witness may turn out to be a record of the chronicle before it reached its final state, which would mean that it — or the copy from which it was made — is older than the Torre do Tombo MS. It is not the only MS where there are differences in the number and extent of chapters by comparison with what may for the moment be regarded as the norm.

The omission of a chapter heading is not, in itself, an indication of a significant divergence from the established tradition of the text, because it can easily be attributed to a decision made by the copyist. This is probably the case with the missing chapter headings of the British Library's MS (MS Add. 15175). This witness was copied in the late sixteenth or early seventeenth century,

---

[24] Francisco Leite de Faria, *Uma relação de Rui de Pina*, pp. 13-14.

as its Latinizing orthography attests. Chs 170 and 171 are apparently missing from it, but only apparently, because the text of these two short chapters runs straight on from Ch. 169 without a break. The last sentence of Ch. 169 begins 'E neste ano...', and the two following chapters, each of which consist of a single sentence, open in a way which is very similar: 'Neste ano' [This year]' and 'E no ano seguinte' [And in the following year]. The copyist may have felt that there was no need to break up what was a lucid structure.

A more significant case is that of BNP COD 833, where the hand and orthography suggest an early sixteenth-century date. In this MS some chapters are run together, not simply by the omission of a heading, but by linking text. An example is Ch. 9, which in the great majority of the MSS so far inspected has the heading 'De como se fez o saimento d'el-rei no Mosteiro da Batalha' [How the funeral of the king took place in the Monastery of Batalha]. However, instead of a chapter heading, COD 833, fol. 7^v, has a sentence beginning: 'Acabado tudo, logo nos dias seguintes ordenaram como se fizesse o saimento d'el-rei no Mosteiro da Batalha [...]' [When all was done, they gave orders over the next few days as to how the funeral of the king should take place in the Monastery of Batalha]. This MS very much seems to suggest a work in draft, a stage in an editorial process that would eventually end with the royal MS of the Torre do Tombo. Part of that editorial process would include the writing of additional chapters, their positioning in the text, and the sub-division of already existing chapters. In their different ways, therefore, both the Oxford MS and BNP COD 833 may reveal something of Rui de Pina's working methods. More importantly, if these two MSS — and there may well turn out to be others — predate the elaboration of what seems to be the definitive version of the chronicle, then they will be the source of alternative readings which can be attributed to Rui de Pina, rather than to the errors or inventions of later copyists.

Divergent Readings of OB

Examples of readings which a future editor of the chronicle might wish to take into account include the following:

Chapter 5, fol. 6^r: 'Acabou o ifante sua prática em que não foram necessárias mais razões que as suas pera se louvar e haver por justa e bõa sua tenção' [The prince finished his speech, in which no arguments other than his were necessary for his plan to be praised and regarded as just and good]. This can be contrasted with the MS of the Torre do Tombo, fol. 9^r: 'Acabou o ifante sua preposição, em que não foram necessárias mais razões persuasivas pera se louvar e haver por justa e boa sua tençom' and with that of the printed text: 'Acabou o infante sua proposição, em que não foram necessárias mais razões para suas sinas, para se louvar e haver por justa e boa sua tenção', p. 212.

'Proposição' or 'preposição' may have been an afterthought of Rui de Pina's for 'prática', but both words are acceptable in the context. The case of D. Pedro's 'razões' is more complex. The first edition's 'para suas sinas' is meaningless, though it may derive ultimately from a mis-reading of 'persuasivas'. It is not, however, an error which is confined to the printed text, because it can be found also in Biblioteca Nacional de Portugal ALC-291 fol. 6^r, where the equally poor reading is 'por suas sinas'.[25] The OB's 'que as suas' cannot derive from 'persuasivas', is unlikely to have been the invention of the copyist and perhaps represents an early draft of the passage, by Rui de Pina himself.

Ch. 55. OB, fol. 40^v: 'Mas Lazaraque marim, governador d'el-rei de Fez, não somente não deu lugar que o ifante fosse tirado de Fez pera Arzila ou <u>pera algum outro lugar</u>, como por Mulei Burar lhe fora requerido [...]' TT17, fol. 77: 'Mas Lazaraque, marim e governador d'el-rei de Fez, nom somente nom deu lugar que o ifante fosse tirado de Fez para Arzila <u>ou para algum outro poder</u>, como por Mulei Buquer lhe fora já requerido [...]' ALC-291, fol. 46^v: 'Mas Lazaraque, marim e governador d'el-rei de Fez, não somente não deu lugar que o ifante fosse tirado de Fez para Arzila ou para <u>outro ['lugar' elided] algum poder</u>, como por Muleibucar lhe fora já requerido [...]' [But Lazaraque, *marim* and governor appointed by the king of Fez, not only did not allow the prince to be transferred from Fez to Arzila or to some other place, as Mulei Burar had requested [...]].

Here there is a possibility that OB may have a reading which is superior to that of the MS which, at least in the present state of our knowledge, seems to come closest to Rui de Pina's intention. In the context of the transfer of Prince Fernando, held by the Moors ever since the disastrous expedition to Tangiers of 1437, from his prison in Fez to a place under the control of the Portuguese, 'lugar' might seem a better reading than 'poder'. The fact that ALC-291, a later MS than either OB or TT17, hesitates between the words points to the existence of two textual traditions at this point. There are various considerations to take into account before making a hasty decision in favour of 'lugar', however. One is the generally high level of correctness of TT17, evidenced here by the fact that the copyist knew, as the copyist of OB did not, that the Arabic word transliterated as 'marim' is not a personal name, but an indication of rank. With regard to 'lugar', there is the possibility of unthinking repetition from the line before and also the doctrine of the *difficilior lectio*, by which the harder reading is always to be preferred. Here 'poder' seems awkward, but in the same paragraph Pina informs the reader that D. Álvaro de Castro had been sent from Portugal with 'poderes abastantes' [sufficient powers] to receive the hostage. In that case the difficult phrase, 'tirado de Fez para Arzila ou para algum outro poder', could mean 'removed from [the power of the governor of] Fez to [that of the governor of] Arzila or to any one else with authority'. Here, then, it is possible to conclude once again that both readings are viable.

---

[25] This sixteenth-century MS is in a half italic, half cursive hand, with many insertions and crossings-out. Further research will be needed to determine how often it corresponds with the first edition.

Ch. 121, OB fol. 98ʳ: '[...] o conde, pela certa sabedoria que tinha do prepósito do ifante, que era morrer, e polo consagramento que ambos tinham feito, não lho cometeria, <u>nem consentiria cometer tal cousa</u>, em que ao menos ficava o ifante por fé perjuro e fraco.' TT17 fol. 129ʳ (and the other witnesses quoted above): '[...] o conde, pela certa sabedoria que tinha do propósito do ifante, que era morrer, e pelo consagramento que ambos por isso tinham feito, nom lhe cometeria <u>nem ousaria cometer tal cousa</u>, em que ao menos ficava o ifante por fé perjuro e fraco' [[...] the count, from the certain knowledge which he had of the prince's intention, which was to die, and because of the oath which they had both taken, would not do it, nor would allow [anyone else] to do such a thing, by which at the least the prince would be taken for a faithless weakling].[26]

Here the context is the highly emotive one of the oath taken by D. Pedro and his great friend, D. Álvaro Vaz de Alamada, Count of Abranches, before the battle of Alfarrobeira, to die together if need be. D. Álvaro's refusal to encourage D. Pedro to break that oath can be as well expressed by 'consentir' as by 'ousar', nor is there any reason to suspect that 'consentir' arose either by a decision of the copyist or through error. Once again the conclusion seems to be that OB is the record of a draft of the chronicle to which changes were later made.

That conclusion is supported by the existence of yet another MS which show signs of being work in progress, though in a way different from the cases already discussed. That is Biblioteca Nacional de Portugal Cód. 396, which is undated but was probably written during the reign of D. Manuel (1495–1521), as the text of the chronicle is preceded by a brief prologue, presumably composed by the copyist, which implies that the king was still living. The MS is not lacking chapters, which is the case of OB and BNP Cód 833, discussed above. However, Ch. 15 is repeated, and there is a note in the text to that effect: 'este capítolo está duas vezes tresladado no próprio' [this chapter is copied twice in the original], fol. 24ᵛ. That suggests that the repetition is not a copyist's error but an indication of an original which had not undergone a thorough editorial revision.

However, the most striking feature of this MS is its tendency to omit words and phrases, in a way which normally makes perfectly good sense, but which results in a text which is notably poorer than the general run of versions of the chronicle. In each of the following examples from Ch. 55 a reading from COD 396, fol. 51ᵛ is followed by one from TT17. The extra material to be found in TT17, fol. 77, and, sometimes in a slightly different form, in the other MSS consulted, is underlined.

> foi muitas vezes cometida — foi muitas vezes <u>aos mouros</u> cometida [was many times undertaken — was many times undertaken <u>with the Moors</u>];
>
> que entendiam é de outras cousas, afirmando-lhe finalmente — que entendiam, <u>logo se mudavam</u> em outras sentenças, afirmando-se finalmente [they

---

[26] TT17's reading 'nem ousaria' means 'would not dare'.

understood something different, stating finally — they understood, <u>then they would change the subject</u>, stating finally];

os outros capitães de Tângere — os outros capitães <u>do palanque</u> de Tângere [the other captains at Tangiers — the other captains at the Tangiers <u>barricade</u>];

A rainha e o ifante por satisfazer a vontade d'el-rei D. Duarte que em seu testamento o leixara muito encomendado — A rainha e o ifante <u>D. Pedro ante de seus desvarios</u>, por se satisfazer <u>ao ifante D. Fernando e comprir</u> a vontade d'el-rei D. Duarte, que em seu testamento o leixara muito encomendado [The queen and the prince, in order to satisfy the wishes of D. Duarte, who had insisted on it in his will — The queen and the Prince D. Pedro, <u>before their quarrels</u>, in order <u>to satisfy Prince D. Fernando and comply</u> with the wishes of D. Duarte, who had insisted on it in his will].

Further examples from Ch. 118 appear below. As before, the reading of Cód. 396, fol. 118ᵛ, is printed before that of TT 17, fol. 125:

despois foi a Sé e a Santa Cruz e a Santa Clara — despois <u>de ter suas cousas providas</u> se foi à Sé e a Santa Cruz e a Santa Clara <u>por serem casas em que tinha singular devoção</u> [Then he went to the Cathedral and Santa Cruz and Santa Clara — after <u>putting his affairs in order</u>, he went to the Cathedral and to Santa Cruz and to Santa Clara, <u>religious houses for which he had a special devotion</u>];
da sua mulher — de sua molher e <u>dos que com ela ficaram</u> [of his wife — of his wife and <u>those who remained with her</u>];
cabeça da comenda de Christus — cabeça da comenda <u>mor</u> de Christus [head of the commandery of Christ — head of <u>the principal</u> commandery of Christ].

There was a vogue for epitomes of historical works in the fifteenth century, but the MS, with its 219 folios, can hardly be said to be one.[27] Rather it seems to reflect an early stage in the composition of the chronicle, a relatively plain outline of the narrative which would later be filled with more detail.[28] Usually the detail is factual, though it can also have a rhetorical function, most obviously in the example of Ch. 118 in which D. Pedro, before his last, fatal journey to Alfarrobeira, visits the churches in Coimbra for which he had 'singular devoção'. Throughout Pina is anxious to present his hero as a man of true devotion, to God as well as to duty and country.

---

[27] See José L. Moure, 'Sobre la cuestión de la prioridad de la composición en las dos versiones de las Crónicas del canciller Ayala', *Incipit*, 12 (1992), 21–49 (p. 32).
[28] In an interesting article, Barry Taylor discusses this phenomenon in relation to chronicles written in Spain, 'Versiones largas y breves de textos castellanos medievales y áureos: la cuestión de la prioridad', in *Text and Manuscript in Medieval Spain*, ed. by D. Hook (London: King's College London, 2000), pp. 103–20 (pp. 104–07).

Conclusion

The *Crónica de D. Afonso V* is a long work, which may have taken as much as fourteen or fifteen years to write. During this lengthy process copies leaked from Pina's office, perhaps into the hands of aristocratic families anxious to read about their forefathers, and these copies, or copies derived from them, still survive. Two of them are held in the Biblioteca Nacional de Portugal. They are Códs 833, in which division into chapters had not yet been definitively determined, and 396, still at a relatively early stage in the stylistic elaboration of the text. The Oxford MS, OB, shares characteristics with both of them, though to a lesser degree, suggesting that it — or the copy from which it was made — was put together near the end of the compositional process. OB, which, apart from anything else, has suffered physical damage over the course of history, is unlikely ever to be the base text for a new edition of the chronicle. However, it contains some interesting readings, which may represent Pina's early thoughts about his work, and which should at least be taken into account by a future editor.

Damião de Góis's *Livro de Linhagens*: An Untold (Hi)Story

CATARINA BARCELÓ FOUTO

King's College London

Damião de Góis is amongst the most accomplished writers and intellectuals of sixteenth-century Portugal and is one of the most cosmopolitan for his personal trajectory and engagement with the wider European Republic of Letters. His life is well documented and his work has been the object of a number of important critical studies.[1] But for all the critical attention that his vast work has attracted, virtually nothing has been written about his *Livro de Linhagens*.[2] This is most likely because the *Livro de Linhagens* was never published, surviving only in manuscript copies, and because genealogy enjoys a minor status as an ancillary discipline.

This article is a critical approach to the *Livro de Linhagens* (henceforward *LL*): it will discuss the problems surrounding the authorship of the work and contextualize the writing of the *LL*, proposing a dating and sources for some of its sections. It will also place the *LL* in the public and literary career of the Portuguese humanist and situate it within the thriving tradition of the writing of books of lineage in late medieval and Renaissance Portugal. In the discussion that follows, I will include the transcription and translation of selected passages of the *LL*, such as its Prologue, shedding light on whom Góis was addressing in his work and how he perceived the task of the writer of genealogies.

---

[1] Amongst these are Elisabeth Feist Hirsch, *Damião de Góis: The Life and Thought of a Portuguese Humanist (1502-1574)* (The Hague: Martin Nijhoff, 1967); *Damião de Góis: humaniste européen*, ed. by José V. de Pina Martins (Braga: Barbosa & Xavier; Paris: J. Touzot, 1982); idem, 'Damião de Góis e o pacifismo erasmiano', in *Humanismo e Erasmismo na cultura portuguesa* (Paris: Centro Cultural Português–Fundação Calouste Gulbenkian, 1973), pp. 63–73; Francisco Leite de Faria, *Estudos bibliográficos sobre Damião de Góis e a sua época* (Lisbon: Secretaria de Estado da Cultura, 1977); Amadeu Torres, *Noese e crise na epistolografia latina Goesiana*, 2 vols (Paris: Fundação Calouste Gulbenkian, Centro Cultural Português, 1982).

[2] There are few exceptions to this: Joaquim de Vasconcelos, *Goesiana* (Porto: Imprensa Internacional, 1879), pp. 29–31; Guilherme J. C. Henriques, *Ineditos Goesianos* (Lisbon: V. da Silva, 1896–98), pp. 246–47; Teresa Andrade e Sousa, 'Lenda da Rainha D. Isabel: códice iluminado da B.N.', *Revista da Biblioteca Nacional*, 2nd series, 2.1 (1987), 23–48 (pp. 29–30); and, more recently, Amadeu Torres, José Baptista de Sousa and Luís Augusto Costa Dias, *Damião de Góis: humanista português na Europa do Renascimento* (Lisbon: Biblioteca Nacional, 2002), pp. 96–98. This article was submitted to the editors before the publication of the *Livro de linhagens de Portugal de Damião de Góis*, ed. by António Maria Falcão Pestana de Vasconcelos (Lisbon: Instituto Português de Heráldica, 2014).

Portuguese Studies vol. 31 no. 2 (2015), 235–49
© Modern Humanities Research Association 2015

Tracing the Text: Problems and Pitfalls

There are doubts surrounding the authorship of the *LL*, first attributed to Damião de Góis by two important seventeenth-century scholars, Diogo Barbosa Machado and António Caetano de Sousa.[3] Amongst the reasons to doubt that Góis ever wrote such a work is that the *LL* was never published during his lifetime, unlike a number of other important historiographical texts such as the *Crónica do Felicíssimo Rei D. Manuel* (in four parts, published in Lisbon, 1566–67) or the *Crónica do Príncipe D. João* (Lisbon, 1567).[4] As a well-established humanist with access to the archival materials deposited at the Torre do Tombo of which he was *guarda-mor* between 1548 and 1571, and the recipient of important commissions by the Crown, Góis had easy access to those involved in the printing trade in Portugal and abroad.

The other reason to doubt whether Góis actually wrote such a work derives from the analysis of the seventeenth-century manuscript copies of the *LL*. In his *A nobreza medieval portuguesa*, the historian José Mattoso raises some concerns about the authenticity of Góis's work, while admitting to never having seen any of the extant manuscript copies.[5] Before Mattoso, G. J. C. Henriques had pointed out the various chronological impossibilities which exist in the manuscript copies that have survived.[6] Amongst these is the existence of a chapter on the family of the 'Dias de Goes' which includes a biography of Damião de Góis, complete with his family ancestry, his travels in Europe and service to the Portuguese crown, and his death.[7] However, the existence of such a biography in the surviving copies of the *LL* alone should not be reason to reject the attribution of its authorship to the humanist. G. J. C. Henriques also proposes, rightly in my view, that the initial part of the chapter on the 'Dias de Goes' may have been commenced by Damião de Góis, and that after the author's death someone else had taken on the task of updating it, completing the biography of the humanist. As will be seen below, the work that Góis carried out on the *LL* is to some extent a recompilation of the work of others before him, and the readers of the *LL* would certainly have been sensitive to the task

---

[3] Diogo Barbosa Machado, *Bibliotheca lusitana*, 4 vols (Coimbra: Atlântida Editora, 1965), I, 621; António Caetano de Sousa, *História genealógica da casa real portuguesa* (Lisbon: Officina Silviana da Academia Real, 1739–48), Aparato vol. I, pp. xxx–xxxiv.

[4] All quotations from both chronicles follow these editions: *Crónica do Príncipe D. João*, ed. by Graça Almeida Rodrigues (Lisbon: Universidade Nova de Lisboa, 1977); *Crónica do Felicíssimo Rei D. Manuel*, ed. by J. M. Teixeira de Carvalho and David Lopes (Coimbra: Universidade de Coimbra, 1949–55).

[5] José Mattoso, *A nobreza medieval portuguesa: a família e o poder* (Lisbon: Editorial Estampa, 1987), p. 49 and p. 49 n. 30.

[6] This objection was formulated in his *Ineditos Goesianos*, 2 vols (Lisbon: V. da Silva, 1896–98), II, 246–47, and was also printed later in *A bibliographia goesiana* (Lisbon: Imprensa Libanio da Silva, 1911), pp. 62–63. Teresa Andrade e Sousa, 'Lenda da Rainha D. Isabel', p. 30, revisits Henriques's objections, but makes no further contribution to the discussion surrounding the authorship of the *LL*.

[7] In the copy of the Biblioteca Nacional, COD 977, this passage of the text occupies folios 267^v–272^r.

of bringing the lineages contained in Góis's manuscript up to date — including even the biography of its author.

There are, in fact, solid reasons to attribute the *LL* to Damião de Góis. We know that the *LL* was deposited in the Torre do Tombo as having been written by Góis, and that it still existed there on 15 February 1622, thanks to the inventory of Manuel Jácome Bravo (*guarda-mor* of the Torre do Tombo). This inventory registered the *assento* of Góis's manuscript made by Gaspar Álvares Lousada (a temporary replacement of Diogo de Castilho, Bravo's predecessor as *guarda-mor* of the royal archive), who identified it as *Livro das linhagens novas de Damião de Goes, que segue ao Conde D. Pedro, que tem cento, e noventa, e cinco folhas com seu alfabeto encadernado como os demais*.[8]

However, before its disappearance, sometime after 1622, several copies were made from the autograph. António Caetano de Sousa, author of the *História genealógica da casa real portuguesa*, offers valuable information to ascertain the context of the production of these copies. He indicates that the decision to carry these out had been made at the request of the king himself (Philip III of Spain) and indicates that at least three copies were made and that their recipients were: the Duke of Braganza, Teodósio II; the Marquis of Castelo Rodrigo, Manuel de Moura Corte-Real, son of the influential Cristóvão de Moura; and, finally, a João Pereira, identified simply as 'hum Fidalgo do Minho'.[9] These copies were signed by Diogo de Castilho, then *guarda-mor* of the Torre do Tombo. Of these three copies, only that belonging to Manuel de Moura Corte-Real has been identified and is held in the Biblioteca Nacional de Portugal, shelfmark COD 977 (former C-1-17). This copy later came into the possession of the clergyman and historian Manuel Caetano de Sousa.[10] He then offered the copy of the *LL* and many other books to his relative António Caetano de Sousa, author of the *História genealógica*, so that he could pursue his genealogical and historiographical interests. In my discussion of the *LL* I will, therefore, refer to this copy and quote from its text.

We know that more copies were made in the first half of the seventeenth century:[11] António Caetano de Sousa himself says so, but is vague about their chronology and number ('alguns mais' [some more]), and omits the names of their recipients.[12] Amongst the other seventeenth-century copies of the *LL* is

---

[8] There is a detailed description of this manuscript copy in Amadeu Torres et al., *Damião de Góis: humanista português*, pp. 96–98.
[9] António Caetano de Sousa, *História genealógica*, p. xxxiii.
[10] For the intellectual career of this clergyman, see Esteves Pereira and Guilherme Rodrigues, *Portugal: dicionário histórico, corográfico, heráldico, biográfico, bibliográfico, numismático e artístico*, 7 vols (Lisbon: João Romano Torres Ed., 1904–15), VI, 1059–60.
[11] There are eighteenth-century copies of the *LL*: two of them can be found at the Biblioteca Nacional, shelfmark PBA. 323 and COD 6835; there are two other copies at the Torre do Tombo: one, dated from 1713, is identified as Genealogias Manuscritas, 21-E-13 (also available in microfilm mf. 4316); the other bears the title *Livro de Linhagens de Portugal, de Damião de Góis* (reference: Livros de Linhagens, n.º 157). I did not consult these eighteenth-century copies.
[12] António Caetano de Sousa, *História genealógica*, p. xxxiii.

Cod. 49-xiii-19, currently held in the Biblioteca da Ajuda in Lisbon — but it is not known if this corresponds to one of the copies mentioned by Caetano de Sousa. This copy, which belonged to the Real Bibliotheca, contains 377 folios and was copied by seventeenth-century scribes (there are two identifiably different hands).[13] The text of Cod. 49-xiii-19 coincides with the material preserved in the copy of the Biblioteca Nacional, COD 977, and its disposition.[14]

This copy contains material of relevance to those with an interest in the *LL*: appended at the beginning are two pages which contain a copy of the prologue of the *LL* according to COD 977 held in the Biblioteca Nacional (which bears some important differences, as I explain below) and additional comments on that copy of the text. The copy of the prologue and the notes are clearly dated, but their author is not identified: 'Copiado em 1-3-1921 de uma folha de papel collada no Codice 977 azul (C-1-17) da Biblioteca Nacional, o qual é o exemplar do apographo que pertenceu ao Marquez de Castelo Rodrigo' [Copied on 1-3-1921 from a sheet of paper glued onto Codex 977 (C-1-17) from the Biblioteca Nacional, which is the apograph which belonged to the Marquis of Castelo Rodrigo]. More interesting, however, is the loose folio which reproduces a note identified as having been written by Damião de Góis himself, and which was originally appended to the autograph of the *LL*: 'Esta memoria estaua escripta da Letra de Damião de Goes no original donde se trasladou este Liuro' [This note was written in Damião de Góis's handwriting in the autograph from which this book was copied]. The text of this loose folio presents numerous lacunae which can only be overcome with the help of the anonymous twentieth-century scholar who notes that the text of Góis's own hand had been included by António Caetano de Sousa in the Apparatus to his *História genealógica da casa real portuguesa* ('Esta declaração vem na Historia Genealogica — Aparato tomo I xxviii'). This note is relevant as it sheds light on the motivations of the author to have embarked on such a project and it points to potential sources of the work of Damião de Góis:

> Este livro das linhagens houve eu Damião de Goes, Guarda mor da Torre do Tombo, per mandado delRey D. João nosso Senhor, terceiro deste nome,

---

[13] For a complete description of this copy, see Carlos Alberto Ferreira, 'Índice abreviado das Genealogias da Ajuda', p. 10, n. 47. This index was never published, but it is available at the Biblioteca da Ajuda and the information is now available on the online catalogue of the Ajuda Library.

[14] I do not think that the manuscript identified as 'Copia das Várias Famílias', shelfmark Cod. 49-xiii-20 is the same text as Cod. 49-xiii-19. Even though Góis is identified as its author on the spine of the binding of this manuscript, there is no doubt that this is very different in several respects. It is markedly longer (997 folios, vs 377 folios) and its index is also different from that contained in Cod. 49-xiii-19. This begins with the genealogies of the Portuguese kings, and moves on to the noble families of Portugal. The index of Cod. 49-xiii-20 does not identify any material concerning the royal families of the first and second dynasties (because there is none). The index also starts with (in alphabetical order) 'Abreus de Regallados' and finishes with 'Vasconcellos', but in Cod. 49-xiii-19, 'Abreus' features only in fourth place, after 'Anriquez', 'Anriques e Noronhas' and 'Alvaro paiz linhagem'. Carlos Alberto Ferreira, 'Índice abreviado', n. 48, ventures the possibility that Cod. 49-xiii-20 may, in fact, be the continuation of the text contained in Cod. 49-xiii-19, but this is unlikely, as all of the material identified in the alphabetical index of the latter is contained in it.

da Livraria de Sisto Tavares, que Deus perdoe, Quartanario, que foy na Sé de Lisboa, e paguey por elle, e por estoutros dous manuaes pequenos, que com elle estão atados, dez cruzados, aos herdeiros do dito Sisto Tavares, que tudo compilou com muito trabalho, e diligencia. Dos quaes livros, e papeis, e do antigo das linhagens do Conde D. Pedro com seu appendix, e o que fez o Doutor Pacheco, que ao presente está em poder de D. Jeronymo de Castro; e das memorias, que compilou Alfonso de Lugo sobre as linhagens, que, segundo me disse Antonio de Teive, recolheu D. Antonio, filho herdeiro de D. Antonio de Taide, Conde da Castanheira despois do seu falecimento, se poderia de novo compilar, e fazer hum outro livro, do qual as linhagens deste Reyno fossem mais alluminadas do que estão. E este livro com os dous pequenos, e outros papeis, tudo atado, e junto lancey na Torre do Tombo, 7 de Junho de 1528, Damião de Goes.[15]

[I, Damião de Góis, guarda-mor at the Torre do Tombo, at the orders of D. João III, acquired this book of lineages from the library of Xisto Tavares, may he rest in peace, prebendary at the Cathedral of Lisbon, and I have paid for it and for these other two small books which are tied up with it, ten cruzados to the heirs of the said Xisto Tavares, who compiled all this material with great persistence and diligence. These books, and papers, and the old book of lineages written by count Pedro with its appendix; and that which was written by Pacheco, doctor in Law, which is now in possession of Jeronimo de Castro; and the memories which Alfonso de Lugo wrote down on the lineages and which, according to what Antonio de Teive has told me, have been compiled by Antonio, the heir of Antonio de Ataíde, count of Castanheira, after his death; they could be compiled once again, and a new book could be written to make the lineages of this Kingdom clearer than what they presently are. And I have tied up this book with the other two smaller books and other papers and deposited them together in the Torre do Tombo, on 27 June 1528. Damião de Góis.]

The date of 1528 can only be correct if the note was written retrospectively: Góis says that he deposited the manuscripts 'por mandado delRei João o terceiro' (who ruled between 1521 and 1557), but the fact remains that António de Ataíde (1530–1603), second Count of Castanheira, was born after 1528 and inherited his father's title only upon his death, in 1563. It was sometime after that, according to Góis, that Ataíde compiled his *Nobiliario das famílias deste reino*, the title assigned to this work by Barbosa Machado.[16] Therefore, the note was written at a later stage, most likely when Góis was already working on the LL or had, in fact, completed it — note the use of the conditional, not the future, in 'a new book *could be written*'.

The *Crónica do Felicíssimo Rei D. Manuel* may shed some light as to why in 1528 Góis was so interested in collecting writings on the genealogy of Portuguese families. In Part II, §19, Góis informs us that, whilst in the service of the king, D. João III (sometime between 1523 and 1531), he had been commissioned by

---

[15] António Caetano de Sousa, *História genealógica*, p. xxviii.
[16] Diogo Barbosa Machado, *Bibliotheca lusitana*, I, 210–11. Góis does not seem to have known Ataíde's work directly.

D. Manuel's son, Prince Fernando (1507–1534) to gather as many chronicles as possible, both manuscript and in print, and in any language. Góis satisfied the Prince's interest on historiography by spending a considerable amount of money collecting these writings (which, sadly, he never identifies). After that, Prince Fernando sent to Damião de Góis in Flanders a complete genealogical table of the ancestry of all the kings of Portugal, from the time of Noah to the reign of D. Manuel, to be illuminated by Simon Bening, of Bruges — a work which, we are led to believe, was linked to the request for chronicles made by the Prince sometime before.[17]

Narrowing down the time limits or circumstances for the writing of the *LL* will lead to chronological problems arising from the extant text. Without offering evidence to sustain his hypothesis, Joaquim de Vasconcelos suggested that the *LL* was commissioned by Prince Luís (1506–1555), sometime between 1548–49 and 1554–55.[18] However, there is no mention of such a commission in the actual text of the *LL*, despite the references to Prince Luís in it, or even in the *Crónica do Felicíssimo Rei D. Manuel*, namely in Part I, §101, which includes a summary biography of the Prince. If such a commission existed, then it is likely that Góis would have referred to it, as he does in relation to Prince Fernando's request for the chronicles, and even his own involvement in the commission to Simon Bening. Equally significant is the absence of a dedication or even an address to the Prince in the prologue of the *LL* (transcribed below).

It is unlikely that Damião de Góis started his work on the *LL* before his appointment to the post of *guarda-mor* of the Torre do Tombo: after his diplomatic missions on behalf of D. João III, he travelled extensively in central and eastern Europe with two longer periods in Italy (1534–38) and Louvain (1538–44),[19] having remained far from the type of sources required to carry out this kind of intense archival research. If we are right in assuming that Góis had already written or started his work on the *LL* when he wrote the note, then the time window is sometime around 1563 (the year when D. António de Ataíde succeeded his father as Count of Castanheira).

[17] This set of genealogical tables, known as the *Genealogia do infante D. Fernando*, survives to this day, and can be seen in the manuscript section of the British Museum in London (shelfmark Add. Ms. 12531 V det IXb). For a complete description of the manuscript, see Frederico de la Figanière, *Catálogo dos manuscriptos portuguezes existentes no Museu Britanico* (Lisbon: Imprensa Nacional, 1854), pp. 268–76. The most complete study of this work, which includes reproductions of the exquisitely illuminated folios, is that by António de Aguiar, *A genealogia iluminada do Infante D. Fernando por António de Holanda e Simon Bening: estudo histórico e crítico* (Lisbon: Gráfica Santelmo, 1962). The genealogical table was first drawn up by António de Holanda, the father of Francisco de Holanda, and later sent to Simon Bening to be illuminated. The work would have been commissioned in 1530 and was left incomplete due to the death of Prince Fernando in 1534. These genealogical drawings are discussed thoroughly in Sylvie Deswarte, *Les Enluminures de la 'Leitura nova', 1504–1552: étude sur la culture artistique au Portugal au temps de l'Humanisme* (Paris: Fundação Calouste Gulbenkian–Centro Cultural Português, 1977), see especially pp. 107–08, 209–10 for the role of Damião de Góis in this commission.
[18] Joaquim de Vasconcelos, *Damião de Goes: novos estudos* (Porto: Typographia de Artur José de Sousa & Irmão, 1897), p. 106.
[19] This period in Góis's life is discussed by Elisabeth Feist Hirsch, *Damião de Góis*, pp. 90–128.

I believe that the apograph copies reveal that some of the material included in them was added at later stages in Góis's career, or even after his death (as discussed earlier regarding the inclusion of Góis's biography in the *LL*). Importantly, the royal genealogy which opens the *LL* leads us to suppose that it was written after 1554 (the year of the death of Prince João, on 2 January) and before 1557 (the year of the death of D. João III, which is not mentioned).[20] Though the birth of Sebastião (20 January 1554) is not mentioned, this is no reason to assume that the book was finished in that year, as Góis only listed D. João III's sworn heirs to the title in his list of descendants, and could have adopted a similar methodology with regard to the issue of Prince João.

However, the manuscript texts on royal genealogies which occupy the last folios of the *LL* were written and included at a later stage. In Part IV, §37 of the *Crónica do Felicíssimo Rei D. Manuel*, Góis explains that he was commissioned to write this text by the regent, Cardinal Henry, five or six years after the death of D. João III, which situates the commission as having been placed in 1562 or 1563. Parts I and II of the chronicle appeared in 1566 and Part III and IV in 1567. In his later historiographical works, there is (understandably) a marked interest in the writing of genealogy, and both the *Crónica do Felicíssimo Rei D. Manuel* and the *Crónica do Príncipe D. João* contain several passages which discuss the genealogy of the kings of Portugal and other European royal families.[21] In Part IV of this chronicle, after narrating the events leading up to the marriage of Princess Beatriz to Charles, Duke of Savoy (IV, §70), Góis includes two other chapters which contextualize the political significance of this matrimonial alliance and defend the illustrious ancestry of the House of Savoy. §71 explores the 'progenia, & linhagem da Rainha donna Maphalda filha do Conde Amedeu de Moriana em Saboia, molher que foi delRei dom Afonso Henriques' [ancestry and lineage of Queen Mafalda, daughter of Count Amedeus of Maurienne in Savoy, wife of D. Afonso Henriques] and is followed by another chapter discussing the 'progenia & linhagem do Conde dom Anrrique pai delRei dom Afonso Anrriquez' [ancestry and lineage of Count Henrique, father of D. Afonso Henriques]. Both topics are also explored in two different texts contained in the manuscript copies of the *LL*: 'Progenia e linhagem do Conde dom Henrique pai delRei dom Afonso Henriques, copillada, & collegida per Damião de Goes' [ancestry and lineage of Count Henrique, father of D. Afonso Henriques, compiled and collated by Damião de Góis] (fols 274^v–277^r) and 'Progenia e linhagem da Rainha donna Maphalda molher delRei dom Afonso Anriquez primeiro Rei de Portugal, copilada, & colegida per Damião de Goes' [ancestry and lineage of Queen Mafalda, wife of Afonso Henriques, first king of Portugal, compiled and collated by Damião de Góis] (fols 277^v–280^v). Part

---

[20] A point first raised by Luís de Mello Vaz de Sampayo, 'A família de Martim Afonso de Sousa, "o da batalha real"', *Revista de Armas e Troféus*, 2nd series, 6–7 (1965–66); idem, *Subsídios para uma biografia de Pedro Álvares Cabral* (Coimbra: Imprensa de Coimbra, 1971), p. xlviii.

[21] Also, in his manuscript 'Lenda da Rainha D. Isabel' (Biblioteca Nacional, shelfmark il-223), Góis devotes a substantial part of the text clarifying the ancestry of the queen. For a critical edition and study, see Teresa Andrade e Sousa, 'Lenda da Rainha D. Isabel'.

III of the chronicle includes one chapter which illuminates the circumstances surrounding the awarding of the Order of the Garter by King Henry VIII of England to D. Manuel, which Góis explains through an excursus into the 'parentesco que ha ẽtre hos reis destes dous regnos' [kinship that exists between the kings of these two kingdoms] (III,§ 24) and which corresponds in almost its entirety to the 'Discurso do bello parentesco que os Reis de Portugal tem com os Reis de Inglaterra, e Casa de Lencastre, copilado, e colegido per Damião de Góis' [Declaration on the illustrious kinship that the Kings of Portugal share with the Kings of England and the House of Lancaster, compiled and collated by Damião de Góis] (fols 272^r–274^r). The likely *terminus a quo* for these sections of the *LL* will be 1563, the date of the commission of the *Crónica*, and it is safe to assume that these were complete by 1567, the date of the publication of parts III and IV of the *Crónica*.

Anyone who confronts and compares the printed text of these three chapters of the *Crónica do Felicíssimo Rei D. Manuel* to the three manuscript texts included at the end of the *LL* will reach the conclusion that the manuscript texts correspond to an embryonic stage of the three chapters later included in the *Crónica*. It should be noted that the text of the three printed chapters corresponds in almost its entirety to the text of the manuscript copies with the exception of the initial sentences and the references to previous chapters of the *Crónica*. For this reason, one could think that the scribes of the copies of the Biblioteca Nacional and Biblioteca da Ajuda thought that they should copy these passages of the *Crónica* into the *LL* (due to their genealogical content). However, the 'Discurso do Bello Parentesco' negates this hypothesis: both manuscript versions include one final paragraph that is not to be found in the printed text of the *Crónica*.[22] This indicates that the manuscript texts existed independently and that they were not copied into the *LL* from the printed edition of the *Crónica*.

Also, one could think that Góis finished his *LL* with three genealogical texts focusing on the ancestry of the first kings of the first and second dynasties to offer a structural counterpart to the genealogy of kings that opens the *LL*. If that were the case, however, the final line of the 'Discurso do Bello Parentesco' would go against what Góis had achieved with this lengthy *LL*: 'E se algũa pessoa achar este discurso maes breve do que se a tão larga materia requere, saiba que as genealogias se vem melhor por arvores, e pinturas do que se podem declarar por escriptura' [And if anyone thinks that this declaration is briefer than is required for such a lofty theme, may they be advised that genealogies are best seen in trees and drawings than explained in writing] (fol. 274^r). It is, thus, unlikely that the three manuscript texts were originally included in the *LL*. This analysis of selected passages of the *LL* shows the type of problems of textual criticism that a critical approach to the *LL* will inevitably raise.

[22] The paragraph is quite typical of Góis's style and revealing of his understanding of the significance of those in charge of the writing of history. See below for the transcription and discussion of the paragraph.

From Góis's note, we also learn how he perceived his role as a genealogist as that of a *compilador*, drawing from the work of others before him, of which he identifies Pedro, Count of Barcelos (author of the well-known *Livro de Linhagens*, written approximately in 1340-44 and reformulated *c.* 1360-65, and again *c.* 1380-83),[23] the clergyman Xisto Tavares,[24] and Fernão Pacheco — who was alive during the reign of João III, and was doctor in Law.[25] Góis does not identify the two other small books that he had purchased from the heirs of Xisto Tavares for the hefty sum of ten *cruzados*, but we are told that these had been *compiled* by Tavares himself. It is tempting and logical to see in these unnamed books the evidence of previous manuscript writings on the lineages of the Portuguese families — material that Tavares would have used as source for his own work, continuing a tradition of genealogical writing begun centuries before. An example of this type of work is the *Livro de linhagens do século XVI*, which, as will be seen, may also have been one of the sources with which Damião de Góis worked on his own *LL*.

It is clear that Góis's selection of material from the *Livro de Linhagens* by the Count of Barcelos incorporates both historical narratives and purely fictional accounts. For a historian who is so concerned with the historical truth, Góis is interestingly silent when incorporating into his *LL* some well-known legends, such as the story of the 'Dama Pé-de-Cabra' (fol. 100^v). Sadly, the material is copied and Góis never comments on how he reconciles such narratives with his own concerns for accuracy and truth. But whenever using the *Livro de Linhagens*, Góis identifies this clearly in the title of the chapter (e.g. *Do título 8º do Liuro das Linhagens donde decendem os senhores de Biscaya, e de Castella, e de Mendoça, e do Cid Ruy Diaz* [from the eighth part of the *Livro das Linhagens* entitled 'The ancestry of the lords of Biscay, Castile and Mendonza and the Cid Ruy Diaz'], fol. 98^v).

The other text upon which Góis relied for his *LL* was the work by Xisto Tavares. The autograph of Xisto Tavares's book of lineage remains lost, having disappeared from the Torre do Tombo, much like Góis's own manuscript *LL*, but the Biblioteca Nacional de Portugal has two copies of the text. The title of one of these indicates that this may very well be an apograph of the text which Góis had in his possession, as there is reference to the date of its deposit in the Torre do Tombo: *Livro das Prencipaes linhagens de Portugal composto por Sisto Tauares quartanario que fui* [sic] *na se de Lisboa o qual por mandado delRey Dom João o 3º se lançou na Torre do Tombo en 27 de junho do ano de 1608* [sic] [Book containing the principal lineages of Portugal, written by Xisto Tavares, prebendary of Lisbon cathedral, which was deposited at the Torre do Tombo by order of D. João III, on 27 June 1608 [sic]] (shelfmark COD 1328). The

---

[23] José Mattoso, *A nobreza medieval portuguesa*, pp. 57-100.
[24] Tavares (b. ?) died in 1525 according to Barbosa Machado, *Bibliotheca Lusitana*, III, 795. His *Nobiliário* is discussed in António Caetano de Sousa, *História genealógica*, pp. xxviii-xxx.
[25] The work of Fernão Pacheco is discussed by António Caetano de Sousa, *História genealógica*, pp. xxxvii-xxxviii.

seventeenth-century scribe who copied the autograph made a clear error in the title page by identifying the year as 1608: Góis's note identifies the date as 27 June of 1528. Tavares's work has no prologue or dedication, but includes an index. It does not identify the families by alphabetical order, but instead by sequential order in the text. This may be due to the relatively small number of family nuclei whose genealogies the text explores (thirty-eight overall). Yet, there is no way of ascertaining whether the index corresponds to the design of Tavares's autograph. Comparing the *LL* to the *Livro das Prencipaes linhagens de Portugal*, it is possible to note that sections of Góis's work are indebted to Tavares's own manuscript: this is, as far as I could ascertain, the case for portions of chapters dedicated to the Eças (*LL*, fol. 8^v; Tavares, fol. 112^v), the House of Braganza (*LL*, fol. 20^v; Tavares, fol. 55), the Limas (*LL*, fol. 25^v; Tavares, fol. 123), the Castros (*LL*, fol. 140^r; Tavares, fol. 1).

Another useful source for Góis in the writing of the *LL* may have been a text whose authorship still remains to be identified and which has been dated to 1547–55 by its editor, António de Faria.[26] This anonymous book of lineages, preserved in a copy, identifies the lineages of more families (forty-six) than the work of Xisto Tavares. A comparison of the first lines of the chapter dedicated to Gonçalo Mendes da Maia between the text of the *Livro de Linhagens* of Count Pedro, the anonymous book of lineages and Damião de Góis's *LL* reveals that the latter presents more similarities with the anonymous text than with the narrative preserved in the *Livro de Linhagens*.[27] Furthermore, Góis's chapter dedicated to the Cabreiras family corresponds verbatim to the 'Titulo dos Cabreiras donde vem os de Vasconcellos, e os Alvellos, e os Ribeiros' [Chapter on the Cabreiras whence the Vasconcellos, the Alvellos and the Ribeiros descend] in the anonymous book (*LL*, fol. 236^v; Anon. pp. 174 ff.).

But this is not always the case in the *LL*. A close analysis of both texts reveals that Góis had other sources to draw from. The sections dedicated to 'Dom Jorge Mestre de Santiago' (*LL*, fol. 24^v), to the Silveiras (*LL*, fol. 28^v), the Mirandas (*LL*, fol. 31^r), the Sás (fol. 34^r), the Castellos Brancos (*LL*, fol. 42^r), the Nogueiras (*LL*, fol. 44^v) or the Britos (*LL*, fol. 45^r) are not indebted to the anonymous text, for example, and they are not included in Xisto Tavares's *Livro das prencipaes linhagens*.

That Góis was indebted to the work of his predecessors is a fact, and this may very well be the reason for the opinion of Manuel Severim de Faria, according to whom 'o Nobiliario de Damião de Goes fora começado pelos Chronistas antecedentes, e elle o acabara [...] E em algumas partes he taõ identico, que saõ os paragrafos inteiros' [the book of lineages by Damião de Góis had been commenced by the chroniclers who had preceded him, and he had completed it

---

[26] *Livro de Linhagens do século XVI*, ed. by António Faria (Lisbon: Academia Portuguesa da História, 1956). For a discussion of the dating of the text, see pp. xix–xx.
[27] The editor of the *Livro de Linhagens do século XVI* compares this text to the medieval *Livro de Linhagens* in pp. xxiv–xxv; the chapter dedicated to Gonçalo Mendes da Maia corresponds to fol. 165^v ff. in Góis's *LL*.

[...] In some passages of the text, it is so identical to them, that entire paragraphs are taken from them].[28] The identification of Damião de Góis's sources for the *LL* will only be possible if more books of lineages are identified, studied and edited, but Góis's own role as compiler of information available to him as *guarda-mor* at the Torre do Tombo should not be underestimated.

The *LL*: Motivations and Audience

The Prologue of the *LL* lays out important lines for the analysis of this work by Damião de Góis, namely his motivations, his intended audience and the organization of the work. The following is a tentative critical edition of the prologue which has taken into consideration the text of the manuscript copy of the Biblioteca Nacional COD 977, copied directly from the autograph *LL* by Góis:[29]

> Liuro das Linhagens de Portugal de 150 annos e 200 a esta parte tresladado na verdade de tudo o que se pode alcançar dellas, algũas antigas de que trata o Livro antigo que fez o Conde d. Pedro e outras modernas
>
> Porque a memoria dos homens passa tam presto polla breuidade de suas vidas e variedade dos tempos e principalmente nestes Reinos de Portugal que nem de couzas medianas que se nelle acontecem senão escreuem sendo tam dignas de ficarém em lembranças, mas ainda das muito grandes, muitas dellas ficão por escreuer, e juntamente com isto, sam tam misturados os parentescos antre a gente nobre, que muito cedo pareçe que não seram necessarias pediremse dispensações, assi pelos esquecimentos que o tempo cauza, como pelos parentescos serem tam juntos, e misturados que se não poderão entender, pollo que querendo eu d'algũ modo fazer hũa breue declaraçam de algũas linhagens [folio 1ᵛ] *nobres*[30] deste reino terá esta breue leitura deste liuro a maneira seguinte:
> Primeiramente declara a linhagem real desde o conde dom Henrique ate *el Rei Dom João o 3º desse nome*,[31] como se pode alcançar por chronicas e memorias dizendo em cada capitolo de cada Rei com quem casarão e quãtos filhos houuerão e o que se pode alcançar que se delles fez, quão tempo viueram e reinaram, e isto atte ElRei Dom Pedro porque dahi por diante vão somente nomeados os filhos que houueram, declarando a geraçam que socedeo de cada hũ, indo a de hum Rei apos outro assi como socederam, e apos estas vem a declaraçam das linhagens de Portugal de 200 annos a esta parte porque os pais e auoos d'alguns destes nobres se acharam no Livro antigo das Linhagens que fez o Conde Dom Pedro, bastardo d'El Rei Dom Dinis.

---

[28] António Caetano de Sousa, *História genealógica*, p. xxix. Caetano de Sousa's patron was the House of Braganza, which may explain the negative comments on Góis's historiographical work in the *História genealógica*.

[29] The copy held in the Biblioteca da Ajuda, Cod. 49-xiii-19, occasionally preserves a better text, but it is shorter than the one preserved in the copy held in the Biblioteca Nacional, COD 977, and it omits important information on the methodology adopted by Góis in the compilation of this work.

[30] The scribe repeated the syllable *no-* ('*nobres*') at the end of fol. 1ʳ at the beginning of fol. 1ᵛ.

[31] I have corrected the italicized text, which reads in the original: 'desde o conde dom Henrique ate *el Rei Dom Henrique o 1º desse nome*'.

Este Liuro tera esta ordem e declaração que falla em cada capitolo algũa das dignidades que cada pessoa teue e se em algunm faltarem será por esquecimento ou nam terem vindo a nossa noticia.

E assi declara em cada capitolo quantos filhos houue e as filhas e com quem cazaram e não se falla mais dellas porque seguem i a natureza de seus maridos e nella declaram os filhos dellas.

E quãto aos filhos dos machos segue a geração do mais velho atte que ou feneçe ou dar no que ao presente he viuo, e dali torna para cima atte enchar [folio 2^r] dos descendentes do filho mais velho do que aqui he nomeado por primeiro na geração. E despois falla do outro filho segundo atte nomearlhe todos seus descendentes por esta mesma ordem e assi dos outros filhos se mais teve este primeiro progenitor.

E estas linhagens vão humas apoz outras sem nenhum modo de precedencias tirando as que descendem dos reis, e as que aqui nam forem bem declaradas, sera por não se poder alcançar certeza de como sucederam huns aos outros. E muitas pessoas honradas hauera desses appellidos aqui nomeados que aqui nam são, por os tomarem por parte de suas mãis e avos por se não dizer aqui mais dellas como ditto tenho, que nomearlhes os maridos com que cazaram.

[Book of the Lineages of Portugal, from 150 and 200 years ago to the present day, copied truthfully from all that could be found about them, some being old lineages which are discussed in the old book written by Count Pedro and others modern

Given that men's memory passes by so quickly through the brevity of their own lives and the variety of times, and especially in this Kingdom of Portugal where neither events of average importance which take place in it are recorded in writing, despite being so worthy of being remembered, nor even those events of great significance, many of which go unrecorded; and, added to this, given that blood relations amongst the nobility are so mixed that it seems that soon enough it will not be necessary to ask for dispensations, both due to the forgetfulness caused by time, and the fact that blood relations are so mixed and intermingled that they will not be understood; for these reasons, since I wanted to present a brief exposition of some of the noble lineages of this kingdom, this book shall read as follows:

First, it presents the royal lineage from Count Henrique up to D. João III, insofar as it was possible to ascertain from chronicles and accounts, each chapter stating to whom each King was married, and how many children they had and, insofar as it was possible to know, what was made of them, how long they lived and ruled; and this up to King Pedro, because from this point onwards only the names of the children of Kings will be included, indicating the offspring which descended from each of them, one king after the other according to their succession.

And after this, the exposition of the lineages of Portugal from 200 years ago up to the present day will follow, because the parents and grandparents of some of these noblemen were included in the *Livro de Linhagens* by Count Pedro, bastard son of D. Dinis. This book will follow this order, and it will declare in each chapter some of the honours that each person attained, and if they are missing that will be due to having been forgotten or not being known to us.

And so, each chapter states how many sons the person had and to whom their daughters were married, and nothing else is said of the daughters because they follow the blood line of their husbands, and their children are indicated there.

As for the children of the sons, each chapter follows the issue of the eldest until it dies out or reaches the person who is alive at present, and from this the chapter goes back to the descendants of the eldest son which is referred as the first born in their generation. And then it moves onto the other second son until all his descendants are stated according to this order, and in the same manner for all the other sons if this first parent happened to have any more children.

And these lineages are presented one after the other with no manner of precedence with the exception of those which descend from kings; and, if there are lineages which are not well explained in this book, it will be because it was not possible to establish with certainty how they succeeded one after the other. And there will be many honourable people with those family names that are indicated in this book who are not included, because they take the names from their mothers' or grandmothers' side, given that nothing is said about them with the exception of to whom they were married, as I explained above.]

Acting as the keeper of the historical memory of the kingdom, Góis's remark about the lack of interest in the writing of history is symptomatic of his condemnation of the growing dissociation of 'arms and letters' amongst the Portuguese aristocratic class. The prologue echoes some of the concerns identified in the manuscript note which was discussed above, where Góis voices his disappointment at the lack of interest and efforts of the noble Portuguese families in the writing of the deeds of their ancestors, past and recent: 'se poderia de novo compilar, e fazer hum outro livro, do qual as linhagens deste Reyno fossem mais allumiadas do que estão' [a new book could be written to make the lineages of this Kingdom clearer than what they presently are]. Note that, in this context, 'allumiar' signifies 'to clarify', but the associated meaning of 'to render more illustrious' is not far from Góis's mind in the prologue, where he denounces the consignment to oblivion of the achievements of the Portuguese aristocratic elites.

In other aspects, the *LL* would also fulfil the same practical objectives as the *Livro de Linhagens* by Count Pedro of Barcelos, given that Góis sees his work as important because his information will help families avoid marriages that are deemed incestuous if the blood relationship is closer than is sanctioned by the Church.

There are important differences between these two works, nonetheless. In the manuscript *LL* there is a clear distinction between the genealogy of kings and the lineages of aristocratic families: the *LL* commences with the three dynasties of Portuguese monarchs up to D. João III. So, even though Góis had access to the *Livro de Linhagens* by Count Pedro of Barcelos, there is no intention in the prologue to promote 'amor' [friendship] — to use Count Pedro's formulation —

amongst the aristocratic families of the Iberian Peninsula or Portugal, or even to uphold class solidarity, both of which are important objectives in the *Livro de Linhagens*.[32] Góis's *LL* is clearly a work which reflects an effective centralization of royal power, hence the precedence which is highlighted in the prologue, and which is a point of clear departure in relation to the work of Xisto Tavares and the anonymous sixteenth-century book of lineages.

This strict precedence is, however, in tune with one other important poetic celebration of genealogical ancestry and heraldry to be found in the *Cancioneiro Geral* (1516), which was composed by the poet and humanist João Rodrigues de Sá de Meneses.[33] In this sequence of *quintilhas*,[34] written sometime between 1508 and 1516, Sá de Meneses follows a strict hierarchy, commencing with the king and the prince, followed by the coats of arms of the duke, the *mestre d'Avis*, and the marquis. As for the aristocratic families, the house of Braganza is given a position of prominence as the first amongst the noble families of the kingdom for its 'sangue tam poderoso' [very powerful kinship]. Góis, on the other hand, makes no concessions to the status of the house of Braganza (fol. 20^v) in the overall scheme of his *LL*, and includes it after the titles dedicated to the lineages of the Eças (fol. 8^v) and the Noronhas (fol. 13^v).

As one would expect, the prologue situates the writing and the reading of the *LL* in a clear courtly environment, but for Góis's views on the intended audience of his genealogical writings we need to look elsewhere. The following two excerpts are transcribed: the first from the printed text of the *Crónica do Felicíssimo Rei D. Manuel* (of which *only* the italicized text is in the manuscript 'Discurso do Bello parentesco'); and the second from the final paragraph of the 'Discurso do bello parentesco' (fol. 274^r), which was not included in the printed edition of the chronicle:

> [...] me pareceo razão darlhe [to the chapter] outra materia mais apraziuel, & neçessaria ahos que ha lerem: ha qual he tratar nelle o antigo parentesco que ha entre hos Reis destes regnos, & hos de Inglaterra, & *porque hũa das cousas que mais alumea has historias, & satisfaz ahos que dellas são estudiosos, he saberem uerdadeiramēte a origem e linhagē donde procedem os Reis, & senhores, cujas chronicas lem, trabalhei tudo ho que em mi foi pera aqui dizer ho que disso pude alcãçar* [...]

> [[...] it seemed good reason to provide this chapter with a more agreeable, and necessary topic to those who read it: which is to explain in it the kinship which exists between the kings of this kingdom and those of England; and

---

[32] José Mattoso, *A nobreza medieval portuguesa*, pp. 37–55; Luís Krus, *A concepção nobiliárquica do espaço ibérico: geografia dos Livros de Linhagens medievais portugueses (1280–1380)* (Lisbon: Fundação Calouste Gulbenkian, 1994).

[33] For the work and cultural significance of this learned aristocrat, see José da Silva Terra, 'João Rodrigues de Sá de Meneses et l'Humanisme portugais', 5 vols (unpublished doctoral dissertation, University of Sorbonne, 1984); and Luís de Sá Fardilha, *A nobreza das letras: os Sás de Meneses e o Renascimento português* (Lisbon: FCG-FCT, 2008), pp. 43–102.

[34] Garcia de Resende, *Cancioneiro Geral*, ed. by Aida Fernanda Dias, 6 vols (Lisbon: IN-CM, 1990–2003), II, 374–91 (n. 457).

because one of the things which renders history clearer, and pleases those who study it is to know the true origin and lineage from where the kings and aristocrats, whose chronicles they read, come, I have worked as hard as I could to communicate what I have discovered about that topic [...]]

E se algũa pessoa achar este discurso maes breve do que se a tão larga materia requere, saiba que as genealogias se vem melhor por arvores, e pinturas do que se podem declarar por escriptura, e alem disto as cousas desta qualidade não são para pessoas a quem natureza não separou do saber, e condições das alimarias, mais que na forma, e na fala, senão para homẽes doctos, discretos, criados e cursados nas cortes dos Reis, e Principes, e praticos nos negocios dellas.

[And if anyone thinks that this declaration is briefer than is required for such a lofty theme, may they be advised that genealogies are best seen in trees and drawings than explained in writing, and also that topics of such importance are not for people whom nature has not distinguished from beasts in knowledge and condition, other than in shape and use of speech, but they are for learned and refined men, brought up and experienced in the courts of Kings and Princes, and well-versed in their affairs.]

The inclusion of genealogies in the *Chronica* is important not only in that it is necessary to clarify the development of the historical narrative ('allumear has historias') and support Góis's argument, but also in that it fulfils the important aesthetic function of offering 'materia apraziuel' to the readers. Also, Góis promotes his own work, implying in the first excerpt that the chapter is a concession to an audience of experts — those who devote themselves to the *study* of history — and not merely those who enjoy *reading* the chronicles of kings. And the same idea surfaces in the paragraph which was omitted in the printed edition of the *Chronica*: one can say that the ideal reader of this genealogical excursus is modelled upon Góis himself — a courtier raised at court, and someone with direct experience of all aspects of the political life of the kingdom at the service of kings and princes. Significantly, Góis says nothing about the social background of his ideal readers, and, by characterizing them as learned, he is effectively making a nobilitating move which identifies his audience as the intellectual elite of his time, regardless of their ancestry.

The writing of lineages does not make for great prose, as Góis implies in the second extract above, and, as he would know from first-hand involvement in the commission assigned by Prince Fernando, genealogical relations are best explained visually. Was this one of the reasons why the *LL* remained unpublished? Or could the controversy surrounding his *Crónica do Felicíssimo Rei D. Manuel* have impacted on the reception of the *LL*? The jury is still out. But I hope that this article has drawn attention to the need for further research into this work by Damião de Góis. The *LL* will certainly prove to be of interest to those concerned with the political life of late medieval and early modern Portugal, if Góis's historical rigour elsewhere is anything to go by.[35]

---

[35] For Góis's activity as a historian, see Elisabeth Feist Hirsch, *Damião de Góis*, pp. 191–207.

Lusophone Studies:
A Cumulative Area Bibliography, 2013–15

Emilce Rees

Visiting Research Associate at the Department of Spanish, Portuguese & Latin American Studies (SPLAS) at King's College, London

The following pages list publications and theses relating to the Portuguese-speaking world which were published from 2013 to early 2015 in English. **Some items previously omitted have been included here.** Relevant online academic search resources have been used, namely the Copac® library catalogue, WorldCat® and the ProQuest Dissertations and Theses Database and for consultation, the British Library EThOS, for ALL theses produced by UK Higher Education. The Copac® library catalogue contains the merged online catalogues of major University, Specialist, and National Libraries in the UK and Ireland, including the British Library. ABIL (Association of Portuguese and Irish Lusitanists) list members are also thanked for their contribution. WorldCat® is a global catalogue with more than 1.4 billion items available in libraries from around the world.

I. Publications

    1.1   Anthropology and Folklore
    1.2   Arts, Architecture and Music
    1.3   Bibliographies, Directories and Guides
    1.4   Environment
    1.5   History, Politics and Social Science
    1.6   Language
    1.7   Literature
    1.8   Religion

II. Theses

    2.1   African topics
    2.2   Asian Topics
    2.3   Brazilian Topics
    2.4   Portuguese Topics

I. Publications

1.1 Anthropology and Folklore

BATARDA FERNANDES, ANTÓNIO PEDRO (2014), *Natural Processes in the Degradation of Open-Air Rock-Art Sites: An Urgency Intervention Scale to Inform Conservation: The Case of the Côa Valley World Heritage Site, Portugal* (Oxford: Archaeopress) xv, 311 pages.

FORTE, MAXIMILIAN CHRISTIAN (2013), *Who is an Indian?: Race, Place, and the Politics of Indigeneity in the Americas* (Toronto: University of Toronto Press) xii, 254 pages.

KOPENAWA, DAVI ALBERT BRUCE (2013), *The Falling Sky: Words of a Yanomami Shaman* (Cambridge, MA: Belknap Press of Harvard University Press) xvi, 622 pages.

SHWALB, DAVID W., BARBARA J. SHWALB & MICHAEL E. LAMB (eds) (2013), *Fathers in Cultural Context* (New York: Routledge) xxii, 419 pages.

1.2 Arts, Architecture and Music

ADZ, KING (2013), *The Stuff You Can't Bottle: Advertising for the Global Youth Market* (London: Thames & Hudson) 342 pages.

ALONSO, NATALIA (2013), *Dance and Modernist Architecture: The Case of Lina Bo Bardi's SESC Pompéia* (London: London Metropolitan University) 120 pages

BIRKENSTEIN, JEFF, ANNA FROULA & KAREN RANDELL (2013), *The Cinema of Terry Gilliam: It's a Mad World* (New York: Columbia University Press) 256 pages.

BRANDELLERO, SARA (ed) (2013), *Brazilian Road Movie Journeys of (Self) Discovery* (Cardiff: University of Wales Press) 288 pages.

BURNETT, MARK THORNTON (2013), *Shakespeare and World Cinema* (Cambridge and New York: Cambridge University Press) xv, 272 pages.

CAMPBELL, PATRICIA SHEHAN & TREVOR WIGGINS (eds) (2013), *The Oxford Handbook of Children's Musical Cultures* (New York: Oxford University Press) xvii, 636 pages.

CLEVELAND, KIMBERLY (2013), *Black Art in Brazil: Expressions of Identity* (Gainesville: University Press of Florida) xii, 173 pages, [24] pages of plates.

COUTINHO, BÁRBARA (2014), *MUDE: Design and Fashion Museum, Francisco Capelo Collection, Lisbon* (London: Scala Publications) 128 pages.

FOSTER, DAVID WILLIAM (2013), *Latin American Documentary Filmmaking: Major Works* (Tucson: University of Arizona Press) xiv, 215 pages.

GRAY, JOHN (2014), *Afro-Brazilian Music: A Bibliographic Guide* (Nyack, New York: African Diaspora Press) xiv, 585 pages.

HERTZMAN, MARC A. (2013), *Making Samba: A New History of Race and Music in Brazil* (Durham, NC & London: Duke University Press) xvii, 364 pages, [6] pages of plates.

MASCARENHAS CASSIANO NEVES, PEDRO & ANA LUÍSA DA CUNHA DE ALVIM (2014), *Houses and Palaces in Lisbon: Coats of Arms* (Lisbon: Scribe) 287 pages.

PACE, RICHARD & BRIAN P. HINOTE (2013), *Amazon Town TV: An Audience Ethnography in Gurupá, Brazil* (Austin: University of Texas Press) 224 pages.

PARÉS, LUIS NICOLAU (2013), *The Formation of Candomblé: Vodun History and Ritual in Brazil* (Chapel Hill: University of North Carolina Press) 424 pages.

RÊGO, CACILDA & MARCUS BRASILEIRO (eds) (2014), *Migration in Lusophone Cinema* (New York, NY: Palgrave Macmillan) viii, 232 pages.

REGO, PAULA & ADAM FOULDS (writer of added commentary) (2014), *Paula Rego: The Last King of Portugal and Other Stories* (London: Marlborough Fine Art) 36 pages.

RENSHAW, AMANDA (2013), *Art & Place: Site-Specific Art of the Americas* (London & New York: Phaidon) 373 pages.

RODRÍGUEZ, JUAN (2014), *Eduardo Souto Moura: At Work* (Porto: A.mag) 277 pages.

SCHACTER, RAFAEL & JOHN FEKNER (2013), *The World Atlas of Street Art and Graffiti* (New Haven, CT: Yale University Press) 399 pages.

SHARP, DANIEL B. (2014), *Between Nostalgia and Apocalypse: Popular Music and the Staging of Brazil* (Middletown, CT: Wesleyan University Press) xxiii, 159 pages.

1.3 Bibliographies, Directories and Guides

BEZERRA, ALEXANDRE, CARRIE-MARIE BRATLEY, ET AL. (2014), *Fodor's Portugal*, 10th edn (New York: Fodor's Travel) 456 pages.

BRIERLEY, JOHN (2015), *A Pilgrim's Guide to the Camino Portugués: Lisboa, Porto, Santiago: A Practical & Mystical Manual for the Modern Day Pilgrim*, 6th edn (Forres, Scotland: Camino Guides) 207 pages.

BROWN, JULES (2014), *The Rough Guide to Portugal*, 14th edn (London: Rough Guides) 527 pages.

CHIODETTO, EDER, CAROLINA CHAGAS (ed) & Maria Abramo CALDEIRA BRANT (translator) (2014), *Brazil* (London: Phaidon Press) 320 pages.

EDITORS OF TIME OUT (2015), *Time Out Lisbon* (London: Time Out Guides) 256 pages.

INSIGHT GUIDES (2014), *Portugal*, 6th edn (Singapore: APA Publications) 390 pages.

LEZARD, SIÂN (2014), *Portugal, Madeira, the Azores* (Greenville, SC: Michelin Travel) 424 pages.

PALIN, MICHAEL (2013), *Brazil* (New York: Thomas Dunne Books/St Martin's Press) 319 pages.

SARAIVA, CLÁUDIA & SYMA TARIQ (2014), *Lisbon*, rev. and updated edn, Wallpaper city guide (London: Phaidon) 103 pages.

ST. LOUIS, REGIS, KATE ARMSTRONG, ANDY SYMINGTON & ANJA MUTIC (2014), *Lonely Planet Portugal (Travel Guide)*, 9th edn (Footscray, Victoria: Lonely Planet Publications) 535 pages.

ST. LOUIS, REGIS (2013), *South America on a Shoestring*, 12th edn (Footscray, Victoria: Lonely Planet Publications) 1109 pages.

SYMINGTON, MARTIN (2014), *Portugal*, rev. edn, Eyewitness travel guides (London: Dorling Kindersley) 480 pages.

1.4 Environment

ALPERT, DANIEL (2013), *The Age of Oversupply: Overcoming the Greatest Challenge to the Global Economy* (New York: Portfolio/Penguin) 280 pages.
BENACH, NÚRIA & ANDRÉS WALLISER (eds) (2014), *Urban Challenges in Spain and Portugal* (New York: Routledge) viii, 124 pages.
DE JUANA ARANZANA, EDUARDO & ERNEST GARCIA (2015), *The Birds of the Iberian Peninsula* (London: Christopher Helm) 688 pages.
GARFIELD, SETH (2014), *In Search of the Amazon: Brazil, the United States, and the Nature of a Region* (Durham, NC: Duke University Press) 343 pages.
LERNER, JAIME (author), Mac MARGOLIS, Peter MUELLO & Ariadne DAHER (translators) (2014), *Urban Acupuncture* (Washington, DC: Covelo) xvi, 143 pages.
PERRAULT, CELESTE & LEONE BELLAMY (eds) (2013), *Savannas: Climate, Biodiversity and Ecological Significance* (New York: Nova Publishers) 155 pages.
THOROGOOD, CHRIS (2014), *Field Guide to the Wild Flowers of the Algarve* (Richmond, Surrey: Kew Publishing, Royal Botanic Gardens, Kew) vii, 272 pages.
VALENÇA, MÁRCIO MORAES, FERNANDA CRAVIDÃO & JOSÉ ALBERTO RIO FERNANDES (eds) (2014), *Urban Developments in Brazil and Portugal* (New York: Nova Science Publishers) xv, 451 pages.

1.5 History, Politics and Social Science

Africa (general)

FIGUEIRA, CARLA (2013), *Languages at War: External Language Spread Policies in Lusophone Africa: Mozambique and Guinea-Bissau at the Turn of the 21st Century* (Frankfurt am Main: Peter Lang) 355 pages.
HAVIK, PHILIP J., ALEXANDER KEESE & MACIEL SANTOS (2015), *Administration and Taxation in Former Portuguese Africa, 1900–1945* (Newcastle upon Tyne: Cambridge Scholars Publishing) 255 pages.
HODGE, JOSEPH MORGAN, ET AL. (2014), *Developing Africa: Concepts and Practices in Twentieth-Century Colonialism* (Manchester: Manchester University Press) xviii, 414 pages.
MCMAHON, CHRISTINA S. (2013), *Recasting Transnationalism through Performance: Theatre Festivals in Cape Verde, Mozambique, and Brazil* (Basingstoke: Palgrave Macmillan) 248 pages.
NUSSEY, WILF (2014), *Watershed: Angola and Mozambique: A Photo-History: The Portuguese Collapse in Africa, 1974–1975* (Solihull: Helion) 143 pages.
SALGADO, SUSANA (2014), *The Internet and Democracy Building in Lusophone African countries* (Farnham: Ashgate) 198 pages.

Asia

CARREIRA, ERNESTINE (2014), *Globalising Goa (1660–1820): Change and Exchange in a Former Capital of Empire (Goa, India: Goa 1556)* 618 pages.
BIEDERMANN, ZOLTÁN (2014), *The Portuguese in Sri Lanka and South India: Studies in the History of Diplomacy, Empire and Trade, 1500–1650* (Wiesbaden: Harrassowitz Verlag) 205 pages.

GUPTA, PAMILA (2014), *The Relic State: St Francis Xavier and the Politics of Ritual in Portuguese India* (Manchester: Manchester University Press) 304 pages
HENN, ALEXANDER (2014), *Hindu–Catholic Encounters in Goa: Religion, Colonialism, and Modernity* (Bloomington: Indiana University Press) 230 pages.
SOUZA, GEORGE BRYAN (2014), *Portuguese, Dutch and Chinese in Maritime Asia, c.1585–1800: Merchants, Commodities and Commerce* (Farnham: Ashgate) 346 pages.
XAVIER, ÂNGELA BARRETO (2015), *Catholic Orientalism: Portuguese Empire, Indian Knowledge (16th–18th Centuries)* (New Delhi, India: Oxford University Press) xxxvi, 386 pages.

Brazil

CASAS ZAMORA, KEVIN (2013), *Dangerous Liaisons: Organized Crime and Political Finance in Latin America and Beyond* (Washington, DC: Brookings Institution Press) 300 pages.
DÁVILA, JERRY (2013), *Dictatorship in South America* (Hoboken, NJ: Wiley-Blackwell) 224 pages.
DOMÍNGUEZ, JORGE I. & MICHAEL SHIFTER (2013), *Constructing Democratic Governance in Latin America*, 4th edn (Baltimore: Johns Hopkins University Press) xxiii, 377 pages.
FREIRE, PAULO & ANA MARIA ARAÚJO FREIRE (2014), *Pedagogy of Hope: Reliving Pedagogy of the Oppressed* (London: Bloomsbury Academic) 226 pages.
GOLDSTEIN, DONNA (2013), *Laughter Out of Place: Race, Class, Violence, and Sexuality in a Rio Shantytown* (Oakland: University of California Press) 400 pages.
GOMES, LAURENTINO & ANDREW NEVINS (2013), *1808: The Flight of the Emperor: How a Weak Prince, a Mad Queen, and the British Navy Tricked Napoleon and Changed the New World* (Guilford, CT: Lyons Press) xiv, 321 pages.
GRAGNOLATI, MICHELE, MAGNUS LINDELÖW & BERNARD COUTTOLENC (2013), *Twenty Years of Health System Reform in Brazil: An Assessment of the Sistema Único de Saúde* (Washington, DC: World Bank) 130 pages.
GUZMAN, TRACY (2013), *Native and National in Brazil Indigeneity after Independence* (Chapel Hill: University of North Carolina Press) 352 pages.
HERNÁNDEZ, TANYA KATERÍ (2014), *Racial Subordination in Latin America: The Role of the State, Customary Law, and the New Civil Rights Response* (Cambridge: Cambridge University Press) 258 pages.
KNIGHT, ALAN & PAULO DRINOT (eds) (2014), *The Great Depression in Latin America* (Durham, NC: Duke University Press) 376 pages.
KUCINSKI, BERNARDO & SUE BRANFORD (translator) (2013), *K* (London: Latin America Bureau) 192 pages.
MCCANN, BRYAN (2014), *Hard Times in the Marvelous City: From Dictatorship to Democracy in the Favelas of Rio de Janeiro* (Durham, NC: Duke University Press) xi, 249 pages.
MONTERO, ALFRED P. (2014), *Brazil: Reversal of Fortune* (Cambridge: Polity Press) ix, 241 pages.
MORRIS, THERESA (2013), *Cut it Out: The C-Section Epidemic in America* (New York: New York University Press) x, 244 pages.

NIBERT, DAVID ALAN (2013), *Animal Oppression and Human Violence: Domesecration, Capitalism, and Global Conflict*, Critical perspectives on animals: theory, culture, science, and law (New York: Columbia University Press) viii, 336 pages.

RONCADOR, SÔNIA (2014), *Domestic Servants in Literature and Testimony in Brazil, 1889–1999* (New York: Palgrave Macmillan) ix, 240 pages.

SLOCUM, RACHEL B. & ARUN SALDANHA (eds) (2013), *Geographies of Race and Food Fields, Bodies, Markets* (Aldershot: Ashgate) 360 pages.

SUGIYAMA, NATASHA BORGES (2013), *Diffusion of Good Government: Social Sector Reforms in Brazil* (Notre Dame, IN: University of Notre Dame Press) 288 pages.

THURSTON, ROBERT W., ET AL. (2013), *Coffee: A Comprehensive Guide to the Bean, the Beverage, and the Industry* (Lanham, MD: Rowman & Littlefield) xi, 416 pages.

VIDAL LUNA, FRANCISCO & HERBERT S. KLEIN (2014), *The Economic and Social History of Brazil since 1889* (New York: Cambridge University Press) xvi, 439 pages.

Portugal

ABREU-FERREIRA, DARLENE (2015), *Women, Crime, and Forgiveness in Early Modern Portugal* (Farnham, Surrey: Ashgate) xii, 237 pages.

BOROOAH, VANI K. (2014), *Europe in an Age of Austerity* (New York: Palgrave Macmillan) xi, 165 pages.

CHILDS, WENDY ROSEMARY (2014), *Trade and Shipping in the Medieval West: Portugal, Castile and England*, Textes et Études du Moyen Âge (TEMA) (Turnhout: Brepols) 187 pages.

CLEMINSON, RICHARD (2014), *Catholicism, Race and Empire: Eugenics in Portugal, 1900–1950*, Studies in the History of Medicine (Budapest: Central European University Press) 297 pages.

DELBRUGGE, LAURA (2015), *Self-fashioning and Assumptions of Identity in Medieval and Early Modern Iberia* (Leiden: Brill) 320 pages.

GIORGI, KYRA (2014), *Emotions, Language and Identity on the Margins of Europe* (Basingstoke: Palgrave Macmillan) 248 pages.

HEIDER, DANIEL (2014), *Universals in Second Scholasticism: A Comparative Study with Focus on the Theories of Francisco Suárez (1548–1617), João Poinsot O.P. (1589–1644) and Bartolomeo Mastri da Meldola O.F.M. Conv. (1602–1673)/Bonaventura Belluto O.F.M. Conv. (1600–1676)* (Amsterdam: Benjamins) xi, 344 pages.

HERZOG, TAMAR (2015), *Frontiers of Possession: Spain and Portugal in Europe and the Americas* (Cambridge, MA: Harvard University Press) 384 pages.

LOPES, RUI (2014), *West Germany and the Portuguese Dictatorship, 1968–1974: Between Cold War and Colonialism* (Basingstoke: Palgrave Macmillan) xi, 269 pages.

MAGONE, JOSÉ MARIA (2014), *Politics in Contemporary Portugal: Democracy Evolving* (Boulder, CO: Lynne Rienner Publishers) xii, 295 pages.

MAYSON, RICHARD (2014), *Portugal's Wines and Winemakers: Port, Madeira & Regional Wines* (San Francisco: Wine Appreciation Guild) 250 pages.

NICHOLLS, KATE (2015), *Mediating Policy: Greece, Ireland, and Portugal before the Eurozone Crisis* (Abingdon: Routledge) 260 pages.

OLIVAS OSUNA, José (2014), *Iberian Military Politics: Controlling the Armed Forces during Dictatorship and Democratisation* (Basingstoke: Palgrave Macmillan) xiii, 296 pages.

PEREIRA, Carlos (2014), *Roman Lamps of Scallabis (Santarém, Portugal)* (Oxford: Archaeopress) iii, 115 pages.

PORRAS GALLO, María-Isabel & Ryan A. DAVIS (eds) (2014), *The Spanish Influenza Pandemic of 1918–1919: Perspectives from the Iberian Peninsula and the Americas* (Rochester, NY: University of Rochester Press) viii, 282 pages.

RILEY, Jonathon (2014), *The Last Ironsides: The English Expedition to Portugal, 1662–1668* (Solihull: Helion) xix, 222 pages.

THOMSON, Ronald B. (2014), *The Concession of Évora Monte: The Failure of Liberalism in Nineteenth-Century Portugal* (Lanham, MD: Lexington Books) xiii, 185 pages.

Portuguese Discoveries and Empire

ALENCASTRO, Luiz Felipe de (2015), *The South Atlantic, Past and Present* (Dartmouth: Tagus Press/UMass Dartmouth) xii, 287 pages.

BANDEIRA JERÓNIMO, Miguel (2015), *The 'Civilising Mission' of Portuguese Colonialism, 1870–1930* (Basingstoke: Palgrave Macmillan) viii, 269 pages.

COATES, Timothy (2014), *Convict Labor in the Portuguese Empire, 1740–1932: Redefining the Empire with Forced Labor and New Imperialism* (Leiden: Brill) xxvi, 205 pages.

COTTROL, Robert J. (2013), *The Long, Lingering Shadow: Slavery, Race, and Law in the American Hemisphere* (Athens: University of Georgia Press) xii, 370 pages.

FRÓIS, Luís (2014), *The First European Description of Japan, 1585: A Critical English-Language Edition of Striking Contrasts in the Customs of Europe and Japan*. Translated from the Portuguese original and edited and annotated by Richard K. Danford, Robin D. Gill, and Daniel T. Reff; with a critical introduction by Daniel T. Reff (London: Routledge, 2014) 312 pages.

HECHT, Susanna B. (2013), *The Scramble for the Amazon and the 'Lost paradise' of Euclides da Cunha* (Chicago, IL: University of Chicago Press) xv, 612 pages.

NELLIS, Eric Guest (2013), *Shaping the New World: African Slavery in the Americas, 1500–1888* (North York, Ontario, Canada: University of Toronto Press) xix, 183 pages.

OWEN, Hilary & Anna M. KLOBUCKA (eds) (2014), *Gender, Empire, and Postcolony: Luso-Afro-Brazilian Intersections* (New York: Palgrave Macmillan) 240 pages.

PAQUETTE, Gabriel B. (2014), *Imperial Portugal in the Age of Atlantic Revolutions: The Luso-Brazilian World, c.1770–1850* (Cambridge: Cambridge University Press) xiv, 450 pages.

POMERANZ, Kenneth & Steven TOPIK (2013), *The World that Trade Created: Society, Culture, and the World Economy, 1400 to the Present*, 3rd edn (Armonk, NY: M. E. Sharpe) xiii, 329 pages.

RICHARDSON, David & Filipa RIBEIRO DA SILVA (2015), *Networks and Trans-Cultural Exchange: Slave Trading in the South Atlantic, 1590–1867* (Leiden: Brill) xvi, 278 pages.

Overseas Communities

BRETTELL, CAROLINE B. (2014), *Men who Migrate, Women who Wait: Population and History in a Portuguese Parish* (Princeton, NJ: Princeton University Press) 348 pages.

1.6 Language

BERLITZ PUBLISHING (2014), *Brazilian Portuguese: Phrase Book & Dictionary* (London: Berlitz) 224 pages.
CABREDO HOFHER, PATRICIA & ANNE ZRIBI-HERTZ (eds) (2014) *Crosslinguistic Studies on Noun Phrase Structure and Reference* (Leiden: Brill) 400 pages.
CALLAHAN, LAURA (ed.) (2014), *Spanish and Portuguese across Time, Place, and Borders: Studies in Honour of Milton M. Azevedo* (Basingstoke: Palgrave Macmillan) xxi, 239 pages.
JOUET-PASTRE, CLEMENCE, ANNA KLOBUCKA, PATRÍCIA SOBRAL, MARIA LUCI MOREIRA & AMELIA HUTCHINSON (2013), *Ponto de encontro: Portuguese as a World Language* (Harlow: Pearson Education) 660 pages.
KELLER, KAREN (2013), *Portuguese for Dummies* (Hoboken, NJ: John Wiley and Sons) xviii, 360 pages.
MUFWENE, SALIKOKO S. (ed.) (2014), *Iberian Imperialism and Language Evolution in Latin America* (Chicago, IL: University of Chicago Press) 368 pages.
ROCHA, JOÃO CEZAR DE CASTRO (ed.) (2013), *Lusofonia and its Futures* (Dartmouth: Tagus Press/UMass Dartmouth) 256 pages.
SARDINHA, TONY BERBER & TELMA DE LURDES SÃO BENTO FERREIRA (eds) (2014), *Working With Portuguese Corpora* (London: Bloomsbury) 328 pages.
WHITLAM, JOHN (2014), *The Routledge Intermediate Brazilian Portuguese Reader* (Abingdon: Routledge) 144 pages.
ZENNER, ELINE & GITTE KRISTIANSEN (eds) (2013), *New Perspectives on Lexical Borrowing: Onomasiological, Methodological and Phraseological Innovations* (Berlin: De Gruyter Mouton) 252 pages.

1.7 Literature

AIDOO, LAMONTE & DANIEL F. SILVA (eds) (2014), *Lima Barreto: New Critical Perspectives* (Lanham, MD: Lexington Books) vi, 241 pages.
ATKIN, RHIAN (2014), *Lisbon Revisited: Urban Masculinities in Twentieth-Century Portuguese Fiction*, Studies in Hispanic and Lusophone Cultures (Oxford: Legenda) x, 196 pages.
AZEVEDO, FRANCISCO & DANIEL HAHN (translator) (2014), *Once Upon a Time in Rio: A Novel* (New York: Atria Paperback) 308 pages.
BARRETO, LIMA & MARK CARLYON (translator) (2014), *The Sad End of Policarpo Quaresma* (London: Penguin Classics) 271 pages.
BLAS DE ROBLÈS, JEAN-MARIE & MIKE MITCHELL (translator) (2013), *Where Tigers Are at Home* (New York: Other Press) 817 pages.
CAMAYD-FREIXAS, ERIK (2013), *Orientalism and Identity in Latin America: Fashioning Self and Other from the (Post)Colonial Margin* (Tucson: University of Arizona Press) ix, 241 pages.

COELHO, TERESA PINTO (2014), *Eça de Queirós and the Victorian Press* (Woodbridge: Tamesis) xiii, 227 pages.
COELHO, PAULO & MARGARET JULL COSTA (translator) (2013), *Manuscript Found in Accra: A Novel* (New York: Alfred A. Knopf) xiv, 190 pages.
COELHO, PAULO & MARGARET JULL COSTA (translator) (2014), *Veronika Decides to Die* (London: HarperCollins) 208 pages.
FONSECA, RUBEM & CLIFFORD E. LANDERS (translator) (2014), *Crimes of August: A Novel* (Dartmouth: Tagus Press/UMass Dartmouth) 287 pages.
LAUB, MICHEL & MARGARET JULL COSTA (translator) (2014), *Diary of the Fall* (London: Harvill Secker) 192 pages.
LEITE, ANA MAFALDA, SHEILA KHAN, JESSICA FALCONI, KAMILA KRAKOWSKA (eds) & Luis R. MITRAS (translator) (2014), *Speaking the Postcolonial Nation: Interviews with Writers from Angola and Mozambique* (Bern: Peter Lang) 271 pages.
LEITE, ANA MAFALDA, HILARY OWEN, RITA CHAVES & LIVIA APA (eds) (2014), *Narrating the Postcolonial Nation: Mapping Angola and Mozambique* (Bern: Peter Lang) 304 pages.
LISPECTOR, CLARICE & ALISON ENTREKIN (translator), edited and with an introduction by Benjamin MOSER (2014), *Near to the Wild Heart* (London: Penguin Classics) 208 pages.
LISPECTOR, CLARICE & STEFAN TOBLER (translator), edited and with an introduction by Benjamin MOSER (2014), *Agua Viva* (London: Penguin Books) 112 pages.
LISPECTOR, CLARICE & IDRA NOVEY (translator), introduction by Caetano VELOSO; edited by Benjamin MOSER (2014), *The Passion According to G.H.* (London: Penguin Books) xi, 193 pages.
LISPECTOR, CLARICE & JOHNNY LORENZ (translator), edited by Benjamin MOSER (2014), *A Breath of Life: Pulsation* (London: Penguin Books) 167 pages.
LISPECTOR, CLARICE & BENJAMIN MOSER (translator), introduction by Colm TÓIBÍN (2014), *The Hour of the Star* (London: Penguin Books) 96 pages.
MACHADO DE ASSIS, JOAQUIM MARIA & RHETT MCNEIL (editor and translator) (2014), *Stories* (London: Dalkey Archive Press) 216 pages.
PAZOS ALONSO, CLÁUDIA & STEPHEN PARKINSON (eds) (2013), *Reading Literature in Portuguese: Commentaries in Honour of Tom Earle* (Oxford: Legenda) 294 pages.
PRADO, ADÉLIA & ELLEN DORÉ WATSON (translator) (2014), *The Mystical Rose: Selected Poems* (Hexham, England: Bloodaxe Books) 160 pages.
RIBEIRO, EDGARD TELLES & KIM M. HASTINGS (translator) (2014), *His Own Man* (Melbourne: Scribe) 352 pages.
ROCHA, JOÃO CEZAR DE CASTRO (ed.) (2014), *Literary Histories in Portuguese* (Dartmouth: Tagus Press/UMass Dartmouth) 276 pages.
SABINO, MARIO (2014), *The Day I Killed my Father* (Melbourne: Scribe) 192 pages.
SARAMAGO, JOSÉ & MARGARET JULL COSTA (translator) (2014), *Skylight* (London: Harvill Secker) 320 pages.
SILVESTRE, EDNEY & NICK CAISTOR (translator) (2014), *Happiness Is Easy* (London: Doubleday) 190 pages.
SILVESTRE, EDNEY & NICK CAISTOR (translator) (2014), *If I Close My Eyes Now* (London: Black Swan) 317 pages.

SOUSA, RONALD W. (2014), *On Emerging from Hyper-Nation: Saramago's 'Historical' Trilogy* (West Lafayette, IN: Purdue University Press) xi, 198 pages.

SPIRK, JAROSLAV (2014), *Censorship, Indirect Translations and Non-Translation: The (Fateful) Adventures of Czech Literature in 20th-Century Portugal* (Newcastle upon Tyne: Cambridge Scholars Publishing) xii, 190 pages.

TORRES, RUI & SANDY BALDWIN (eds) (2014), *PO.EX: Essays from Portugal on Cyberliterature & Intermedia* (Morgantown, WV: Center for Literary Computing) xxiv, 262 pages.

WELGE, JOBST (2014), *Genealogical Fictions: Cultural Periphery and Historical Change in the Modern Novel* (Baltimore, MD: Johns Hopkins University Press) 254 pages.

ZEPP, SUSANNE & INSA KUMMER (translator) (2014), *An Early Self: Jewish Belonging in Romance Literature, 1499-1627* (Stanford, CA: Stanford University Press) ix, 261 pages.

1.8 Religion

TRIVELLATO, FRANCESCA, LEOR HALEVI & CATIA ANTUNES (eds) (2014), *Religion and Trade: Cross-Cultural Exchanges in World History, 1000-1900* (Oxford: Oxford University Press) 296 pages.

VERKAAIK, OSKAR (2013), *Religious Architecture: Anthropological Perspectives* (Amsterdam: Amsterdam University Press) 210 pages.

II. Theses

2.1. African Topics

GLEASON, TIFFANY KATHLEEN, *Coastal Islam: Religion and Identity among Minority Muslims in the French Colonial City of Porto-Novo, 1889-1939*. Ph.D. (University of California, Los Angeles) 2014. 288 pages.

MULIRA, SANYU RUTH, *Yearning for Transformation: Women Living in the Margins of Senegal and France, 1958-2003*. MA. (UCLA) 2014. 64 pages.

STALLER, JARED GLENN, *Island of Imaginations: The Historical Dialectics between Experience and Observation in the Creation of São Tomé (1472-1953)*. Ph.D. (University of Virginia) 2013. 1 CD-ROM; 4 3/4 in.

2.2 Asian Topics

BEUS, ANNALYN, *Translation and Transcription of a Passage from the Baduem Manuscript: An Eighteenth-Century Portuguese Embassy to China*. MA. (Brigham Young University-Provo, UT) 2013. 186 pages.

HUBERT, MARIA DEL ROSARIO, *Disorientations: Latin American Fictions of East Asia*. Ph.D. (Harvard University) 2014. 206 pages.

LEE, ANA PAULINA, *Luso-Hispanic Archipelagos: The Imaginary of Asia in Brazilian and Cuban Literary and Visual Culture*. Ph.D. (University of Southern California, Los Angeles) 2014. 173 pages.

PENDSE, LILADHAR RAMCHANDRA, *19th Century Periodicals of Portuguese India: An Assessment of Documentary Evidence and Indo-Portuguese Identity*. Ph.D. (University of California, Los Angeles) 2013. 294 pages.

2.3. Brazilian Topics

ALLEN, ALICE LOUISA, *Sites of Transformation: Urban Space and Social Difference in Contemporary Brazilian Visual Culture*. Ph.D. (University of Cambridge) 2013. xiii, 201 leaves.

ALLEN, KOYA C., *Cultural Embeddedness and the International Traveler: Influences on Travel Behavior for the Prevention of Imported Dengue*. Ph.D. (Kent State University) 2013. 281 pages.

ARDIGÓ, FABIANO, *Close Together but a World Apart: A Comparative History of Research Practices during the Formative Years of Brazilian Academic Science (1934–1955)*. Ph.D. (University of Oxford) 2014. 331 pages.

BEYER, BETHANY RENEE, *Performable Nations: Music and Literature in Late Nineteenth- and Early Twentieth-Century Cuba, Brazil, and the United States*. Ph.D. (University of California Los Angeles) 2013. 163 pages.

BRAEHLER, VERENA BARBARA, *Inequality of Security: Exploring Violent Pluralism and Territory in Six Neighbourhoods in Rio de Janeiro, Brazil*. Ph.D. (University College London) 2014. 291 pages.

BROEKMAN, KIRSTEN, *The Meaning of Aesthetics within the Field of Applied Theatre in Development Settings*. Ph.D. (University of Manchester) 2014. 251 pages.

BURRIER, GRANT, *Ordem e Progresso: The Programa de Aceleração do Crescimento, Developmentalism, and Democracy in Brazil*. Ph.D. (University of New Mexico) 2014. 204 leaves.

CABRELLI AMARO, JENNIFER, *The Phonological Permeability Hypothesis: Measuring Regressive L3 Influence to Test L1 and L2 Phonological Representations*. Ph.D. (University of Florida) 2013. 265 pages.

CAIRUS, JOSE, *The Gracie Clan and the Making of Brazilian Jiu-Jitsu: National Identity, Culture and Performance, 1905–2003*. Ph.D. (York University, Canada) 2013. 269 pages.

CHILD, MICHAEL W., *Cross-Linguistic Influence in L3 Portuguese Acquisition: Language Learning Perceptions and the Knowledge and Transfer of Mood Distinctions by Three Groups of English-Spanish Bilinguals*. Ph.D. (University of Arizona) 2014. 243 pages.

COHON, ADAM JOSEPH, *Building Regulatory Bodies in the Brazilian States*. Ph.D. (University of California, Berkeley) 2013. 212 pages.

D'ABREU, Lylla, *Sexual Aggression and Victimization among College Students in Brazil: Prevalence and Vulnerability Factors*. Ph.D. (Potsdam University) 2013. 227 pages.

DE LIMA, KALINA, *Continuing Professional Development and Reflective Practice for English Teachers in the Municipal Schools in Northeast Brazil*. Ph.D. (University of Southampton) 2014. 350 pages.

FORCELINI, JAMILE MARMITT, *When More is Less: The Effect of a Third Language on a Second Language*. MA. (Florida State University) 2013. 64 pages.

FRAJTAG SAUMA, JULIA, *The Deep and the Erepecuru: Tracing Transgressions in an Amazonian Quilombola Territory*. Ph.D. (University College London) 2014. 282 leaves.

GALVAO, JIZELDA F., *Upon the Plains of the Soul .'. The Liberating Logos of João Guimarães Rosa in 'Grande Sertão: Veredas'*. Ph.D. (City University of New York, Graduate Center) 2014. 350 pages.

GHARAVI, MARYAM MONALISA, *Be an Outlaw, Be a Hero: Cinematic Figures of Transgression and Urban Banditry*. Ph.D. (Harvard University) 2013. 242 pages.

GIMBERNAT, JAVIER GONZALEZ, *New Cultural Identities through Literature and Rock Music in Latin America (Mexico, Colombia, Argentina, Brazil)*. Ph.D. (University of Colorado at Boulder) 2013. 342 pages.

GUYTON ACOSTA, KILEY JEANELLE, *Azucar negra: (Re)Envisioning Race, Representation, and Resistance in the Afrofeminista Imaginary*. Ph.D. (University of New Mexico) 2013. 313 pages.

HESS, HANS MICHAEL ANSELMO, *Uses of Samba in Brazilian Films, 1943-2011*. Ph.D. (Bristol University) 2014. 300 pages

HORNIKE, DAFNA, *Orientation towards Home or the Boundaries of the Nomad*. Ph.D. (Cornell University) 2013. 227 pages.

KANEYASU-MARANHAO, BRENNO KENJI, *The Dialectics of Formation and Conformation: The Politics of Fiction in Brazil and Argentina*. Ph.D. (University of California, Berkeley) 2013. 134 pages.

KAROSS, LUCIANA, *The Amateur Translation of Song Lyrics: A Study of Morrissey in Brazilian Media (1985-2012)*. Ph.D. (University of Manchester) 2014. 480 pages.

LATHEY FARACINI, ELIZABETH, *Caipira Dialect Stylization and the Representation of Modernity in Brazilian Telenovelas*. M.A. (University of Colorado at Boulder) 2013. 66 pages.

LEE, ALEXANDER F., *Chouriço, please! Portuguese in Massachusetts Service Encounters: A Dissertation in Luso-Afro-Brazilian Studies and Theory*. Ph.D. (University of Massachusetts Dartmouth) 2013. x, 195 leaves.

LEITE, EDUARDO LYCURGO, *The Fair Use Doctrine as a Limitation to Copyright and a Comparative Analysis of the Three-Step Test in the Copyright Systems of Brazil and the U.S*. Ph.D. Doctor of Juridical Science (S.J.D.) (Washington College of Law. American University) 2014. 485 pages.

LIMA, PAULO PEREIRA, *Candomble and its Living Garments*. Ph.D. (University of California, Los Angeles) 2014. 239 pages.

LIMA DE SOUSA, HELEN MARIE, *Beyond Indianism: The Different Faces (and Races) of Civilization and Primitiveness in Brazilian Romanticism*. Ph.D. (University of Cambridge) 2013. iii, 236 pages.

LIU, LANG MARIA, *Bimba's Rhythm is One, Two, Three: From Resistance to Transformation through Brazilian Capoeira*. Ph.D. (Ontario Institute for Studies in Education, University of Toronto) 2013. 347 pages.

MACKIN, ANNA ELIZABETH, *Protest and Repression in Democratic Systems: A Comparative Analysis with a Focus on Brazil*. Ph.D. (University of Oxford) 2014. xiii, 193 leaves.

MAGIE, NICOLE JEAN, *A Pearl in a World on the Move: Italians and Brazilians in Caxias, Brazil (1870-1910)*. Ph.D. (Michigan State University) 2014. 230 pages.

MERA, JANINA, *Does Solidarity Matter? Social Capital in Land Reform Settlements in the Northeast of Brazil*. Ph.D. (University of Wisconsin–Madison) 2013. 230 pages.

MONTES, AMANDA LIRA GORDENSTEIN, *The Use and Perception of English in Brazilian Magazine Advertisements*. Ph.D. (Arizona State University) 2014. 217 pages.

MURRAY, Eric A., *Tradition and Innovation in the Pedagogy of Brazilian Instrumental Choro.* Ph.D. (Kent State University) 2013. 214 pages.

NARITA, Flávia M., *Music, Informal Learning, and the Distance Education of Teachers in Brazil: A Self-Study Action Research Project in Search of Conscientization.* Ph.D. (Institute of Education, University of London) 2014. 335 pages.

NAVARRO BARNARD, Doris Graziela, *The Role of Social Capital in Household Economy and Land-Use / Land-Cover Change in Areas of Land Reform in Santarem, Brazilian Amazon.* Ph.D. (Indiana University) 2014. 390 pages.

NONATO, Rafael, *Clause Chaining, Switch Reference and Coordination.* Ph.D. (Massachusetts Institute of Technology) 2014. 152 pages.

OLMEDA, Juan C. *(Dis)united They Stand? The Politics of Governors' Coalition Building in Argentina, Brazil and Mexico.* Ph.D. (Northwestern University) 2013. 326 pages.

OLSEN, Michael L., *The Realization of Final Stops in Interlanguage: More Evidence for Universal Grammar.* MA. (Southern Illinois University at Carbondale) 2014. 72 pages.

PAVESE, Carolina B., *Level-Linkage in European Union–Brazil Relations: An Analysis of Cooperation on Climate Change, Trade, and Human Rights.* Ph.D. (London School of Economics and Political Science, University of London) 2014. 342 pages.

PIERINI, Emily, *The Journey of the Jaguares: Spirit Mediumship in the Brazilian Vale do Amanhecer.* Ph.D. (University of Bristol) 2014. 291 pages.

PORTO FONSECA, Juliana Soares, *How much say do you have on their pay?: An Analysis of the Regulation of Director and Executive Compensation in the United States and Brazil.* Thesis (LL. M.) (Harvard Law School) 2013. 100 pages.

POTTER, Berit, *Grace McCann Morley and the Dialectical Exchange of Modern Art in the Americas, 1935–1958.* Ph.D. (New York University) 2015. 404 pages.

SANTOS, Helade Scutti, *Cross-linguistic Influence in the Acquisition of Brazilian Portuguese as a Third Language.* Ph.D. (University of Illinois at Urbana-Champaign) 2013. 263 pages.

SMITH, S. Daniel, *Pro-drop and Word-Order Variation in Brazilian Portuguese: A Corpus Study.* MA. (Brigham Young University) 2013. vii, 102 pages.

SOLER, Patricia A., *Sleek Words: Art Deco and Brazilian Modernism.* Ph.D. (Georgetown University) 2014. 208 leaves.

SOUZA, Valeria M., *Challenging Bodies: Representations and the Aesthetics of Disability in João Guimarães Rosa's Grande* Sertão: Veredas *(1956): A Dissertation in Luso-Afro- Brazilian Studies and Theory.* Ph.D. (University of Massachusetts Dartmouth) 2013. ix, 286 leaves.

SOUZA E PAULA, Leonora Soledad, *Critical Geographies of Globalization: Buenos Aires and São Paulo in the 21st century.* Ph.D. (University of California, San Diego) 2013. 145 pages.

SOUZA HOGAN, Maria Leda, *Novels of Decolonization in Modernity: Malambo, Um defeito de cor, and Fe en disfraz.* Ph.D. (University of Massachusetts Amherst) 2014. 243 pages.

STEPHEN, Matthew David, *Pivotal Rising Powers: India, Brazil, South Africa and Contestation in Global Governance.* Ph.D. (Freie Universität Berlin, Otto-Suhr-Institut für Politikwissenschaft) 2013. 337 pages.

STORELLI, ELIZANGELA, *Support Transfers and Well-Being among Older Adults in Latin America*. Ph.D. (Boston College) 2014. 185 pages.
TERRIE, P. LARKIN, *State Building and Political Regimes: The Nineteenth-Century Origins of Liberal Democracy in Latin America*. Ph.D. (Northwestern University) 2014. 330 pages.
TORRES NUNEZ, CINTHYA EVELYN, *Mapping the Amazon: Territory, Identity, and Modernity in the Literatures of Peru and Brazil (1900-1930)*. Ph.D. (Harvard University) 2014. 311 pages.
TREMBLAY, CRYSTAL, *Empowerment and Communication in São Paulo, Brazil: Participatory Video with Recycling Cooperatives*. Ph.D. (University of Victoria, Canada) 2013. 191 pages.
VALDEZ, TERESA, *The Benefits of a Portuguese Heritage Language Textbook: Possibilities and Approaches: A Dissertation in Luso-Afro-Brazillian Studies and Theory*. Ph.D. (University of Massachusetts Dartmouth) 2014. xi, 173 leaves.
VARGAS DE FREITAS CRUZ LEITE, MARIANNA, *From Rhetoric to Reality in Improving Maternal Health Outcomes: An Analysis of Women's Rights Activism in Brazil*. Ph.D. (Birkbeck, University of London) 2014. 325 pages.
WADDELL GILLIAM, DORIS, *'I have to know who I am.': An Africana Womanist Analysis of Afro-Brazilian Identity in the Literature of Miriam Alves, Esmeralda Ribeiro and Conceição Evaristo*. Ph.D. (Florida State University) 2013. 150 pages.
WALTER, WOLFGANG K., *Recommendations for Small Water Supply Systems in Newly Industrialized Countries on the Example of Assessments in the State of Minas Gerais, Brazil*. Ph.D. (Universität der Bundeswehr München) 2013. 418 pages.
WHITWORTH-SMITH, ANDREW C., *Solidarity Economies, Networks and the Positioning of Power in Alternative Cultural Production and Activism in Brazil: The Case of Fora do Eixo*. Ph.D. (University of California, San Diego) 2014. 293 pages.
ZHANG, JIHUI, *Financial Development, Political Instability and Growth: Evidence for Brazil since 1870*. Ph.D. (Brunel University) 2014. 163 pages.

2.4. Portuguese Topics

FERREIRA CAMPOS, ÂNGELA DA CONCEIÇÃO, *Shifting Silence, Enduring Shame, Ambivalent Memories: An Oral History of the Portuguese Colonial War (1961-1974)*. Ph.D. (University of Sussex) 2014. 312 pages.
FRANCO, RAFAEL ANTONIO SERRALHEIRO, *Exploring Marketing Managers' Use of Accounting Information: A Case Study of the Portuguese Fashion Retail Sector*. Ph.D. (D.B.A.) — (University of Manchester) 2014. 338 pages.
GANT, ALIA CHANEL, *Europeanization in the European Union: The Case of Portugal during the Sovereign Debt Crisis*. MA. (University of Iowa) 2014. 126 pages.
GONTIJO, VIVIANE, *'I start to sweat, I crack my fingers and I hold my hand': The Impact of Anxiety on the Learning of Portuguese: A Dissertation in Luso-Afro-Brazilian Studies and Theory*. Ph.D. (University of Massachusetts Dartmouth) 2013. ix, 151 pages.
GRADOVILLE, MICHAEL STEPHEN, *A Comparative Usage-Based Approach to the Reduction of the Spanish and Portuguese Preposition Para*. Ph.D. (Indiana University) 2013. 320 pages.

INFANTE, GUSTAVO, *When the Mountains Speak: The Voices of Rural Landscape in the Short Stories of Miguel Torga and Han Shaogong*. Ph.D. (University of Bristol) 2014. 271 pages.

KUNTZ, DANIELLE M., *'Appropriate Musics for that Time': Oratorio in the Exchange of Power at the Portuguese Court (1707-1807)*. Ph.D. (University of Minnesota) 2014. 299 pages.

LARSON, JARED D., *Bringing the Outside in: The Comparative Politics of Immigration in Spain and Portugal after Democratic and Migration Transition*. Ph.D. (University of Delaware) 2014. 473 pages.

MONTGOMERY, ZAK K., *The Reception and Legacy of the Portuguese Generation of 1870 in Spain*. Ph.D. (Indiana University) 2013. vii, 239 pages.

PIRES, SONIA G., *Salazar's Case for Dictatorship through Nationalism in Three Speeches: A Thesis in Portuguese Studies*. Ph.D. (University of Massachusetts Dartmouth) 2013. vii, 139 leaves.

ROBINSON, STEVEN, *Assessing the Europeanisation of Portuguese Foreign and Security Policy*. Ph.D. (University of Newcastle upon Tyne) 2013. xiii, 313 pages.

SAIVE, DENISE, *Challenging Masculinities: The Role of Gender in Os Lusíadas by Luís Vaz de Camões*. Ph.D. (University of Wisconsin–Madison) 2013. 212 pages.

STEIN, NAOMI E. G., *Spatial Dimensions of High-Speed Rail: Intermediate Cities, Inter-Jurisdictional Planning, and the Implications for High-Speed Rail in Portugal*. Master of Science (Massachusetts Institute of Technology) 2013. 204 pages.

WEIZ, FRANKA, *Idioms of Racism: Discourses on Race and Black Slavery in the Lusophone Atlantic, 15th-19th centuries*. Ph.D. (University of Essex) 2013. 594 pages.

ABSTRACTS

Sanctity and Alienation in Twelfth-Century Braga as Portrayed in the Vita Sancti Geraldi
STEPHEN LAY

ABSTRACT. The *Vita Sancti Geraldi* is an account of the life of Gerald of Moissac, a French Cluniac monk who became Archbishop of Braga in the early years of the twelfth century. The *vita* was composed by another French immigrant clergyman, Bernard, archdeacon of Braga. A primary aim of the medieval hagiographer was to construct an iconic portrait of human sanctity and the image of saintly piety presented in the *Vita Sancti Geraldi* is firmly based in hagiographical convention. Yet Bernard was also able to individualize his account by including a wealth of historical detail, while at the same time revealing the sense of alienation both he and Gerald experienced as outsiders in a sometimes hostile land. These elements are woven together to produce a vivid insight into a Portuguese society in the throes of fundamental cultural change.

KEYWORDS. Medieval hagiography, Portuguese Church, St Gerald, Braga, Gregorian Reform, Cluny.

RESUMO. A *Vita Sancti Geraldi* oferece um relato da vida de Gerald de Moissac, monge da ordem de Cluny que veio a tornar-se arcebispo de Braga nos primeiros anos do século XII. A *Vita* foi composta por outro clérigo imigrante francês, Bernard, arcediago de Braga. Um objetivo principal deste hagiógrafo medieval era construir um retrato icónico da santidade humana e, por isso, a imagem de piedade do santo apresentada em *Vita Sancti Geraldi* é firmemente baseada em convenções hagiográficas. Mesmo assim, Bernard foi também capaz de individualizar o seu relato incluindo uma profusão de detalhes históricos, sem esconder o sentimento de alienação que tanto ele como Geraldo experimentaram enquanto estranhos numa terra por vezes hostil. Tais elementos são alinhavados de forma a produzir uma imagem muito viva duma sociedade portuguesa em vias de mudanças culturais fundamentais.

PALAVRAS-CHAVE. Hagiografia medieval, igreja portuguesa, São Geraldo, Braga, reforma gregoriana, Cluny.

Seeing is Believing: The Miniatures in the Cantigas de Santa Maria *and Medieval Devotional Practices*
KIRSTIN KENNEDY

ABSTRACT. The miniatures that accompany the *Cantigas de Santa Maria* have been examined in terms of their content, relationship to the text, method of creation and political and religious ideology. In this article I refer to recent research about the medieval practice of Christian devotion to draw out some of the doctrinal messages inherent in the miniatures, messages that have previously been overlooked in favour of stylistic, narrative or archaeological interpretations. I will argue that the miniatures reflect contemporary ideas about the physical effect of vision, and that they illustrate fundamental arguments of Christian theology with reference to the sense of sight.

KEYWORDS. Alfonso X, *Cantigas de Santa Maria*, Christian church, Middle Ages, material culture — religious aspects, miracles — Europe, reliquaries, Virgin Mary, five senses.

RESUMO. As miniaturas que acompanham as *Cantigas de Santa Maria* já foram analisadas em termos de conteúdo, da sua relação com o texto, do método de criação e da sua ideologia política e religiosa. No presente artigo baseio-me em pesquisas recentes sobre a prática medieval de devoção cristã no intuito de extrair algumas das mensagens doutrinárias inerentes às miniaturas, que têm sido negligenciadas no passado em favor de interpretações estilísticas, narrativas ou arqueológicas. Avanço que as miniaturas refletem ideias contemporâneas sobre o efeito físico da visão, e que ilustram argumentos fundamentais da teologia cristã com referência ao sentido da visão.

PALAVRAS-CHAVE. Alfonso X, Cantigas de Santa Maria, igreja cristã, Idade Média, cultura material — aspetos religiosos, milagres — Europa, relicários, Virgem Maria, cinco sentidos.

Early Modern Marginalia in the Cancioneiro da Ajuda
ANDRÉ B. PENAFIEL

ABSTRACT. The history of literary reception, within Galician-Portuguese scholarship, remains a relatively unexplored field, largely due to the scarcity of sources. On the other hand, codicological studies tend to privilege the original features of a given manuscript over later additions. The present article, instead, focuses on the late medieval and early-modern marginalia to be found in the thirteenth-century, Iberian manuscript, the *Cancioneiro da Ajuda*. It includes a comprehensive catalogue and edition of these notes, presented in a partially modernized spelling, accompanied by a short study. It is hoped that both will pave the way for future studies on literary reception that could make use of textual evidence available but so far little explored.

KEYWORDS. *Cancioneiro da Ajuda*, marginalia, edition, literary reception.

RESUMO. Estudos de recepção literária da lírica galego-portuguesa ainda são raros, em grande parte devido à escassez de fontes históricas. Ao mesmo tempo, estudos codicológicos tendem a valorizar os elementos originais dos manuscritos em detrimento de acréscimos posteriores. O presente artigo concentra-se em anotações marginais encontradas no Cancioneiro da Ajuda, manuscrito do século XIII, e datáveis do fim do período medieval ou início da Idade Moderna. Além de breve estudo, incluiu-se um catálogo destas anotações que se pretende exaustivo, devidamente editadas em grafia parcialmente modernizada. Espera-se que tanto a edição como a análise revelem-se instrumentos úteis para estudos futuros sobre recepção literária que poderão assim fazer uso destes elementos até agora pouco explorados.

PALAVRAS-CHAVE. Cancioneiro da Ajuda, *marginalia*, edição, recepção literária.

The Manuscript Tradition of the Regula Benedicti *in Portuguese*
IVO CASTRO

ABSTRACT. The *Regula Benedicti* [Rule of St. Benedict] in Portugal in the Middle Ages is notable for the number of translations done of it and for the number of manuscripts which still survive. Today, almost all of these manuscripts have been edited and ordered chronologically, making it possible to identify and group the relevant translations and, by comparing the different versions, to establish a timeline of the diachronic evolution of the Portuguese language.

KEYWORDS. Old Portuguese, medieval manuscripts, translation, Rule of St Benedict.

RESUMO. A transmissão da *Regula Benedicti* na Idade Média portuguesa é notável pela quantidade de traduções feitas e pela quantidade de manuscritos que ainda sobrevivem. Hoje estão editados praticamente todos esses manuscritos e ordenados cronologicamente; torna-se possível identificar o agrupamento das traduções e, comparando versões, estabelecer uma diacronia real da evolução da língua portuguesa.

PALAVRAS-CHAVE. Português medieval, manuscritos medievais, tradução, *Regula Benedicti*.

Service, not Subservience: Chapter 98 of D. Duarte's Leal Conselheiro
JULIET PERKINS

ABSTRACT. Chapter 98 of the king D. Duarte's moral treatise, *Leal Conselheiro*, recounts the good relations enjoyed by him and his siblings with their father, D. João I. When detached from the overall context, it reads as a somewhat rosy portrait of family harmony, appropriate to a panegyric of the Avis dynasty. However, when read within the coherent moral framework of the treatise, the chapter reveals a quasi-monastical striving towards obedience, humility and service on the part of D. Duarte, which may be traced in large part to the influence that John Cassian's writings had on his moral and spiritual development.

KEYWORDS. King D. Duarte of Portugal, *Leal Conselheiro*, family relations, Christian teaching.

RESUMO. O Capítulo 98 do tratado moral *Leal Conselheiro*, da autoria do rei D. Duarte, relata as boas relações gozadas pelo próprio e seus irmãos com o pai, D. João I. Quando desligado do contexto geral, o capítulo aparenta ser um retrato algo idealizado de harmonia familiar, adequado para um panegírico da dinastia de Avis. No entanto, quando lido dentro do quadro moral coerente do tratado, o capítulo revela por parte de D. Duarte um esforço quase monástico no sentido de obediência, humildade e serviço, que pode ser atribuído, em grande medida, à influência que os escritos de João Cassiano tiveram sobre o seu desenvolvimento moral e espiritual.

PALAVRAS-CHAVE. Rei Dom Duarte, *Leal Conselheiro*, relações familiais, preceitos cristãos.

Rui de Pina, Crónica de D. Afonso V *and Bodleian MS Don. c. 230*
T. F. EARLE

ABSTRACT. The Bodleian Library has recently acquired a manuscript of the chronicle, one of around forty. The MS is described, and its relationship to the manuscript tradition discussed. The chronicle has never been edited critically, despite its historical importance. Rui de Pina has often been accused of plagiarism, and there is some discussion of this issue and of the date of composition of the work. There are some omissions in the Oxford MS and also some readings which diverge from what might be thought of as the official version. However, the Oxford MS is unlikely to form the basis of a new edition.

KEYWORDS. Chronicle, Rui de Pina, Portuguese history, plagiarism, textual criticism.

RESUMO. A biblioteca bodleiana, da Universidade de Oxford, adquiriu recentemente um dos aproximadamente quarenta manuscritos existentes da *Crónica de D. Afonso V* de Rui de Pina. Apesar da sua importância, esta obra nunca foi editada criticamente. O autor foi muitas vezes acusado de plagiário, tópico abordado no artigo, que inclui também uma discussão acerca da data de composição da crónica. O manuscrito de Oxford omite certas passagens e possui também algumas leituras que divergem da versão considerada definitiva da obra (guardada na Torre do Tombo). O manuscrito de Oxford, porém, dificilmente poderá ser utilizado como texto-base de uma nova edição.

PALAVRAS-CHAVE. Crónica, Rui de Pina, história portuguesa, plágio, crítica textual.

Damião de Góis's Livro de Linhagens: *An Untold (Hi)Story*
CATARINA FOUTO

ABSTRACT. This paper is a first critical approach to the *Livro de Linhagens* by Damião de Góis (currently preserved in several manuscript copies). It discusses the problems surrounding the authorship of the work and proposes a dating and sources for some of its sections. The article places the *Livro de Linhagens* in the public and literary career of Góis (especially the *Crónica do Felicíssimo Rei D. Manuel*) and situates it within the thriving tradition of books of lineage in late medieval and Renaissance Portugal. The analysis of selected passages of the text (including its prologue) sheds light on whom Góis was addressing in his work and how he perceived the task of the writer of genealogies.

KEYWORDS. Damião de Góis, Portuguese early-modern historiography, genealogy, *Livro de Linhagens, Crónica do Felicíssimo Rei D. Manuel*.

RESUMO. Este artigo é uma abordagem crítica do *Livro de Linhagens* de Damião de Góis (atualmente preservado em várias cópias manuscritas). Discutem-se aqui os problemas em torno da autoria desta obra e sugere-se uma data e fontes para algumas das suas secções. O artigo situa o *Livro de Linhagens* na carreira pública e literária de Góis (especialmente face à *Crónica do Felicíssimo Rei D. Manuel*) e igualmente na próspera tradição literária dos livros de linhagens em território português no final da Idade Média e no Renascimento. Através da análise de trechos do texto (incluindo o prólogo) discute-se o público-alvo da obra de Góis e como o humanista português concebia o trabalho do escritor de genealogias.

PALAVRAS-CHAVE. Damião de Góis, historiografia portuguesa do Renascimento, genealogia, *Livro de Linhagens, Crónica do Felicíssimo Rei D. Manuel*.

www.ingramcontent.com/pod-product-compliance
Lightning Source LLC
Chambersburg PA
CBHW061418300426
44114CB00015B/1981